MEMOIRS

Reginald Maudling

MEMOIRS

SIDGWICK & JACKSON

LONDON

First published in Great Britain in 1978
by Sidgwick and Jackson Limited

Copyright © 1978 by Reginald Maudling

ISBN 0 283 98446 5

Printed in Great Britain by
The Anchor Press Ltd and bound by
Wm Brendon & Son Ltd, both of
Tiptree, Essex
for Sidgwick and Jackson Limited
1 Tavistock Chambers, Bloomsbury Way
London WC1A 2SG

TO BERYL

in gratitude for thirty-eight years of happiness

'Les années qui avaient passé sur sa tête ne lui avaient laissé que leur printemps.'

CHATEAUBRIAND

PROLOGUE

From quiet homes and first beginning,
Out to the undiscovered ends,
There's nothing worth the wear of winning,
But laughter and the love of friends.

I FIRST read these words of Belloc very many years ago. (By a strange coincidence it was in Edward Marsh's *Memoir* which opens the Sidgwick and Jackson edition of Rupert Brooke's collected works published in 1936.) They struck me as being profoundly true; nothing that has happened since has led me to doubt this. Every book should have a theme, and this will be the underlying theme of the one you are now reading. We shall see how it stands up to half a century of experience, most of it in the practice of politics.

I think it needs, at this initial stage, just some qualification. The wear of winning is not the same as the wear of doing. Many things are profoundly worth doing by reason of the results they produce for human happiness. But you do those things, you make those efforts, you carry those responsibilities, not for their own sake, but as a means to some other end. It is the end itself, and not the means, that is involved in the wear of winning.

The love of friends is a fascinating phrase, for it underlines both the identity and the difference of love and friendship. What they have in common is that they are an end in themselves and, I believe, the greatest end of human life. I have had many friends, as this book will show, powerful and modest, eminent and raffish, and I have rejoiced in the friendship of all of them.

When I come to the end of my story, I will try to reassess, in the light of experience, my initial reaction to Belloc's lines.

REGINALD MAUDLING

February 1978

CONTENTS

ILLUSTRATIONS

The cartoons on pp. 68 and 70 are reproduced courtesy of the *Daily Mail;* those on pp. 135, 190, and 208 courtesy of the *Daily Express;* and those on pp. 138 and 181 courtesy of Mr Les Gibbard.

INTRODUCTION

IT was in February 1977 that Frank Longford invited me to lunch with him at the Garrick, with his colleague, William Armstrong, to discuss the possibility that Sidgwick and Jackson might publish a book of my composition. It was a very good lunch, as I had expected, because although I am somewhat awed by Frank's principles, I have always found his company most agreeable. He embarrassed me by declaring that as I was a known expert on claret he intended to order the best the club had available. I told him my reputation was pretty bogus, and that I was an enthusiastic amateur rather than an expert, but I never denied the suggestion that I was an expert, because it meant that I was given some very pleasant clarets to drink. As it was we had a Rausan-Ségla 1962, which was excellent, and enabled me to score one of the few points I can make in this field because I had visited the château itself years ago and had seen the remarkable selection of historic relics which Christian Cruse had established in the museum there. However, the point was to talk about a book. I said it had always seemed to me there were only three reasons for writing a book: talent, malice or money. I didn't claim the first, I hoped I had little of the second, and as for the third, it was hard to believe that I was likely to produce a best seller. William Armstrong suggested that there was in fact a fourth reason, namely the satisfaction one can obtain from self-expression. So I thought I would have a go.

What I want to try to produce is not so much an autobiography as an expression of some ideas which I have developed over the last half-century about politics and the vast range of related subjects. It occurs to me that some account of how I came to reach these views, and the experience I have had in the practice of politics, might help to define and sharpen them. So this is what I am going to try to do.

I am certainly not going to try to produce a historical record. That is for the historians, in so far as they are interested. I have never kept detailed records myself of my activities; it always seemed to me a rather cold-blooded activity to do so, and I much prefer to get on with the job and let the results speak for themselves. Clearly after more than twenty-five years of Government or Opposition Front Bench responsibility there is much that I can and no doubt should remember. I have been fortunate in having responsibility for a number of Departments, and it is astonishing how wide is the range of matters in which Ministers have to take an interest and for which they may be held responsible. Did you know, for example, that wild ginger is a substance much used in the seduction of young women in the Seychelles? I certainly didn't until I had to answer a question about it in the House of Commons when I was Colonial Secretary. So inevitably what I have to say will be impressionistic and selective. It may well at times be inaccurate, though I have done my best to avoid that where I can.

It is extraordinary how selective the human memory is. Why do we remember some things and not others? Is there any reason behind it? Take a no doubt trivial example, golf, on which I spent years ago a great part of my life. I must have played thousands of rounds of golf, yet more than ninety-nine per cent of them have vanished from my memory. Certain things remain. I can remember Fred Robson's professional shop at Cooden Beach over fifty years ago, where the professional made his own clubs out of hickory shafts and twine, and the smell of the warm gluepot. I can see the long fifteenth at Cooden Beach, where at the age of seven or eight I scored by some strange chance my first bogey. I can still see the astonished look on the face of an elderly sheep when a wild slice of mine landed full toss on its cranium. I can see every shot I played at the last four holes of the Wildernesse Club, Sevenoaks, when I finished 4, 4, 4, 3, to record a 75, thereby beating 80, and winning a pot, for the first time. I can recall three-putting on the first green at Lytham St Annes, starting my disastrous progress to a 10 and 8 defeat in the first round of the Boys' Championship well over forty years ago, and I can even recall my French opponent sucking oranges and spitting out the pips on every alternate tee. I can recall being given a golf ball to play with in the U.S.A. called a Wilson, and asking whether it was true that this was the only golf ball that was capable of swerving left and right simultaneously. Why should one remember this tiny selection out of a totality of experience? Moments of success one understands, moments of failure, occasions of triumph, occasions of disaster, but there is more to it than that. I only wish I knew what it was. Suffice it to say I have a strong suspicion that one's recollections of past experiences, though perhaps less accurate than the records, may in some strange way be more true.

Most of what I shall be writing about concerns politics, political issues, Government decisions, Opposition attitudes: this, after all, at the time was my working life. I do not intend to dwell to any extent on life outside politics, though in the long run I suspect it was far more important. I will refer to friends, to business life, the enjoyments and experiences, only as they make some contribution to the main theme. About my family life you will find little in this book. I still feel, though it is unfashionable, that there is virtue in reticence and that some things matter too deeply to parade them in print. I share the view of a famous British actress, who said many years ago that she agreed with the Japanese, how strange it was that we in England should express such disapproval of the baring of the body and so little of the baring of the soul.

So what I am aiming at is a pattern of reminiscences woven into a theme, putting them, broadly speaking, in a chronological order, because order in point of time and order in point of logic, different as they be, to some extent coincide in an exercise such as this. I want to express as best I can an outlook on political life that I have held for a very long time, that has developed over the years in Government and in Opposition, but has not I think in any way fundamentally changed since the days when I was at Oxford. I start with an article which I wrote for *The Spectator* in 1943. It was my first essay into public print. I was twenty-six at the time and working in the Air Ministry. The War was at its height. What I said then and what the editor of *The Spectator* was good enough to print, from a wholly unknown correspondent, has remained my consistent belief ever since.

The full text of the article I have, on my publisher's insistence, consigned to Appendix 1, but the theme was broadly this. The main political issue of the nineteenth century had been a struggle against political privilege. This struggle had been won largely by the Liberal Party, whose principle had been that of *laissez-faire*. The Liberals stood in political matters for both liberty and equality, and they were successful because where political issues are concerned liberty and equality coincide – one man, one vote. But in economic matters it is a different thing indeed. Complete liberty will lead to extreme inequalities, complete equality can be achieved only by the extinction of liberty. It was for this reason I argued that the once great Liberal

Party had effectively run out of steam and a new political impulse was required to solve twentieth-century economic problems. Socialism accepted that equality can only be achieved at the sacrifice of liberty, *laissez-faire* Liberalism accepted the sacrifice of equality as the price of liberty. My argument was that both of them were wrong, because they were thinking of liberty solely in negative terms, in other words freedom 'from' not freedom 'for'. Freedom from political control had meant for so many people nothing more than freedom to be poor, to be workless, to live in discomfort, insecurity, squalor.

I was calling for a new concept of freedom that would be positive, not negative, a concept of freedom in which the power of the State would not conflict with the freedom of the individual but would underpin it and enable it to develop in the truest possible sense. I said, 'Freedom for civilized man is not a mere negative, not just freedom *from*; it is freedom . . . to think, speak, work and worship and to develop his individual personality in conditions that befit the dignity and greatness of the human race.' I said that the Conservative Party appeared at that time divided. There were those who were against all controls, and their appeal during the War was considerable. There were those, on the other hand, who were beginning to think in terms of a freedom that was positive and constructive, not purely negative.

What I said in detail is in the Appendix. It has been my political philosophy throughout my life, strengthened and developed by experience. Were I writing that article again today I would not wish to change a word of it.

How has what I said been borne out in practice? Economic equality has certainly increased within Britain, if not between the nations of the world, but it should be recorded that the narrowing of differentials between high and low incomes has been achieved more by penalizing the successful than by encouraging the others, more by bringing people down to a common standard than by elevating them to it. Nothing has done more to promote this development than the system of taxation under which we have laboured and continue to labour. The shackles of poverty on the exercise of freedom have been reduced. Real privation is now confined to a very small section of Britain's population, mainly among the elderly. Few people now are cold or hungry. It is to our shame that any at all should be so. But this reduction in the inability to enjoy freedom, what I described as negative freedom, freedom from want and privation, has not been accompanied by any noticeable increase in the ability to enjoy positive freedom.

The economic monopoly powers to which I referred remain, though they have changed their nature. The monopoly of capital has been cut back very severely but it has been replaced by a monopoly of labour exercised by the great Trade Unions. The political Parties continue to fight over the distribution of a national income which, in relative terms, has been diminishing. They have continued virtually to ignore the basic requirement, which is to increase its total. The Conservative Party has not solved its dilemma. There are still adherents of either point of view, those on the one hand who wish to abolish virtually all Government and return to the glories of a Victorian economy, those, on the other hand, who still argue that the enjoyment of true freedom requires an adequate measure of Government control.

In Government, pressed by the realities of life which face Ministers, the Conservative Party has moved steadily in the latter direction. Yet each time the progress has been opposed by the Party fundamentalists when in Government and set back by the same influences when we have been in Opposition. We had Selsdon Man, and it took some while to get over that. We do not yet know the full measure of Selsdon Woman.

I wish I could have done more in these last decades to follow the logic of that old article of 1943 and to persuade my Party to move along those lines. My analysis of the problem remains unchanged, and the fact that the problem is still with us is sad evidence of efforts that have borne inadequate result. The story of this book will be a story of those efforts over those years, and of the conclusions I have drawn from their progress.

1

Early Days

1917–1939

I WAS born in London in 1917, and shortly afterwards my parents moved to Bexhill on the South Coast, because of the German air raids on London. I was an only child, and from that I both derived the advantages and suffered the disabilities that are the normal portion of only children. It is hard to tell what is the balance between the two, but suffice it to say that my wife and I, both having been only children, are happy that we have a family of four ourselves. Only children get many advantages which parents cannot provide for a large family, but they are constantly in danger of being spoiled and attracting too much attention to themselves, and taking too much for granted. This is fine while it lasts, but when you grow older and move out into the world, it sometimes calls for rather painful adjustment.

We were what I suppose would be described in modern sociological jargon as an upper- or middle-middle-class family. My father was a consulting actuary, who had built up his own firm with considerable distinction and great hard work and integrity. We led a comfortable life. Sometimes we had a house with a tennis court. We even had the services of a full-time maid for the greater part of those early years.

It was a society which, like all societies, had its virtues and its short-comings. It was narrow, closed, and class-conscious in both directions, up and down. But it had high standards of integrity, and a deep belief in patriotism, in honest hard work, and in the virtues of saving. No doubt it was in many ways intolerant, and could be described as complacent. Certainly one acquired a consciousness of that class structure which is so often the target of criticism in British society.

I always remember at the age of six winning, with the help of a substantial handicap, a swimming race at the local baths on the occasion of some fête, beating the favourite by a narrow margin. Afterwards I was asked by a woman working in the café, 'Why didn't you let him win? After all, he is only a poor boy.' It is strange how one carries that sort of memory along, like my only memory of the General Strike, which took place when I was at my preparatory school. The headmaster – whom I recall particularly for his bald head and walrus whiskers and who rejoiced in the perfect name for a headmaster, Mr Whicker, nearly a pun but not quite – came in at lunchtime in a state of great excitement to tell us the General Strike was over. We all felt that civil war at least, if not something worse, had been averted. We didn't understand the issues, but this was a feeling with which we had grown up. Oh, incidentally, there is one other vivid recollection. In those days the West Indies were making, I think, their first tour in the U.K. and the terror of their fast bowlers had spread far and wide in advance of their coming. We were all queuing for lunch, when some master, with the awful habit that some of them have of teasing small boys about really serious matters, announced that in the first Test Britain were all out for twenty and Constantine had taken eight wickets for no runs.

In general I think the first influences I encountered in early school-days were of those whose standards embraced a strong belief in Britain and the established system, who were somewhat fearful and not wholly comprehending of the new social pressures that were developing from organized labour, but who believed that the basic principles of middle-class morality, integrity, effort, ambition and caution were permanent and would endure.

My life on the coast gave me a feeling for the sea which has lingered on. In the summer we were able to spend many long hours on the beach. I do not know whether the summers were really warmer then, or whether it was just that we were younger, but one came to know and love the sea and feel entirely at home in it, not on the surface in a boat, but just swimming, lazing and floating. Familiarity bred not contempt but confidence and affection. Some of the loveliest lines I recall are about the waves of the sea in all their moods, and they still invoke memories of the happiest kind. Here is Aeschylus :

ποταμῶυ τε πηγαί, πουτιωυ τε κυμάτωυ
ἀνήριθμου γέλασμα

–'O, ye river-waters, and numberless laughter of the waves of ocean';

or Shelley,
Like light dissolved in star-showers, thrown

George Meredith,
Mark where the pressing wind shoots javelin-like
Its skeleton shadow on the broad-backed wave!
....
... where the ponderous breakers plunge and strike,
And dart their hissing tongues high up the sand

Rupert Brooke,
the little dulling edge of foam
That browns and dwindles as the wave goes home

We moved back to London and lived in Bickley, where I went to school at Bickley Hall, a typical preparatory school for day boys run by the brothers Farnfield, who did their best to instil an adequate mixture of scholarship, exercise and discipline. My own performance was, I think, a mixed one. I found the scholarship relatively easy, because I had a quick mind and an ability to absorb facts, and that was what was then meant by scholarship. I found the exercise unattractive as I was grossly overweight. We were all compelled to play rugby, and, as the fattest boy in the school, I was always placed in the second row of the forwards, where, as far as I recall, I spent most of my time being sat on by everyone else. Never, till some years later, when I came to watch rugby as opposed to playing it, did I discover how a three-quarter line operated. As for discipline, that was not difficult as I was far too scared of authority to transgress on many occasions.

But here there is one very interesting difference between today's world and the world of fifty years ago. Parents then were on the side of discipline and parental authority was considerable. I and my friends would have been far more worried about displeasing our parents than displeasing our teachers. This was not because our parents were tyrants in any sense whatsoever : it was simply because we had a deep feeling that if we misbehaved we would be letting them down. It is hard to believe the same sentiments operate today. I cannot help feeling that a great deal of the emergence of crime in our society and the general decay of social discipline are caused by the withering of this relationship between parent and child, and the unwillingness in so many cases of parents to use their authority to ensure that their children accept the disciplines which a free society must expect of its members.

From Bickley Hall I moved with a scholarship to Merchant Taylors' School, again as a day boy, and I was lucky to come across some remarkable men as schoolmasters. Spencer Leeson was the headmaster, an extraordinary, rather unworldly man of haggard and troubled appearance when headmaster, but who subsequently took Holy Orders and acquired the rotundity that came with peace. He was not a great scholar, but he was an enthusiastic one. On one occasion he was trying to teach us ancient history, and there was some reference in the text to a hundred denarii. 'How much,' we asked, 'was this in English money?' Well, he said, a denarius was worth nine pence, whereupon he turned his back to the class, seized the chalk and proceeded to divide 900 pence by 360 to produce an answer in pounds. This, I must confess, shook the faith of some of us in his mathematics. He had, nevertheless, a way of impressing his own fervour and sincerity on the younger mind. One phrase he used has lingered always with me, 'ἀρχή φιλοσοφίας χάσκω' – 'The beginning of philosophy is a gape.' Certainly I owe him a great debt for some advice he once gave me. He used, as headmaster, to see every boy at the end of term briefly. I arrived in my turn expecting, as I had done well in exams, some words of praise. Not a bit of it, all he had to say was, 'Maudling, you suffer from two dangers, vanity and selfishness, beware of them both.' I have never had better advice from anyone, or briefer for that matter.

The Classical Lower Sixth Form was in the hands of a remarkable man known to all his pupils as 'Billy'. He was a clergyman of singularly plain appearance, who normally wore a pretty grubby clerical collar, but he was a remarkable teacher, with a great capacity for getting boys to see what the Classics were all about. He had strong aversions as well as strong enthusiasms. Top of his list of aversions came Bernard Shaw, G. K. Chesterton and the Pope, not, I hasten to add, any particular Pope, but just the Papacy in general. I well remember him starting one lesson with the words, 'Ever since the first Pope stank in the Chair of St Peter's'. However, he had a profound knowledge of and love for the Classics. He always argued that ῥοδοδάκτυλος Ἠώς meant not the rosy-fingered dawn but the rosy-toed dawn, which, after all, is in line with 'The dawn in russet mantle clad walks o'er the dew of yon high Eastern hill'. His opinion of my Greek verse was both scathing and justified. 'Well, boy, how long did it take you to whack that lot out – two minutes eh?' But I am grateful to him for introducing me to so many things that otherwise I might have missed – above all, Catullus – and he did once say something that I have never forgotten, 'The purpose of an education is to learn how to learn.' It would not be a bad idea to have that written up in many modern classrooms.

As a participant in the collective school activities I am afraid I was a considerable failure. I was no good at moving-ball games because of my short sight, and that meant, of course, that I was an outcast so far as team games, which mattered so much in our school community, were concerned. Nor, quite frankly, was I a very commendable member of the school Officers' Training Corps. I was quite unable to get my puttees to stay up, and I could not run fast enough to maintain a proper place in my platoon. I think my sole distinction was fainting on parade one afternoon, no doubt after excessive enjoyment of the lunch-hour at the school tuckshop.

Non-team activities in which I indulged were not at that time regarded as being wholly acceptable. Things have changed since then. Golf, for example, is now highly regarded; it certainly was not then. Nor, indeed, was ice skating, to which, incongruously enough for my bulk, I was greatly attracted. In fact I still hold the bronze medal for figure skating of the National Skating Association, and I gave two exhibitions on London ice rinks.

One, for no reason I can honestly recall, consisted of a brief spell of skating entirely on one foot with the other skate covered by a leather guard. It was the left foot; I always found myself more at home on the left foot than on the right (some of my political colleagues might say, 'Just as we would have expected').

The other was at a Hallowe'en charity ball at the then Grosvenor House ice rink, where I performed a duet with a charming young woman to the tune of 'I Met Her in Monterey'. I was dressed, presumably because it was Hallowe'en, as a brown owl. Perhaps this was the first occasion on which I began to acquire my reputation for sleeping, if not, alas, for wisdom. I do not recall any comparable occasion, save when in the 1960s I found myself dancing a foxtrot in Sochi on the shores of the Black Sea, with the wife of the local Commissar, to the tune of 'Smoke Gets in Your Eyes' (and the same colleagues might say, 'Reggie always has had smoke in his eyes when it comes to Russia').

Then I spent the years from 1935 to 1938 at Oxford, having won a Postmastership at Merton College, where I had the enormous good fortune of being tutored by a very remarkable man, Geoffrey Mure. Geoffrey was the last remaining Hegelian and of all the minds I have met in a long career his was certainly the most acute and the most perceptive. I have no doubt at all that anyone who was fortunate enough to read Greats at Oxford, and certainly anyone who sat at the feet of Geoffrey Mure, had the opportunity of acquiring a mental discipline and a system of thought which is of immense value in any occupation in life.

For anyone who was lucky enough to win his way there, life in Oxford in the mid-1930s was extremely agreeable. It was to some extent overshadowed by the growing menace of Hitler and I think we all felt at the bottom of our hearts that before many years were out we would be engaged in another war with Germany. But this did not inhibit either our intellectual activities or our practical enjoyment of life.

The freedom of Oxford was a tonic to those who had recently left school. The contact with other keen questing minds, the fact that among the Dons were to be found some of the most distinguished intellects in Europe, provided inspiration. I believe we all did work hard – at any rate, most of us – and we argued hard, often long into the night. We also enjoyed ourselves pretty vigorously. We consumed vast quantities of beer, we got tight from time to time, when we made a lot of noise and probably made a nuisance of ourselves, but in those days there was no student violence in the modern sense. As for the police, we respected them; we did not try to remove their helmets, even on Guy Fawkes' night. The worst behaviour towards policemen that I recall was the chanting of a tune, 'All Policemen Have Big Feet', which had been invented by the son of a distinguished cleric who was then at Oxford with us. Afternoons were spent by and large in one sporting pursuit or another : some rowed, some played cricket or football, some, like myself, took to golf. Evenings were a mixture of studying and enjoyment, with a good deal of visiting public houses, to which, theoretically, we were not entitled to go. In practice, however, we were not impeded. After all, had not the Roman poet declared,

meum est propositum in taberna mori

– 'I propose to end my days in a tavern.'

There was a great deal of pleasure to be had in English pubs in those days, not so much in the city of Oxford itself as in the surrounding villages, which we could then visit by car because it was in the days before the breathalyser. I do not think we made a nuisance of ourselves to the local inhabitants. In fact, I believe they welcomed us.

There was one evening in the Seven Stars at Marsh Baldon, a few miles from Oxford, when a group of us, including the recent Permanent Under Secretary at the Home Office, Sir Arthur Peterson, were engaged in lustily singing our own version of 'Green Grow the Rushes, O' in the public bar, when we were interrupted. We thought for a moment it was a complaint. Far from it. A charming man said, 'We are giving a party for the village children down at the school hall, a little way down the road. We like your singing so much, would you come and sing to them?' And so we did, much to the amazement of the children, and certainly to our own embarrassed surprise. Michael Clapham, who has just read this, and who was present, avers that in fact the man concerned was the local vicar, and that the audience were the village Mothers' Union, who had booked a professional entertainer for their social evening who had failed to turn up. He also tells me that we lost our amateur status by accepting a single bottle of beer as our collective remuneration for the performance.

Merton then was a small college, which I still believe to be a virtue, with only some 200 undergraduates, but they came from many different backgrounds and many different countries. The presence of so many men from the Commonwealth and from America, many of them Rhodes Scholars, was a great enrichment to our college life. From Australia and New Zealand came Hew Roberts; also Eric Dobson and Norman Davis, both to become distinguished Professors of English. There was Paul Engle, the American poet, and other Americans too of considerable scholastic attainment and other gifts as well. One in particular had a remarkable resemblance to a gorilla and his feats in climbing the college railings were quite remarkable. Elvis Stahr, subsequently to become head of one of America's greatest universities, was known as the Colonel because he came from Kentucky, while another, now a distinguished public servant, who should remain nameless, rejoiced in the evening when he danced down Holywell Street in only the top of his pyjamas. There was Vinicius de Moraes, later to become Brazil's leading poet.

From China there came the son of a well-known general, who displayed a remarkable subtlety at table tennis. He also showed remarkable calm on the occasion when the then Warden Bowman received all the new undergraduates of the year one by one. He was an elderly man, and his grasp was less clear than it had been. He shook hands with us one by one, occasionally making such remarks as 'How is your father?' until he was confronted with this charming Chinese undergraduate. He shook his hand, then realizing something unusual was happening, stared closely into his face and said, 'Young man do you understand English?'

Warden Bowman was a considerable character. There was a time, so rumour has it, when the college was on fire and the Bursar sent him a note to the effect, 'Warden, the College is on fire.' He received a prompt reply, 'Bursar, put it out.'

The British undergraduates were a mixture, some from boarding schools, others, like myself, from day schools. All of them, I believe, were happy to be there, and all of them had a loyalty to the college and college life, which existed without being provoked. None, so far as I can recall, took part in any political demonstrations. There was Airey Neave, now a leading figure in the Conservative Party, then an old Etonian of great elegance and chairman of an esoteric dining club called the Myrmidons, to whose membership I never aspired. There was Arthur Peterson, or rather Bill, as we called him (because there was another Arthur already around), a formidable scholar with the deceptive appearance of a dissipated parrot, whose rooms were always wrapped in semi-darkness and a lingering smell of prime Stilton. He took a brilliant degree in Greats and subsequently went on to a distinguished career in local and national Government.

Geoffrey Mure once lectured for two terms on Hegel, each Tuesday and Thursday morning. He started with an audience of twenty or thirty, including Bill Peterson and myself and some Americans, but they rapidly fell by the wayside, and his audience was reduced to us two. It was a mark of his composure that he used to arrive nevertheless every Tuesday and Thursday, and address his assembled audience of the two of us as if the lecture room had been full to the brim. I think Bill would agree with me, that the people who missed those lectures were very foolish, though he and I had qualms from time to time when the other was late, and we feared we might be reduced to an audience of one. Another contemporary was Leonard Cheshire, who, as a young man, was full of life and a rather controversial figure, but who subsequently displayed the utmost gallantry in wartime, and in the years of peace thereafter, a deep sense of service to and compassion for his fellow men. These and many others one remembers, Kenneth Holloway, Arthur Headley, Jimmy James, Stewart Lusk and Art Harvie from New Zealand, and above all, my closest friend, Michael Clapham, godfather to my eldest son Martin, with whom I have kept in constant friendly touch ever since.

There is no doubt in my mind that in the 1930s, at any rate, Greats was a remarkable school. Being of a rather lazy disposition, and not a meticulous scholar in any sense at all, I took Pass Moderations instead of Classical Honour Moderations, and went straight on to the ancient history and philosophy which constituted Greats. Fortunately one was not expected to do well in both of them. Examples of people who could were rare, though I do remember William Armstrong, now Lord Armstrong of Sanderstead, who took his degree and his oral examination at the same time as I did, being congratulated by the examiners on 'The consistent excellence of his papers throughout the examination'. Was there ever a man more clearly destined to become Head of the Treasury?

The elements in philosophy were logic, metaphysics and moral philosophy, all of which I found enjoyable, but, above all, logic. Geoffrey Mure was a superb tutor and brought us all through the transition from Plato and Aristotle through Kant and Hegel, to the more modern philosophers. The way he taught us was to see everything as a logical development, from the Platonic forms through the Hegelian dialectic, to Bradley's 'unearthly ballet of bloodless categories'. However, he stopped abruptly at Bertrand Russell and A. J. Ayer. He had the ability to make philosophy live and real and warm. It may be true, as Hegel said, that the owl of Minerva spreads her wings only with the approach of twilight, but nothing was so apparent in Geoffrey's teaching.

The principles one acquired from him were many : the need to distinguish between differences of degree and differences of kind; the essential relationship between substance and accident; the view of a community whose unity lay in the differentiation of its parts; above all, the equation of the good, the true and the beautiful. In this he added to Keats,

> *Beauty is truth, truth beauty – that is all*
> *Ye know on earth, and all ye need to know.*

Looking back on it I can think of several principles which I acquired from Geoffrey Mure which have stood me in good stead. First, the relation between the individual and the community, between freedom and order, and the connection of the one with the other. Secondly, his belief that philosophy progresses not by finding the answers but by progressively clarifying the questions. Thirdly, the impartiality of logic and the utter need to apply the test of logic to any proposition.

This does not mean that formal logic alone is enough. In the late 1940s, when sharing an office with Enoch Powell, I tried to persuade him that he was too logical, a concept which he could neither accept nor understand. But somehow or other to be too logical in form was to accept as logical what is in substance illogical and this has always seemed to me impossible.

Perhaps, as a good friend once told me, my addiction to logic was why I could not make more progress as Home Secretary in the tangled affairs of Northern Ireland. Muriel Bowen, it was, I think, who said, 'It is no good, Reggie, trying to find the logical solution; neither the Irish people nor the Irish situation are controlled by logic.' The trouble was, as I had to point out to her, there is generally only one logical solution to a problem, and it is possible to work towards that, but the illogical alternatives are numerous, and on what principle is one to choose which one to adopt?

There are many problems that do not yield to logic, but there are few that can be solved by methods that are blatantly illogical. This is one reason why I have always disliked the extreme in politics. The present truth always lies somewhere in between, as Party Conferences are never prepared to recognize, and future progress should be the purpose of current contradiction. The Hegelian process of thesis and antithesis leading to synthesis is the essential principle of human progress. In politics it may be called the Middle Way, Butskellism, or Consensus. By any name it makes sense to me.

It was in those years that I had my first opportunities to travel widely. I have seized every opportunity of doing so since, and I have been very fortunate in the extent and variety of my travels. They have been a source of great enjoyment and of considerable political education.

My first long trip abroad was to Canada. I had previously visited

Europe with my parents, and seen a certain amount of France, Switzerland and Hungary, but Canada was a different matter. I left school a term early, much to the fury of the school authorities, who felt that anything exceptional was disruptive, in order to visit Canada and stay with the Dalley family, who lived in Hamilton, Ontario. My connection with them once again was through golf, and I was a close friend of Sam Dalley, their younger son. Most of the time I spent in Canada was devoted to playing golf on one course or another with varying degrees of success. I think my particular recollection is taking part in the Hiram Walker Open on one of those delightful courses near Toronto, when each competitor was announced by loudspeaker as he stepped onto the first tee. I was a little disconcerted as I moved forward to hear the announcement that 'Mr Mangling of London is about to drive', and the result, needless to say, was disastrous. But the times were pleasant, the Canadians in general and the Dalleys in particular were extremely hospitable people, and it was an experience at the age of eighteen between school and university which was of great value.

I came back via New York, where I spent a day or two on my own and learnt how lonely you can be in a big city when you are young and mystified. Then back home on the old German liner, the *Bremen,* on which I shared a cabin immediately over the propeller with three New Yorkers, one of whom, a Hungarian barber, had spent several years working in New York but still could speak virtually nothing but Hungarian. That taught me quite a lot about America too.

I travelled in the long vacations from university by cargo boat, first on an extensive tour round the Mediterranean, and second, to the east coast of South America. It was a good way of travelling. There were usually only a few cabins on board and not more than ten passengers. The passengers were a very mixed bunch, and the crew, both officers and men, were fairly mixed also, save that the chief engineers were invariably Scots. It was, for a young man, enormously exciting and, indeed, heart-warming. The many days at sea with no duties to perform provided an admirable stimulus to the study of books which had remained unread during the university term. I think it was a worthwhile series of ventures. I only remember one moment of despair, when I was studying Adam Smith, and came to one of his most intricate chapters. At this stage I fear temptation was too great, and Adam Smith went through the open porthole. No doubt many would say this is one of the reasons why I did not make a better Chancellor of the Exchequer.

There was something immensely attractive to a Londoner like myself, with little experience of the world, in the men one met on those so-called cargo liners, especially the junior officers. They had a freedom and a frankness, a self-confidence and a pride in their country, which was altogether admirable. No doubt it led them at times to be improperly condescending to the inhabitants in the ports of the countries they visited. No doubt their behaviour in ports sometimes left much to be desired, but their hearts were warm and their personalities strong. They readily accepted a young city-bred classical scholar, not only as a passenger but, far more important, as a friend, and they taught me a great deal. I am afraid some of the lessons were of a kind that would draw the disapprobation of my more respectable constituents.

I remember the first time I visited a casino, I think it was called the Casino Utca, in Rio. It lay, unhappily for me, at the far end of the harbour where my ship was docked, unhappily because I swiftly lost all of the very small amount of money I had with me, and had to walk the whole way home. But it was a useful lesson, and much as I enjoy casinos, and preferably watching other people gamble, I have never since entered one with more than I can afford to lose, on the assumption, which has normally proved to be right, that I would lose the lot anyway.

There was an occasion when I was returning from Buenos Aires on a rather large liner called *The Highland Patriot*, and we docked in Santos alongside the much smaller cargo liner on which I had gone out to South America. A very pleasant evening was spent at the local night-club with the crew of the cargo liner, and I woke the next morning rather stiff and uncomfortable on the floor of the second mate's cabin; unfortunately it was the wrong ship. I had to take the train to São Paulo and then fly up to Rio to catch my own ship again, a journey not made any the more comfortable or agreeable by the fact that I had been sitting in the aircraft next to a group of American tourists who were blithely discussing the rumour that a European war had broken out the night before. They were, as it happened, wrong, but only by twelve months.

A lesson I learnt from that occasion was always to take care that you know where you are before you go to sleep. A lesson which is not without its value, so tradition would have it, in either House of

Parliament. Of course everyone knows the story of the elderly Peer who dreamed that he was addressing the House of Lords, and woke up to find that he was! I cherish the memory too of a time when James Stuart, then Secretary of State for Scotland, was addressing the House in his usual mild quiet way, when someone from the Back Benches called out, 'Speak up!'

'I am sorry,' replied James, 'I didn't think anyone was listening.'

For my own part I forgot this lesson once when I was Minister of Supply. I had been giving dinner to my scientific advisers, and we had been conducting a scientific analysis of the relative merits of various vintage ports. I had to return to the House of Commons for a vote and then remain on the Front Bench to listen to a Motion moved by Sir Gerald Nabarro. Gradually I became aware that something was amiss. I opened one eye cautiously trying to pretend that I had been awake all the time, only to hear some Member putting to the Chair as a Point of Order, 'Mr Speaker, is it in order for the Minister of Supply to snore so loudly that we cannot hear Sir Gerald Nabarro?' I am afraid Gerald never really forgave me, nor did I easily forgive the Whip on duty on the Front Bench who failed to wake me up in time.

The other valuable experience I had was being arrested in Buenos Aires by a local customs officer. On the way out I had been in São Paulo where I had bought two very small semiprecious stones for Beryl. Incidentally, I remember, possibly for the last time, saying to the shopkeeper that I was very sorry I had no Brazilian money, would he be prepared to take pounds sterling? To which he replied, he would rather have pounds sterling than anything else. That was indeed a long time ago. I left the ship in Buenos Aires, along with a German student, and we were stopped by the customs officers at the dock gate, who spoke to us in Spanish, which neither of us understood, and when they received no satisfactory reply to their incomprehensible questions, they took us into the police post and searched us. Then my two semi-precious stones, the total value of which must have been slightly over £10, were revealed. The excitement that ensued was worthy of a major jewel smuggler, not helped by my German companion who insisted on saying that they were diamonds. Our arguments took place in Spanish, but tempers were restored when I managed to produce the phrase, 'Señorita en Inglaterra'. So several hours later, after signing a long statement in Spanish, which I certainly did not understand, I was released, and through the good offices of the local agent of I.C.I. I eventually got the stones restored. But there was a clear lesson here. When in trouble with the police, particularly in a foreign country, patience, amiability and an infinite desire to please are the essential ingredients of escape.

My other main recollection of Buenos Aires is going to lunch there with some friends of my father's, called, I think, Martin, an English family of accountants, who had gone some years ago to set up in practice there. He was a very pleasant man, and he had the most charming wife, who was Irish, and they explained to me that from the moment she had married him her Irish relatives in Argentina had refused ever to talk to her again. Such was their recollection of the 'Troubles', and by Troubles they meant not what happened in the twentieth century, but in the nineteenth century. Many years later, when I came to try to deal with the problems of Northern Ireland, I often recalled Mrs Martin and her family.

Another voyage I made was round the Mediterranean ports, again in a cargo liner, and again largely in the company of the admirable members of the British crew. I saw a lot of things that would have been beyond the comprehension of anyone confined to the life of London. Above all, for the first time, I saw poverty and squalor in their starkest form. There were lovely things to see, contrasted with ugliness. The canal between Bizerta and Tunis, where the memory of the beauty of the flamingoes mingles with the not forgotten stench of the canal waters. The streets of Tunis and the bars crammed with every known form of French liquor, and the sweet scent of the jasmine that boys were selling from bar to bar. The majesty of the Pyramids and the Sphinx, and the luxury of the Mena House Hotel alongside them, contrasting so violently with the abject poverty of so many of the people, and the widespread afflictions of the children, who still had to beg in the streets.

When the boss called for tea
– 1948

The 1951 Election with Anthony Eden and Archie Stone,
President of Barnet Conservatives

At the Commonwealth
Trade and Economic
Conference, Montreal,
September 1958

The signing of the
E.F.T.A. Convention by
Chancellor Heathcote
Amory, December 1959

2

Into Politics

1939—1950

I T was in the course of the War that I made up my mind to go
into politics. Previously I had been looking forward to a career at
the Bar, and I had qualified as a barrister during the early months of
the War. But much changed in the years from 1939 to 1945. The
problems of personal finance were one consideration. In those days it
was very difficult for a young man starting at the Bar to earn a reasonable income for several years. This had been quite possible to contemplate in the late 1930s, while one was single, but it was clear when
1945 came that for a married man with a son to wait several years
before earning any means of sustaining his family was no longer
practicable. I had, moreover, become increasingly interested in the
whole process of Government during the war years, which I spent at
the Air Ministry. At the outbreak of war I volunteered for active
service, but I was rejected by all Services because of my poor eyesight.
I then managed to obtain a commission in R.A.F. Intelligence, and
went to work at the Air Ministry in a branch dealing with the Italian
Air Force. It was a fascinating time, and I learnt a great deal about
the methods of Intelligence, and particularly the remarkable achievements of the British cipher-breakers. A team led by Professor Last,
Professor of Ancient History at Brasenose College, Oxford, had learnt

how to crack the Italian Air Force ciphers, and we were able to predict their activities in advance with remarkable accuracy. Those were the days of what Churchill described as 'the wizard war', when British technology was achieving great triumphs.

After a fairly short spell at Fighter Command in their Operational Research Division, and some time as a pilot officer, later acting flight lieutenant, in Air Intelligence, I was asked by Ronnie Melville, then Principal Private Secretary to the Secretary of State for Air, Sir Archibald Sinclair, to join him in his office, and towards the end of the War I moved on to a branch known as S6, which was the Secretariat for the Air Staff.

This series of posts held much fascination, and I was extremely lucky, both in the people I encountered and in the insight I was able to obtain into the workings of a Government Department and a great Service. Sir Charles Portal, Sir Wilfred Freeman and Sir Maurice Dean are a few examples of the men of extraordinary talent and determination who were at the centre of our war effort. But my own particular master was Archie Sinclair, then Leader of the Liberal Party. He was an unusual man, I do not think a great Minister, or necessarily a great politician. But he was a man of principle and integrity to whom I owe a debt, above all, because he convinced me that politics was a profession that could be pursued with honour. This was a question which, in the minds of young men at that time, was not always easy to answer.

Archie Sinclair had a way of working very late into the night which did not suit me, because I preferred the early-morning hours. He was not very decisive, being inclined to answer a minute from the Chief of Air Staff, asking for a decision between A and B, roughly on the lines that 'Of course A is of the utmost importance, but, on the other hand, let us not neglect B'. In fact this worked pretty well and the relationship between him and Sir Charles Portal who was Chief of Air Staff and really ran the Air Force, between politician and practitioner, was a good one. Archie was meticulous in his relations with Members of Parliament, and from him I learnt a proper respect for them when they were acting in the interest of their constituents, together with a certain amount of technique in replying to their enquiries. He explained to me on one occasion, when I had drafted a letter saying 'No' to one request that a Member of Parliament had made but 'Yes' to the other, that I had made a deep psychological error by getting them the wrong way round. Always begin, he said, with the affirmative, with the agreement, then, regretfully, at the second stage come to your inability to meet the other point.

One rather bizarre episode took place while I was in his private office. A number of distinguished Air Force commanders overseas were to receive honours in the 1942 New Year's honours list, and I dutifully sent to them congratulations on behalf of the Secretary of State. As this was prior to publication I arranged for them to be sent in cipher, but I had not reckoned with the effect of New Year's Eve on the cipher officers. It was then the practice, in order to baffle the enemy cipher-breakers, to add some bits of a nursery rhyme at either end of the official message, and these normally would not appear in the decoded message. Alas, on this occasion, all did not go well. So Sir Arthur Tedder, C.-in-C. R.A.F. Middle East, received the following message: 'Little Boy Blue, Congratulations on your K.C.B. Go blow your horn. Signed Archibald Sinclair.' This naturally was not very well received. Tedder's reply was restrained, though to us baffling. It read, 'Secretary of State, Thank you very much for your congratulations; unfortunately the trumpet is not my favourite instrument. Signed Tedder.' I must say we had not the faintest idea what it was all about when it arrived, but we got to the bottom of the mystery and started to find what other messages had been treated the same way. A lot of time was spent, and a lot of faces were pretty red, before it was all sorted out.

In the course of working both in the Secretary of State's Private Office and in S6, I came to be more and more interested in the relationship between Government and private industry. It seemed to me increasingly clear that we should not return, after the War, to the previous relationship, and the Government was bound to play a much larger part than it had in the past.

There was no doubt that great adjustments would be required on both sides. Before the War bureaucrats and businessmen had always been very much at arm's length: there was a deep suspicion between them, bred largely of ignorance of each other's virtues. Clearly industry would have to cooperate far more closely in future. This would be made possible by the contacts that had been established between leading businessmen and the Civil Servants in whose Departments they had come to serve in a wartime role.

It was at that time that I first myself began to appreciate some of the great virtues of the British Civil Service, and how these could be developed after the War in a combined effort to increase Britain's prosperity. Also I learnt something of how remote bureaucracy could be from everyday life. I was in the fortunate position of being able to see Cabinet papers, which was, incidentally, an instruction in itself. I always remember one splendid example of the bureaucratic mind. There was a Committee appointed at a very high level indeed to report to the Cabinet on what arrangements should be made for 'Celebrating the termination of hostilities in Europe'. Some of the phrases remain in my mind still. The Cabinet was advised that a course should be steered between 'suppressing legitimate celebration' and 'organized mafficking'. One particular recommendation stood out. The Committee commented that it was a well-known fact that on such occasions the British public were inclined to light bonfires; this, they pointed out, with sagacity and perception, could give rise to danger of fires, so something should be done about it. They thought, on the whole, that it would be impracticable to try to impose a ban on the lighting of bonfires in celebration of the defeat of Hitler, and they offered to the Cabinet, as a practical alternative, the suggestion that bonfires should be lit officially and at safe intervals throughout the country by the National Fire Service.

The interface between Government and industry was going to present fascinating problems and exciting opportunities, and here I could see real opportunities in the future to use what ability I possessed on problems that really mattered. This I have always believed to be the real attraction of politics. Certainly financial gain is not the attraction, when you compare what a man may expect to earn in politics and what he could hope to earn in finance or industry. Public acclaim, the desire for publicity, is a possible motive. I always remember Iain Macleod once saying to me, 'Fame is the spur', but I am not sure that this is adequate in itself. In any case, as one comes to learn from bitter experience, fame carries its own handicaps with it, and a life led in public may do much to intrude on the happiness of a private life. No, I believe the real attraction of politics to the vast majority of those who are engaged is the opportunity to use one's talents in the tackling of major problems which really affect not only oneself and one's family, but one's whole country. The sense of service still runs deep in British politics as does the sense of principle. There can be few who enter politics without the ambition to become a Minister at least, and that is an ambition to carry responsibility on a scale greater than can be seen in any other walk of life. It can lead to great fulfilment. It can lead to great strain. It can lead to great unhappiness if you think that by your error you have damaged the lives of thousands. As Heine said, '*Du stolzes Herz! Du hast es ja gewollt! Du wolltest glücklich sein, unendlich glücklich, oder unendlich elend, stolzes Herz. Und jetzo bist du elend.*' – 'Proud heart! It was your desire! You wanted to be happy, eternally happy, or eternally sorry, proud heart. And now you are sorry.' – The governing of men is still an endless adventure, and it will be a sad day when there are no longer those who see it in that light.

So I set about trying to become a candidate for Parliament in the 1945 election. Beryl and I went from one selection committee to another, until finally I was chosen for Heston and Isleworth. Things were very different in those days because, on Churchill's instructions, the Conservative Party organization had virtually closed down during the War, and there remained active in each constituency only a handful of loyal enthusiasts. The Chairman of Heston and Isleworth was a man called Bob Salisbury, a cheerful extrovert who had built up a substantial business in cinema display advertising and who gave me an early warning that I should disregard anything he said after nine o'clock at night. We got on very well. We started by hiring a shop in the High Street as our offices, and buying the blotting paper and drawing pins and other stationery requirements. Then we tried to get a few helpers together. It was not easy, and the Conservative Party had a great disadvantage compared with our opponents, because the Trade-Union organization had remained intact and operating throughout the War. The people were friendly and helpful, though one could not help being angered from time to time by the superior people who were doing nothing themselves to help, but who approached one saying, 'Young man, where are all your canvassers? They have not called on me yet.'

Heston and Isleworth was a suburban West London constituency which would normally have been a good bet for the Conservatives but in fact, as a result of wartime movements, the population was far greater than normal, many houses were in shared occupation, and there were a surprising number of people who had moved there from Wales during the Depression bringing with them a deep radical Welsh tradition.

On the whole I enjoyed my first experiences of public meetings and canvassing. You get used to the charming woman who says, 'Well, young man, I think I would like to vote for you but I will have to ask Dad what he says,' and who then returns from the parlour a minute later to say, 'Sorry, Dad says we're Labour.' You get used to the people who say, 'Of course I vote Labour, when I'm out of work I go to the Labour Exchange, there aren't any Conservative Exchanges are there?' But, overwhelmingly, the impression I received from canvassing was one of warmth and friendship. I have always insisted on shaking hands with every elector on whom I call, whatever his Party views, and only in a handful of cases, over a span of ten elections now, have I met anyone who has refused to shake my hand. I still cling to the belief that there is importance in this, and that this is part of the contact between the elector and his Member of Parliament which still means a great deal for democracy in this country.

In the result we were heavily defeated. I suppose we should have expected this. Certainly when the Forces' vote, which on that occasion was counted early, came through, we could see the way things were going. There was a desire for change, a determination not to go back to the pre-war days. The Conservative Party had not much to offer at that time to those who wished to see change, and we relied heavily on the personality of Winston Churchill. There was no doubt about his popularity, or, indeed, the reverence, in which people held him, but as it turned out we overestimated the effect this would have on their voting. People distinguished between Churchill the War Leader, and the Conservative Party as a peacetime Government. It may well be that the strange political instinct of the British people proved right again on that occasion. When I was working for Winston in the late 1940s, he told me that after his defeat in the 1945 election, Lady Churchill had said to him, 'Well, Winston, it may be a blessing in disguise,' and how he had replied, 'If it is, it is a pretty effective disguise.' But, he added, 'On looking back on it, I think she was probably right.' There had not been an overthrow of individual liberty, which many, including Winston, had feared, and while he fought tooth and nail against the Socialists, I think he realized, as other lesser minds do not, that this country cannot permanently be governed by one Party, that we must operate within a framework where change is possible, and that what is essential is to ensure that change takes place within an agreed acceptance of basic political liberty, thereby leaving the opportunity always for further change when the electorate so desire.

Shortly after the election two things happened which confirmed my commitment to politics. One was my adoption as prospective Conservative candidate for Barnet, which was one of the most fortunate events of my life. The relations which Beryl and I have had with the Conservatives of Barnet for more than thirty years have been invariably happy and friendly.

The constituency of Barnet had been lost to Labour during the General Election, to most people's surprise. Our candidate had not been very effective, whereas the Labour man, Dr Stephen Taylor, later Lord Taylor, had impressed everyone very much. It was clearly a seat that was likely to return to the Conservative faith and there was a good deal of competition for the selection. The local association were determined to have a candidate who contrasted with the previous one, who had been a barrister of considerable distinction but had a certain excessive formality of manner. They were looking for someone young, fairly vigorous and who understood the feelings of the kind of people who lived in Barnet. We went through a whole series of processes, being interviewed by a selection committee, until finally the field was reduced to three, Robert Carr, Ian Orr-Ewing and myself. We appeared before a crowded meeting of association members at the main hall in Barnet, where we had in turn to address them and to answer questions. The final decision was taken by a ballot, in which I was fortunate enough to be chosen. This is the traditional procedure of the Conservative Party, and I still think that it is one that is hard to beat : it was certainly fair and simple.

My two opponents in the final vote, Robert Carr and Ian Orr-Ewing, now both adorning the House of Lords, became lifelong, and in the case of Ian and Joanie Orr-Ewing especially, very intimate friends.

However, Winston Churchill cast one slight doubt upon my adoption for Barnet : he said to me one day, 'Maudling, I hear you have been adopted for a constituency. Where is it ?'

'Barnet, sir,' I replied, 'where I live.'

'Oh,' he said, 'young man, great mistake, you will have a row with the bloody laundry first week.' As usual he was not all that wrong, because, although I never had a row with the laundry, I do recall setting out on polling day in the 1950 election, when the laundry basket had just arrived, and I opened it to find on top a very large piece of paper, with the words 'Vote Labour' on it in brilliant red ink.

Barnet suited me very well. I had been born in neighbouring Finchley and the people of Barnet were just the sort of people with whom I had been brought up, sharing a similar outlook and similar values : people who believed in integrity and in individual effort, but, at the same time, in personal responsibility. People of humour, friendliness, kindliness and patriotism. We have many friends there now, and have fought many elections.

The first Maudling to fight an election in Barnet in fact was not I but Beryl, who won a seat on the Hertfordshire County Council in 1949, for which she fought very hard, and in which capacity she worked very hard.

Throughout the many Parliamentary elections since my adoption I have had unfailing support. There are many people I should like to mention who have held office in the Barnet Conservative Association and its branches, but a list covering thirty years would demand a volume in itself, and to pick out any particular name would be invidious. There is only one exception I think I can make, Captain A. W. P. Fawcett, M.B.E., T.D., who has been my Agent now for over a quarter of a century and for whom I have the deepest respect and gratitude. Relations between an M.P. and his constituency association vary very much, not merely in different parts of the country, or between town and country, but even between adjoining constituencies. Habits and traditions vary. My belief has always been that success depends upon complete mutual confidence and frankness, and a desire not to interfere in one another's business or to confuse or blur responsibility. The association choose their candidate to represent them in Parliament, and when they have achieved his victory they expect him to represent them not as a delegate but as a representative who declares at all times sincerely his own views, after taking fully into account what they think, and of course the views of his constituents generally. The M.P. has no right to interfere in the working of the association, or the appointment of its officers. Of course there is always close and friendly contact and discussion, but the association have their place and the M.P. has his, and the more clear the distinction the better for the friendship and understanding between them. Incidentally, I think much the same is true about relations between an M.P. and the local authorities in his area : they both have their own job to do.

An M.P. represents his constituents in Parliament in two ways, first, by his participation in the conduct of national affairs, and, secondly, by making representations on behalf of his constituents to Ministers if at any time he thinks that any of them have been unjustly treated. It is not his job to interfere or attempt to interfere in the activities or decisions of local authorities, still less should he try to parade himself as the first citizen of the borough, if he be a borough member. That is the privilege of the Mayor, and over the last thirty years we have been very lucky in Barnet in the quality of our Mayors, and of the Chairmen of Council before them. I know that other M.P.s often think differently, and are consequently more active and prominent in local activities than I have been. I would not presume to argue who is right. We must each one of us follow our own judgement. But I do remember that after the count at the last election my defeated Liberal opponent, in what was supposed to be a speech of thanks to the returning officer, made a strong attack on me for 'neglecting the constituency'. I could not resist saying to her that if she were right and I had been neglecting my constituents, it was fairly clear from the voting that they liked being neglected.

The other development which confirmed my commitment to politics was the invitation to become a member of the Conservative Parliamentary Secretariat, later to become the Conservative Research Department. Ralph Assheton, subsequently Lord Clitheroe, extended the invitation to me, and I owe him a permanent debt of gratitude for it. It was a wonderful opportunity to join what was a very remarkable organization at its very beginning. Since then the Research Department has gone from strength to strength, and its influence on Conservative policy and thinking has been remarkable and, in my belief, invariably beneficial.

After the War politics had become much more professional. The days of the amateur who could argue entirely from his own personal knowledge were passing. Parliamentary spokesmen for the Opposition needed a sort of unofficial Civil Service to back them up with facts and arguments. I remember an occasion when a distinguished Backbench M.P. of long standing had been successful in the ballot for Private Members' Motions, and found somewhat to his dismay that he had to move a Motion on the state of the economy. He asked me for help and suggestions, which I gladly gave him, but as our conversation continued he seemed to grow more uneasy. Finally, he burst out, 'That is all very well, Reggie, I am sure, but answer me this one. I am told the National Debt is more than £2,000 million. When on earth are we going to pay it back?' Something more systematic was required to furnish Opposition spokesmen with a factual basis for their policies, and their arguments, and inevitably with this 'Shadow Civil Service', as with the official Civil Service, those whose duty was to provide the facts and figures found themselves drawn into the business of advising on and influencing policy itself.

David Clarke was head of the organization. He had considerable experience and knowledge, and made a very good head of a Shadow Civil Service. My main colleagues under him were Enoch Powell and Iain Macleod. Between us we divided the business. Iain was particularly responsible for social problems, in which he had a close interest. I was detailed to look after economic and financial matters, and Enoch did a variety of jobs, including town and country planning.

We were none of us experts and did not pretend to be. It would have been a great mistake to do so. It has always seemed to me that any Minister who claims to be an expert in his own right is bound to run into trouble, for experts always disagree, and the Minister cannot be more professional than his own professionals. You have only to contrast as Chancellors of the Exchequer Hugh Dalton and R. A. Butler. Dalton knew a good deal about economics from the academic point of view, but I do not think that anyone would regard him as having been a good Chancellor. Rab, on the other hand, knew little about economics but a great deal about people. He based his judgement on individual issues not so much on an intellectual appreciation of the factors involved, as an assessment of the merits of his various advisers. 'Do you not think,' he would say, 'that in these matters Edwin is more sound than Robert?' Not a very scientific method perhaps, but in practice a very effective one, and certainly the reason why he was about the most successful Chancellor of recent years.

The great advantage of the position I held, as a non-economist, was that I had to learn what the economists were saying and try to interpret it in lay terms. Advice was not lacking from the academic world, from business, from the City. A flood of advice came in from people of great distinction. The job really was to interpret this in political terms, by which I mean terms that can be understood by the ordinary elector. It certainly was a good training and the basic lesson was that there are really no economic problems, only political ones, and that you should rely on no one who is unable to explain in simple practical terms the technical ideas which he is trying to develop.

I shared a room with Enoch Powell for two years, and I look back on those times with considerable affection. I do not recall meeting anyone else with a mind that had such a power of acquiring knowledge. At one stage when Enoch was detailed to become the expert on town and country planning, he acquired the standard textbook and read it from page to page, as an ordinary mortal would read a novel. Within a matter of weeks he had fully grasped both the principles of the problem and the details of the legal situation. Within a matter of a few months he was writing to the author of the textbook, pointing out the errors that he had made. I do not think I had any real arguments with Enoch in those days. They came later.

Iain Macleod was my closest friend. I have missed his presence in politics enormously. He had colour and spirit, and a humanity which was unique, and the gap his passing left in the Tory Party has never been filled. We talked, and argued, and thought, and discussed about politics day after day, but we were never, I believe, solemn, because we realized that you do not have to be solemn in order to be serious. Often we went to lunch at Iain's club, Crockford's, and I marvelled at his facility with cards, and his astonishing memory. There were occasions in the bar at Crockford's before lunch when he would suddenly see a fellow enthusiast and say, 'What do you think about this hand I had three weeks ago?' and then detail from memory all four hands dealt, and the way the sequence of play had taken place. He was godfather to one of my sons, and a very good godfather too. I remember him saying one day at lunch to his godson, 'Here is a quid for you, and here is another quid if you undertake to put it on the favourite in the 3.30 tomorrow at Newmarket.' Iain had humour and humanity, and warmth, a passionate sense of purpose, and a deep understanding of his fellow men and women. I can think of no other politician in my experience who has had those qualities in such a combination. 'ὃν οἱ θεοὶ φιλοῦσιν ἀποθνῄσκει νέος' – 'Whom the gods love dies young.'

The greatest good fortune I had at the Research Department was the contact with Anthony Eden and Winston Churchill. It was exciting for a young and inexperienced man to meet the great names, and interesting to assess them. It meant a lot if a member of the Shadow Cabinet took you seriously and showed an interest in you. Sir David Maxwell-Fyfe and Oliver Lyttelton were good examples. Others were a little more precious, and one could assess how one was doing oneself by the degree and quality of attention which one received from them. But taking it all in all, it really was a remarkable experience which could only happen within a Party in Opposition, for a young man without any previously established Party service, whose qualification was mainly measured in terms of enthusiasm, to be able to deal on such intimate terms with the great figures of the day.

One of my early tasks was to help Anthony Eden in the drafting of the speeches he was making on financial and economic matters. He was, of course, the supreme expert in Foreign Affairs, but his know-

ledge of domestic subjects was more limited and, therefore, the scope
for helping him was more considerable. No one could have been more
considerate or more helpful, and, happily for me, the sort of ideas
which I was developing coincided with his own. Two themes were
developed. One was the idea of a property-owning democracy, the
other, the basic relationship between freedom and order. Indeed he
chose the phrase 'Freedom and Order', the theme of my first *Spectator*
article, as the title for his collected volume of speeches. I believe the
speeches that he made on these subjects had some considerable influence on the development of postwar Conservative thinking, and it
was a privilege to make some contribution to them.

But, of course, the great experience was Winston Churchill. I have
never met, and I am sure I shall never meet, a man cast in the same
mould. Perhaps it was an age of titans – Bob Menzies, for example, or
Smuts. Perhaps one is merely deluding oneself in thinking that the
personalities then were on a larger scale than one meets today. But
whatever the truth or falsehood of the generality, Winston stood alone.
There was a power, a vision and a magic about the man which I have
encountered nowhere else.

My job as a member of the Research Department was to help him
with the background work on his speeches, providing facts, checking
references – occasionally, with great daring, criticizing what he proposed to say. I remember so well our first meeting. I was sent down to
Chartwell, bidden to appear at 4 p.m., and I was duly waiting in his
Private Secretary's office. In came the great man, clad in his famous
boiler suit. 'Ah, Maudling,' he said, 'I see you have arrived, come
and have a whisky and soda. Of course,' he said, after a moment's
reflection, 'there is tea if you would prefer it.' I did not prefer it,
and my relation with the great man thereby got off to a satisfactory
start.

We were at that time developing a new postwar economic policy for
the Conservative Party. A group headed by Rab, of which I was
secretary, produced a statement called the Industrial Charter, which
included a workers' charter, dealing specifically with industrial relations. On the whole it marked a substantially different approach for
postwar Conservative philosophy. The role of the Government in
industry was accepted on a far greater scale than before. While the
philosophy was still essentially one of private enterprise, the Party had
come to recognize that private enterprise alone was not enough, that
the Government had a very definite role to play and that indeed if the

Government did not play that role then private enterprise could not develop its full potential in the interests of the country. Though in line with the thinking of Rab in particular, and of Harold Macmillan, it marked a certain new departure, and while it was welcomed by many people, particularly by the men with industrial experience, who had come to play a larger part in the Conservative Party as the influence of the old knights of the shires and landed gentry declined, there was still a good deal of antipathy to it among the traditionalists.

Winston did not play much part in it. His attitude to economic problems was a fairly cavalier one. These things, he felt, should take care of themselves, and who is to say, in the light of experience, that he was wrong? I remember a dinner he gave once just before he was due to make a speech on economic policy in the House of Commons. Lord Cherwell was there in the capacity Winston described as 'The scientific lobe of my brain'. I was there as assistant, to take notes. The main guest was Geoffrey Crowther, who, someone had explained to Winston, was as editor of *The Economist* a bit of a dab hand at these economic problems. Over dinner Winston explained the lines of the speech he was going to make, which, of course, was robust and straightforward. Then he invited Geoffrey to give his views, which he did, as always, with coherence and eloquence. He dwelt at some length on the then fashionable economic controversy, namely, the relative merits of cheap money and dear money. Winston grew steadily more impatient, till finally, interrupting his guest, he said, 'Mr Crowther, this is all very interesting, but I should tell you that although I was Chancellor of the Exchequer for five years, I never understood that bucket-shop side of the Treasury.' Sometimes when I hear the long and intricate arguments about the money supply, M_1 and M_3, and how it should be managed and controlled, I look back to the simple wisdom Winston then expressed.

But, as for the Industrial Charter, he played no part in its formation. It was approved at a Party Conference in Brighton in 1947; I had, in fact, myself, as candidate for Barnet, moved the resolution that the Charter be adopted as Conservative policy. I was working for Winston on his concluding speech to the Conference and we came to the topic of the Industrial Charter. 'Give me five lines, Maudling,' he said, 'explaining what the Industrial Charter says.' This I did. He read it with care, and then said, 'But I do not agree with a word of this.'

'Well, sir,' I said, 'this is what the Conference has adopted.'

'Oh well,' he said, 'leave it in,' and he duly read it out in the course of his speech, with the calculated coolness which he always accorded to those passages in his speeches, rare as they were, which had been drafted by other people, before he went back to the real meat of his own dictation.

For it was his constant practice to dictate his speeches in detail and to read every word of them. They were typed in a peculiar way, on a large typewriter, on octavo paper, with each paragraph slanting to the right. His spectacles were such that he was able to stand well back from the desk on which his notes were perched, and appear to be improvising, but, in fact, he rarely, if ever, did. His habit varied little. The night before any speech he would retire to bed fairly late, saying, 'Tomorrow, Maudling, I will need no notes. After all, I have been brutalized by many years of politics, why should I need a long text?' Invariably the next day at an early hour, the buzzer from his bedroom went for his secretary, and a series of them were summoned to take dictation.

He composed his speeches not as a coherent whole, but in individual sections on various topics. Section A, for example, would be six pages on the iniquity of the Labour Government, section B might be something to do with agriculture, section C could be a dissertation about Foreign Affairs (in particular relationships with the United States). All these sections were dictated separately, then, at the end of the morning, when he had dictated enough and it had been typed, he would sit in bed shuffling the various sections into order. The astonishing thing, and I never discovered the secret of how he did it, was that the result was invariably a speech of total coherence and apparently a perfectly consecutive order of ideas.

It was the same with broadcasts. The text had to be carefully prepared; he accepted ideas with courtesy, but seldom used them, because his own ideas were prolific enough. He accepted criticism too, if it was tactfully made and based on some substance. We had a conversation once when he was drafting a broadcast, in which he was going to say, 'The Socialists spend your money with a song in their hearts.' I said to him, 'Sir, that is not entirely fair, you are quoting the Chancellor of the Exchequer, Hugh Dalton, and when he used the phrase he was referring specifically to expenditure upon the depressed areas and to nothing else.'

'Maudling,' said the great man, 'I have been in politics since long before you were born, and I have never yet been deterred by any consideration of what is fair.'

'Yes, sir,' I was constrained to reply, 'but you know people will think that this is unfair.'

'Maudling,' he said, 'my boy, that is a totally different matter, strike it out.'

And so one learnt many things simply by contact with the world's greatest man. Though possibly the phrase I remember best had nothing to do with me. There was a debate in the House in which Winston was taking part, and he was interrupted by Nye Bevan, an opponent for whom, incidentally, he had both a deep respect and genuine affection, though he did his best to conceal both. Bevan's point was this, 'Why should the House trust the judgement of the Right Honourable Gentleman when three days before the fall of France he said to us that he had full confidence in the French Army?' Winston rose slowly to his feet, with the simple but devastating comment, 'Should I that day have said the opposite?'

Both Churchill and Bevan had a mastery of the House of Commons that few people, save Iain Macleod at his best and Harold Macmillan, have since displayed. I remember when Bevan was being attacked as Minister of Health by the Tory Front-bench spokesman, who made a passionate but not altogether effective speech about the iniquities of the National Health Service. Bevan's opening sentence in his reply was a killer. 'Mr Speaker,' he said, 'I have always thought it a great mistake for a weak man to use strong adjectives.' That was a comment on a level with Harold Macmillan's famous rebuke to George Brown after he had lost the Leadership battle with Harold Wilson : 'The Right Honourable Gentleman should not allow defeat to go to his head.' Maybe it is the passing of the years which affects one's judgement, but I do not remember hearing in recent years dialectical blows of that formidable quality.

And there are so many other recollections of Winston. Two particularly concern Oliver Lyttelton. The first is the story he told about one of the Cabinet meetings towards the end of the War, when minds were turning towards peacetime reconstruction and Lord Woolton was in charge of this. Winston was not all that interested at the moment in postwar reconstruction; he reckoned that he still had to win the War. He had a technique when things which he found rather boring were on the Cabinet agenda of deferring them till the end, and then claiming pressure of lunchtime, or, as apparently he used to say when that well-known vegetarian Lord Cherwell was holding forth, 'Beetroot time.' Lord Woolton had apparently prepared a splendid thesis in the best traditions of Keynes, on how in future to deal with booms and slumps. In future when there was a boom the Government should spend less and so reduce public demand, when there was a slump the Government should arrange for more to be spent and so increase demand and prevent unemployment. Winston apparently listened patiently to this exegesis as the minutes of lunchtime ticked by, and when it came to an end he finished the discussion quite simply by saying, 'I understand quite clearly what you mean. We should arrange to have a salute the slump week every now and again.'

The other Churchillism I remember in connection with Oliver Lyttelton was when I was working for Winston in his room in the House of Commons during the 1945 Parliament, when Attlee was Prime Minister. Attlee had been making a speech, and Oliver came in to tell Winston that it had really been quite a good one, and the House had been impressed. 'Ah,' said Winston, 'they tell me that if you feed a grub on royal jelly it becomes a Queen Bee.' In fact he had a great and sincere respect for Attlee. But I wonder how many subsequent Heads of Governments in different countries could be described in those terms?

Winston had a strange relationship, almost a love/hate relationship, with Parliament and public life in the Opposition years of the late 1940s. He hated being in Opposition, yet he could not withdraw from the conflict. Once I was lunching with him at Chartwell, after working for him on a speech he was due to make. He said, 'I hate having to go to London to make these speeches.' Then, after a few moments' reflection, he added, 'I would hate even more not having to go to London to make these speeches,' and with that he fortified himself by pouring part of his glass of champagne over his cold ham, a traditional practice which he always observed.

It is said of Winston, of course, that he drank a great deal of alcohol: in fact this is not true. He loved good wine and brandy, he had champagne, port and brandy at every lunch or dinner, but the amount he drank was very modest, and although he often had a whisky and soda at hand when he was working, it was always a very small whisky with a large amount of soda, and he drank it slowly. His tastes were simple and definite. The champagne was always Pol-Roger 34. When he died Mme Pol-Roger decreed that henceforth all the labels on her champagne should carry a black band in memory of the great man, which I believe they do to this day. His port was from a pipe given him by some Spanish grandee. His brandy varied, but was always good. Wherever he went in the late 1940s in Opposition he took with him, along with personal staff and the apparatus of composing his books – typewriters, red boxes and documents – a simple wine case containing the champagne, the port and the brandy, with all of which he was generous to all around him.

Of course supplies of the comforts of life were very restricted at that time. When Winston came back from a meeting with Stalin, a large consignment of caviare and vodka was found in the back compartment of the R.A.F. bomber in which he was travelling. The Prime Minister was informed. 'A magnificent gift,' he said, 'please arrange for it to be shared among my friends and colleagues.' Two days later in the Air Ministry department where I was, we received a call from the Soviet embassy, 'Where,' they said, 'is the caviare and vodka for our National Day celebration tomorrow which you kindly transported back in the Prime Minister's aircraft?' A rapid search throughout London was conducted, and a fair amount was recovered, but it was a hair-raising moment.

Looking back on that time, I have no doubt that of all the joys that have come to me in my political career, none surpasses, or matches, the privilege of working with Winston Churchill. He was, as I have said, a man set apart, a man of Titanic stature and deep humanity. Few generations have seen such a man.

3

Back-bencher to Economic Secretary

1950–1955

I W A S elected to the House of Commons in February 1950 and
I made my maiden speech on 10 March 1950. I was followed by
another maiden speaker, Desmond Donnelly. We were then both
formally congratulated by Sir Hartley (now Lord) Shawcross, then
Attorney-General, who was speaking for the Government. The theme
I adopted was one that I have pursued consistently ever since, namely,
the danger of inflation and the need to deal with it by reducing taxation, increasing incentive and encouraging production. I stressed that
inflation was then the most important of the economic difficulties
facing us, though the inflation rate in those days was laughably small
compared with recent experience. In those days the problem was
genuinely one of demand inflation, of 'too much money chasing too
few goods' – the Labour Chancellor's phrase. The problem of wage
inflation as we now know it had still not emerged and everyone was
concentrating, in line with good Keynesian principles, on the need to
reduce purchasing power, particularly by a Budget surplus. I commented on this concept as follows:

In dealing with the problem of inflation much emphasis is nowadays laid on the need for a Budget surplus. That is a rather novel idea but it is one which is now accepted, I believe, on both sides of the House. The point I wish to make is that a Budget surplus is not necessarily the best way, in every case, to counter the danger of inflation. It depends partly on how the surplus is achieved. A surplus based on increased taxation rather than on decreased Government expenditure may be positively harmful; and if we are mesmerized by the idea of a Budget surplus we may tend to forget the other methods of countering inflation, such as increased personal savings or increased production.

I then went on to advocate some measures to increase savings and to encourage production by reducing direct taxation, particularly on average earnings, using the following phrase, 'I advance these statistical considerations, therefore, as some backing for the argument, which I believe has much validity, that the impact of P.A.Y.E. on weekly earnings is a very great disincentive to production.' The measure I specially recommended was a reduction in the rate of marginal taxation falling on lower incomes, and I supported it with this argument :

I know that any such alteration would involve the Treasury in a substantial loss of revenue, but the point is that that loss of revenue might be more than counterbalanced by the gain in production which would arise from such relief.

The main point I want to make is that a Budget surplus is, in many cases, a good way of tackling the problem of inflation, but not always, and not irrespective of the means by which it is achieved. The method of applying leeches, when first used by the medical profession was a great advance, but it became customary to apply leeches whatever the patient or the complaint. I think there is some analogy here. If financial leeches, if I may use such an expression to describe tax gatherers, are applied they may be very useful indeed with a patient suffering from galloping inflation, but if applied too long and too assiduously the effect may be not to increase production or reduce inflationary pressure, but to drain strength from the patient and make ultimate recovery more painful and more prolonged. We cannot, in this country, tax ourselves into prosperity.

I was very fortunate thirteen years later, when Chancellor of the Exchequer, to be able to carry out my own suggestions, both in principle and in a fair degree of detail. They still seem to me relevant today after the passage of more than twenty-eight years.

My first eighteen months in Parliament under the dying rule of Clement Attlee were interesting and instructive, if somewhat frustrating. It is always more agreeable to be a Back-bencher in Opposition than in Government, because the opportunities are infinitely greater, and I think those of us who entered in 1950, a few of whom still remain, took full advantage of it. We had also a certain independence of mind. There was an occasion when Attlee was visiting America and the Tory Whips had decided in his absence to call a snap Division which could have defeated the Government. Robert Carr and I and one or two others went to the Chief Whip and told him that we were not prepared to vote against the Government when the Prime Minister was abroad on national business. We were given fairly clearly to understand that ours was not to reason why. Nevertheless, I think that our representations were not ineffective.

With the autumn of 1951 came another election and the return of a Conservative Government. This was the opportunity for which many of us had been waiting, though it took a little time to make itself felt. It was in early 1952 that I was dining with the 1950 Dining Club of M.P.s elected that year and a senior messenger from the Whips' Office came to say that I was wanted by the Prime Minister. I found it hard to believe him until he returned fairly shortly afterwards to say quite simply, 'The Boss wants you, sharpish like.' So I went. He offered me the post of Parliamentary Secretary to the Ministry of Civil Aviation. I was in two minds about accepting it and asked for a little time to think it over. It was, of course, a great honour to be offered any position in the Government, but my interests lay in the mainstream of financial and economic policy, and I felt I could be of more service in a Back-bench capacity in dealing with these problems than by going, albeit as a Parliamentary Secretary, to a highly specialized Ministry. However, Rab, as so often, gave me wise advice. He indicated that by accepting this position I would be making a first step in the direction of the Treasury, over which he was then presiding. So I accepted the Prime Minister's offer.

The Minister of Transport and Civil Aviation then was Jack Maclay, one of the kindest and best people I have ever met. I was slightly embarrassed by the encounter we then had. I went and knocked on the door of his room and was bidden to enter. 'Hello, Reggie,' he said. 'What can I do for you?'

'Well, Jack,' I replied, 'I am your new Parliamentary Secretary.'

'Oh,' he said, somewhat aghast, 'are you?' The truth is that Winston had not bothered to tell him. However, he acquiesced readily in the appointment and for the short time we were together I enjoyed his leadership enormously. He was replaced by Alan Lennox-Boyd, a man of different character but equal quality. Alan brought enormous enthusiasm to the jobs he did in Government, though I think that of all he did the Colonial Office was closest to his heart. He was an ideal senior Minister to work for, for the basic reason that he treated his juniors as human beings, was absolutely open with them, sought and listened to their views, and so cultivated in them the confidence without arrogance which is essential to Ministerial success.

At that time we were still in the throes of unwinding from a World War and the danger of American domination of world civil flying was the main concern of my Department. Indeed, so deeply was this felt in Whitehall, that towards the end of the war a scheme had been solemnly canvassed in parts of the Air Ministry for total Governmental or military control of air transport, in the early years after the War, ostensibly as a means of dealing with the practical difficulties that still hung over the recent battlefield, but in fact in order to prevent the Americans using their overwhelming position of practical superiority to scoop the whole pool.

It was not long before I found myself involved with the Treasury. I was instructed to speak for the Government in the course of the debates on the Finance Bill, which were then all on the floor of the House and, consequently, extremely protracted. It was the first time that a Parliamentary Secretary for another Department had been allowed to speak on behalf of the Treasury.

In November 1952, Sir Arthur Salter left the Treasury, and I was appointed Economic Secretary, a post which I held for some three years. I think on the whole it was the most exciting and most satisfying time of my political career. This was for three reasons, first, the personality of the Chancellor, second, the quality of the Treasury Civil Servants, and, third, the fascinating nature of the problems in which the Economic Secretary was involved.

Rab was, as I have stressed already, one of the great postwar Chancellors. During the period in which he held the office a real advance was made in the prosperity of the British people, which is as good a standard to judge by as any other. His great strength lay in his ability to bring the best out of those who were working for him. I had noticed this in the days of the Research Department, and I noticed it even more at the Treasury. If you went to talk to Rab about some complicated problem with your own view on it still unclear, it was remarkable how in the course of discussion with him your own ideas clarified and seemed to fall into place. It is a great gift to be able to inspire people to think with you, as well as work with you, and to bring out of them more than they could have produced unaided. Rab had this gift in full measure.

1952–5 was a period of economic liberalization and progress. There were still wartime restrictions to be dismantled and there was an immense amount of progress to be made. Rab predicted that we could double our standard of living in twenty-five years, which seemed at the time a hopelessly optimistic target, but he was well on the way to achieving it when he ceased to be Chancellor. Public expenditure had been too high and so had taxes. It was a time for reforming both. It was a time for unleashing the enterprise of British industry and business. It was a time of encouragement and inspiration.

As a very young Economic Secretary – I was then only thirty-six – I had the good fortune to undertake some weighty responsibilities. I had to deputize for Rab at the World Bank and I.M.F. meeting in 1953, and although I was provided by the Treasury with the most splendid briefs on every subject, it was a stretching experience. Not only were Britain's interests deeply involved in what happened : we were still the second world power in monetary terms and what we did and said had an influence far beyond our own shores. We had, moreover, a very special responsibility still for the whole Commonwealth.

I remember leading the annual deputation of Commonwealth Finance Ministers to call on the American Secretary of the Treasury. Flanked by a great team of senior and wise Ministers from South Africa to India, I had to put the case, which at that time we put once a year, for an increase in the price of gold. I need not have worried about my task. George Humphrey, the then Secretary of the Treasury, received us with his usual cordiality and listened carefully to what I had to say. At the end of it he said, 'Reggie, I do not quite understand your argument. What you appear to be saying is that the gold I am buying at the present moment I should pay more for than I am doing.'

'But, George,' I said, 'in the last year you have not bought any gold at all, you have been selling it.'

'Oh,' he said, 'have I? That is interesting.' It was an agreeable occasion and vastly reassuring to such an inexperienced Junior Minister.

Not that the post of Economic Secretary was without its difficulties. One of my tasks was to receive, on behalf of the Chancellor, trade deputations who were seeking a reduction of purchase tax on their product. One such deputation came from the piano manufacturing industry. I was much impressed by their arguments, and I forwarded a recommendation to that effect to Rab. It was a little embarrassing a day or two later when my mother-in-law rang me up and said she was thinking of buying a piano and should she do so before the Budget or wait till afterwards. Biting on the bullet I did the only possible thing, and advised her to buy irrespective of any tax considerations. From Budget day onwards I was a little unpopular. But, of course, that is one of the penalties of being a Treasury Minister. On one occasion shortly before a Budget I called at the local garage for some petrol and, seeing a car there that interested me, enquired about the possibilities of part-exchanging my present model in order to acquire it. As I drove away, ruminating on what the garage proprietor had said, I suddenly realized that whatever I did thereafter was bound to be regarded as some hint about which way the Budget was likely to go.

The truth simply expressed is just this, that the life of a Treasury Minister is a lonely one. For many weeks before the Budget he cannot speak to any of his friends and for many weeks afterwards he will be lucky if any of his friends will speak to him.

In fact I have every reason to be grateful, as Economic Secretary, both to Rab as Chancellor, and to the Treasury officials. It really was a remarkable experience to combine responsibility for important matters at a relatively early age, with the experience of working with some of the clearest and most penetrating intellects in the whole of the British Government. For whatever may be said from time to time about Treasury Civil Servants, and often it is far from complimentary, that description is the simple truth. Just as I have found, over the years, in international conferences, that the British Civil Service are intellectually the equal, if not the superior, of any other, save perhaps the French, so it always seemed to me that the Treasury Civil Servant is normally one grade superior in capacity and understanding to his colleagues in other Departments. I suppose on the whole it was not to be wondered at; after all at that time the Permanent Secretary at the Treasury was also head of the Home Civil Service, and it would not be surprising if he kept the brightest men for his own Department.

But the great advantage was to be able to operate in practice with responsibility in fields which I had thought about and talked about previously in purely theoretical terms. One learnt a lot. Exchange control, for example, was the responsibility then of the Economic Secretary, and I soon learnt the difficulty of bureaucratic decision-making when I had to purport to decide which applications for permission to invest in overseas ventures were in the national interest and which were not. I learnt a great deal too about taxation. It surprised me at the time that the Treasury's attitude to taxation was of a rather negative character. There was a pretty clear gap between the Treasury and the Inland Revenue, the heads of both Departments reporting independently direct to the Chancellor, and their independence was jealously guarded. The result was that very little thought in practice was given to the use of taxation, in the volume in which it was necessary, as a positive factor in shaping and encouraging our economic development.

But really I think the greatest benefit I obtained from those years as Economic Secretary was the confirmation of my earlier ideas about economic policy, and the conviction that money should be the servant of human beings not their master, that economics is about people not about ideas, and for that reason there are really no economic problems, only political ones. The purpose of economic policy was to maximize the well-being of the country, and the purpose of fiscal policy in principle was to ensure that so far as possible the national prosperity filtered through to everoyne in shares that were as fair in terms of worth and effort and need as human thought could, in practice, make them. The greatest lesson of all was the limitations upon economic policy, the uncertainty of prediction. One learnt that trying to guide an economy was rather like an amateur trying to steer a ship, the time lags are so great, the detailed consequences often so unpredictable. You turn the wheel in one direction and for a long while the vessel does not appear to respond at all, then suddenly it does, and when it does you realize that you are already too late to make the correction of course that has already become necessary.

My duties as Economic Secretary took me to many countries across the world. The journey I remember best was to the Indian sub-continent, to take part in the 1953 Colombo Plan meeting in Delhi. I went first to Ceylon. It is a superbly beautiful island. I well recall the first sight of it from the aircraft, in its brilliant Indian Ocean setting, and, equally, the extraordinary colours of the whole country from the tropical colours of the vegetation to the clear pinks and blues of the women's clothes and the dramatic yellow of the Buddhist priests. Unfortunately the quality of Government did not entirely live up to the quality of the environment. Politics there hardly followed the accepted English practices. There had been an election just before I visited the island, and they were in the throes of a series of election petitions. One in particular was brought on the grounds that the victorious candidate sensing possible defeat had hired a herd of elephants to trample down the polling booths in the district where his opponent was being too successful. The internal clashes with the Tamils had not then really begun on a serious level, but there appeared to be an unease about the island and a widespread feeling of political uncertainty. It has been much the same since.

Pakistan I had visited on the way. Those were the days when Ghulam Mohammad was in charge. The division of the sub-continent was not all that old and tensions remained. The Pakistanis were coming to grips with the unique problem of running a country divided into two parts separated by more than one thousand miles of territory, which, if not hostile, was at any rate not exactly friendly. Relations with Britain were good and our reception was cordial. We were considering making a substantial contribution to the setting up of the Sui Gas Project, which was very important to the industrial development of the country and which has since proved to be a substantial factor in their economic progress.

From Ceylon we went via Bombay to Delhi. Bombay at that time was governed by the redoubtable Morarji Desai, who was renowned for two things, first the competence and integrity of his Government, and secondly, his passionate opposition to any form of alcohol. Precautions were taken in advance by my thoughtful staff. I was issued with a standard permit, which I still cherish, authorizing me, as a foreigner, to acquire, transport and consume one pint of foreign liquor. There were a number of conditions on the standard form, one of which, in my case, had been struck out. Curiosity aroused I managed to decipher what had been excluded; it was the condition that 'the holder shall not get drunk in a public place'. I wonder how many other people can claim to have received an exclusive licence to get drunk in public in Bombay in the 1950s. My other precaution was to take a bottle of whisky in my official briefcase. This gave rise to slight apprehension when travelling from the airport to the city in the official car. We were stopped at a road block. I asked the A.D.C. who was escorting me, 'What happens here?'

'This is where we search foreigners' bags for whisky,' he replied with an entirely straight face. I was relieved when diplomatic immunity carried us unchecked through the soldiers who were manning the checkpoint.

I have been to Delhi on more than one occasion, staying sometimes with the High Commissioner, sometimes in a hotel and once with our

old friend, Michael Clapham, when he was B.O.A.C.'s manager there.
It is an immensely impressive city. In the 1950s I was struck not only
by its spaciousness and beauty, but by the extraordinary preservation
of some of the British traditions. A garden party was held, for example,
in the grounds of the former Vice-Regal home; the Bengal Lancers
were on duty just as they had been under the British, and when a
banquet was given in the Vice-Regal dining-room, the multiplicity of
servants waiting at table were still controlled by a series of what looked
like traffic lights on the wall which changed colour whenever the
waiters had to serve, to clear away, or what have you.

Some things I must confess were a little different. When the great
Nehru addressed the opening of the Colombo Plan conference in the
Parliament building, one could not help noticing the numerous
pigeons that kept flying round above his head in the vast ceiling of the
building, and wondering whether they were going to behave themselves throughout the proceedings! Equally, though the Indian hospitality was warm and forthcoming, two solid hours of Indian music
after dinner on the Presidential balcony, accompanied only by soda
water, was a fairly rigorous experience.

But to move away from frivolities, the substance was immensely
impressive. There was no doubt of the abiding goodwill between the
Indian and British peoples and it was immensely heartening to sense
and to feel it. Whatever had been said, at the time of independence,
in bitterness and anger, had by then died away, just as Winston had
become reconciled to Nehru to the point at which it was reported they
sang Harrow songs together at a dinner in the House of Commons.
So the British and the Indians had settled down to their new relationship. Indians are infinitely gentle people, as the British sometimes can
be, though not always.

We had left behind us in India some of the things that matter most
of all – not so much the roads and the bridges and the physical
inheritance, but the traditions of democracy, of respect for law and
independent Courts of Justice, and a very high quality indeed of
public servants. Relations between the British and the Indian Civil
Service, and this, of course, includes Pakistan, had always been close
and cordial. They had learnt much from Whitehall, and they appreciated what they had learnt.

It is very hard until you go there to appreciate the enormous difficulty which the sheer facts of size and geography impose on those who
try to govern a country the size of India on a democratic basis. It is

eternally to their credit that they made so much progress and I believe we can claim some credit for what we left behind.

What is true of the Civil Service is true of the armed forces also, and this is not unimportant in the progress of a developing country. To have an army that the people respect but do not fear is an asset that is as rare as it is valuable. One of my happiest moments in India was when my train was waiting in a station between Delhi and Agra (not an uncommon experience, true), and I saw among the crowd of poor peasants and their families squatting on the opposite platform a young Indian soldier walking along in uniform, smart, erect, obviously self-confident, and apparently conscious of the responsibility that rested on him and his colleagues. He was a man, one felt instinctively, who understood what was meant by discipline, and understood that the purpose of discipline was service to others. Perhaps it was starry-eyed of me, but he appeared to personify the best of the British tradition that was still cherished in India. It will take a long time before it can be seen whether this judgement was right, but I am still hopeful that it was not all that far wrong.

4

Minister of Supply

1955–1957

W H E N Anthony Eden became Prime Minister in 1955, he promoted me to Minister of Supply, which was my first full Ministerial post, and which carried with it the privilege of becoming a member of the Privy Council. This was a great honour at the age of thirty-eight and after only five years in the House of Commons, and I was deeply grateful to Anthony for the confidence he thereby showed in me. I have always been happy to know that he never came to regret it. It was a strange Department, and the target of a good deal of criticism, much of it justified. It was supposed to be concerned mainly with the supply of munitions to the three Services, and this was a large part of the routine work of the Department, but in addition it had responsibility for the aircraft-production industry generally. The Government exercised a great deal of influence over the industry because, with the scale of modern projects and the vast amount of research expenditure involved, the industry had to rely heavily on the Government for contracts and for support. In addition, the Ministry of Supply was responsible for the Royal Aircraft Establishment at Farnborough, a quite remarkable institution, upon which the industry relied heavily for scientific and technical support.

Inevitably we got caught in the middle in all disputes that went on between manufacturer and consumer. This was particularly true in the field of military aircraft, with the Air Force always demanding more from the manufacturers and complaining they were not getting their requirements met, while the manufacturers were saying that they were doing all that was possible and the R.A.F. were asking too much. Relations between the Ministry of Supply and the Air Ministry were not ideal, and indeed I had from time to time considerable battles with Nigel Birch, who was then Secretary of State for Air. There were some very alarming occasions. For example, once it was found that the Hunter fighters in their latest model experienced a complete engine stall when their guns were fired. On another occasion a small flap in the front of the aircraft tended to fly open in flight, and this too took a great deal of urgent correction. I came to the conclusion during the time I was there that the system was a bad one and that the interposition of a third party between customer and supplier, rather than acting as a pacifying agent, merely exacerbated argument. I did, in fact, recommend the abolition of the Ministry of Supply and when Harold Macmillan asked me to continue in that job when he became Prime Minister I naturally refused, because it seemed absurd to continue as Minister in charge of a Department whose existence I did not think was justified.

It is hard to form a judgement about how far Britain lost opportunities in the field of aviation in those years, and if opportunities were lost, why they were. Some blamed British Overseas Airways for clinging too long to turboprop aircraft. Others blamed me for cancelling the V–1000. The sudden unforeseeable and tragic crashes in 1954 of two British Comets – the world's first jet-engined passenger aircraft – were disastrous. Before they occurred it had seemed we were leading the world in a form of air transport which was not only fast but also economically justifiable.

In the long run, however, the biggest problem was the competition of the American industry, which was enormous. Their research and development were on a far larger scale than we could possibly afford. This did not necessarily mean that they came forward with brighter or better ideas, but it did mean that the development process of new aircraft was much more rapid in their case because when a snag occurred, and the process of development of an aircraft is generally from snag to snag, they could deploy vastly greater engineering resources to smooth it out.

It seemed to me that we were making a fundamental mistake if we tried to compete with the Americans across the whole range of aircraft types, and our interest as a country was better served by choosing particular fields of endeavour and concentrating on them. The Viscount was a conspicuous example of the success which British aircraft could achieve in a particularly suitable field. The bigger the aircraft the greater the difficulties, and our greatest difficulty was in competing with the Americans in the big inter-continental airliners.

Engines were another matter. Rolls-Royce could stand up to any American competitor, and as the value of engines plus spares over the life of an aircraft represents so much of the total cost, this was a very important factor indeed. When it came to airframes the Americans had two great advantages. First, the great support they got from the military – for example, in the development of the Boeing tanker, which enormously helped the Boeing Company in the development of its jet liners. Second, the enormous size of the domestic American airline industry, where the sheer facts of geography seemed likely to present America in this generation with the geographical advantages in competition which our island had had in previous maritime ages.

The Britannia was a good aircraft, though we had some panics about its development, particularly when it developed a nasty habit of letting its engines go out one by one in certain tropical weather conditions. The fault was eventually traced to the design of the air intake, and put right, but there were some unpleasant moments. The trouble was that by the time the Britannia was fully operational, too many years had passed, and the jet was overtaking the turboprop. Miles Thomas, then Chairman of B.O.A.C., had considerable faith in the Britannia, and persisted with it for some time, but it soon became apparent that the jets were going to win.

It was about that time that we had to take the decision about the Vickers V–1000. This was a project for a four-engine jet aircraft to be used both for military and for civil purposes. Vickers had put a lot of effort into its design, and they looked to the Ministry of Supply for support. My difficulty was that I could not find a customer. The R.A.F. decided they could not afford it within their budget and B.O.A.C. decided that they did not want it. I had, therefore, really no option but to cancel Government support, and this was announced on 11 November 1955. I remember when I told Rab, then Chancellor, that I had done so, his only comment was that I should have done it a long time before. The Vickers people, in particular, George Edwards, then a director, were incensed at the decision and thought it was a mistake. I could quite understand their feelings. Looking back on it I suppose one could argue that they may have been right, who can say? But it was one of those occasions which come to you from time to time as a Minister, when the decision makes itself because really you have no alternative. They sometimes bring the greatest of protests, but they are certainly a lot easier to deal with than the decisions that really have to be made on conflicting merits and conflicting arguments.

I was Minister of Supply at the time of the Suez episode, but being outside the Cabinet I was not aware of all that was going on. The Prime Minister played the cards pretty close to his chest. On the night the whole thing started I was at a dinner given by Anthony Eden for the Prime Minister of Norway. Philip de Zulueta, then one of his Private Secretaries, sat next to me. Halfway through dinner he went out to look at the tape to see what was happening and he came back to say that the Israelis were fifty miles inside Egypt. I remember that my automatic reaction was to ask, 'What on earth are they doing there?' There followed some pretty hectic days. Debates in the House of Commons were continuous and violent – Denis Healey, for example, used to get so worked up that steam could be seen issuing from his ears. Yet I believed that Anthony Eden was doing the right thing and I wrote to him to say so. I have not changed my mind since.

Anthony Eden was brilliant on anything to do with Foreign Affairs and in this field he established a pre-eminent position in both the country and the Cabinet. I remember Anthony telling me once that when he was a very young Foreign Secretary he had a rough time in the Cabinet and afterwards the Prime Minister led him to one side and said: 'Don't worry, Anthony, you'll find in every Cabinet there are twenty-two Foreign Secretaries and only one Minister of Labour.'

By the time of Suez he had had an enormous experience of foreign relations and a considerable acquaintance with the people who mattered in other countries in the world. You might well say how did Suez come about in that case? I still think he was right about Suez and his reaction was correct. Unfortunately, Suez did not succeed, partly because of the Americans.

We had every reason to believe that the relationship we had established with them would hold over Suez. It certainly continued afterwards. Typical of that relationship was one Cabinet meeting late at night when Harold Macmillan was Prime Minister. We were summoned after ten o'clock to the House of Commons and Harold told us that he had had a message from King Hussein to the effect that he was expecting a revolution. Would we fly in some troops to help him? Harold said we had better find out what the Americans thought. He went out of the room and rang up Foster Dulles. He was back in literally five minutes. 'I have spoken to Foster,' he said, 'who says that whatever we do the Americans will back us.' We thus decided to send in our troops. (I remember a humorous sidelight to this occasion : no one knew what the time in Jordan was. All the Chiefs of Staff were there but could not give an answer until finally one of them produced a Boy Scout pocket diary. Also, in the confusion we forgot to inform the Israelis we were over-flying them.)

At any rate, I think the real mistake made at Suez was in the planning. It took too long for our forces to turn up. If we could have acted more quickly and decisively, it probably would have been all right. But the opposition built up and the Americans had no alternative but to bring pressure on us.

I certainly believe it was a morally correct action. It was intended to protect Western interests in a way that was perfectly justifiable.

Of course, Suez destroyed Rab's chances of ever becoming Prime Minister. At the time he gave the impression that he was lifting his skirt to avoid the dirt. The feeling in the Party was that if he would not take responsibility we could not have him as leader. Afterwards Rab was hounded for that very reason, by what I call the 'blue blood and thunder' group, and one or two of them did their best to stop Rab becoming Eden's successor.

My great difficulty in the Suez affair as Minister of Supply was to persuade the military that the politicians really meant business. The job of my Department was to ensure that they would have the necessary munitions to carry out their task, but when we approached them to ask if they had all they needed, their reaction was always calm to the point of scepticism. Looking back on it I still feel that a great misjudgement was made about the strength of the reaction we were likely to meet, and if only the military had been as quick and decisive in their actions as the politicians for once had been, history might have been very different.

In the Kremlin with
Kosygin, 1961

Opening of the British
Trade Fair in Moscow,
1961, with most of the
Praesidium in the front
row; I am hidden behind
the speaker

E.F.T.A. meeting in London, 27 June 1961. From left to right:
Bruno Kreisky, Austria; Fritz Bock, Austria; Jens O. Krag, Denmark;
Karl Gustav Netzen, Sweden; Gunnar Lange, Sweden;
Frank E. Figgures, E.F.T.A. Secretary-General; Friedrich T. Wahlen,
Switzerland; Correira Oliveira, Portugal; The Author, President of
E.F.T.A. Council; Arne Skauga, Norway; Edward Heath, UK;
Hans Schaffner, Switzerland

With Roy Welensky, 29 November 1961

5

Paymaster-General

1957–1959

W H E N Harold Macmillan became Prime Minister in January 1957
I had high hopes of being invited to join his Cabinet, but it was not to
be. Instead, he asked me to continue as Minister of Supply outside the
Cabinet. I did not feel inclined to accept this offer for the reasons
explained in the previous chapter. Harold very kindly made me other
offers. He suggested that I should become Minister of Health, but this
did not appeal to me. It was a field in which I had no experience and,
quite frankly, no great interest. I felt that I could render the greatest
service in one of the economic Departments, for that was where my
experience and my interest lay. The trouble was that the main
economic Departments were already committed. Harold came up with
the suggestion that I should be Paymaster-General and in that capacity
deputize in the Commons for Lord Mills, who had been made Minister
of Fuel and Power. This involved demotion from full Ministerial rank,
but I was happy to take it on because the work was fascinating, the
opportunities in the House of Commons were considerable, and Percy
Mills was a most congenial person. I never had cause to regret the
decision. A great deal was going on in the world of energy, with the
aftermath of Suez and with the development of nuclear power, of
which I had seen something at the Ministry of Supply.

The lesson of recent events had been the dependence of Britain on imported oil, and Percy Mills was determined to tackle the problem vigorously, with the same determination he had shown as Housing Expediter under Harold Macmillan at the Ministry of Housing, when he carried through the famous 300,000 houses programme. Urgent steps were taken to increase the supply of tankers, and Rear-Admiral Sir Matthew Slattery, then Chairman and Managing Director of Short Brothers and Harland, was given a special assignment to oversee this. Alternative sources of oil were explored – shale-oil deposits, for example, or the conversion of coal into oil, which seemed to have achieved some success in South Africa. There were further new processes in the chemical field, such as the Lurgi process and schemes for the underground gasification of coal. We decided also to put a heavy investment into the development of nuclear power, for here was a field where British technology was pre-eminent and where the demand appeared unlimited.

Our plans were carefully laid on the basis of the best estimates available to us from public and private sources. I remember making a long speech in the House of Commons about the future pattern of Britain's energy consumption. It created a considerable impression as I was able to go into very detailed estimates of future consumption trends in a fairly lengthy speech, made, as was my custom then, without any use of notes. The only trouble was that all the figures I gave turned out in the event to be wrong. It was a salutary lesson in the dangers of economic forecasting, but it was also a lesson that private enterprise, in the shape of the great oil companies, could be just as far out in their predictions as Government Departments. We had been warned that there was a threat of a severe shortage of tankers in a few years' time, and this was largely why Admiral Slattery was appointed, but when the plans came to fruition, the whole market position had changed and we virtually had tankers running out of our ears.

By and large I think that Percy Mills' tenure of office was an effective one. The conduct of his Department did lead to a practical development of British energy resources, both technical and commercial, which was of lasting value to the British economy.

In addition to my responsibilities as spokesman for fuel and energy in the House of Commons, Harold asked me, as Paymaster-General, to take on a number of other assignments. I was assigned to help Derick Heathcoat Amory, who had become Chancellor of the Exchequer, over the whole range of his responsibilities, and this I found extremely congenial, both because it meant renewing my contacts with the Treasury and because of Derick's delightful personality. Modest, unassuming, shy, he nevertheless has a mind of clarity and a great strength of character, and I think all who worked for him when he was Chancellor would agree that they could not have had a more pleasant boss. He often seemed the original of the 'downy old bird'.

I was also asked to take on some responsibility for the nuclear energy programme. Harold Macmillan, as Prime Minister, had taken personal responsibility for the Department and he asked me to work under him. I am afraid I did not make much of a contribution here. It was particularly difficult for any politician to try to exercise control over scientists and administrators in a field of such complexity and technicality. One of the main jobs of a Minister is to exercise within his Department a sense of priorities and a control over the volume of expenditure. It is one thing to do this in a social Department such as housing, or health, or education, where the priorities are very much political matters. It is more difficult to exercise such control in an economic Department, where the decisions to be taken are partly political and partly technical, though, in the long run, I believe it is the political factors that must dominate. But in a Department that is wholly technical (and very high technology at that), the lay Minister is at a great disadvantage. He cannot possess anything like the skills of his senior advisers. If he claims to have some degree of their skills, then they can always defeat him on his own ground; if he has none at all, then he really cannot understand what they are talking about most of the time.

The most interesting task that Harold asked me to undertake was to lead the British delegation at the discussions about the creation of a free-trade area in Western Europe, to embrace all the seventeen nations that were then members of the Organization for European Economic Cooperation (O.E.E.C.). Here was an excitement and a real challenge. The chances of getting agreement did not seem very good, particularly because any European free-trade arrangement would inevitably cut across the then existing system of Commonwealth preference, to which the Conservative Party had a very deep attachment. As Harold made it clear when appointing me, in August 1957, the alternative results appeared to be either that I should fail and be blamed for the failure, or that I should succeed at the expense of the Commonwealth and be blamed by the Party for sacrificing our traditions and our heritage.

The negotiations at the Château de la Muette were long, arduous and fascinating. The main problem rested between us and the French. Indeed, the course of events can fairly be described by saying that when we started there was a French Government who wanted to say 'Yes' but had not the political authority to do so, and we finished with General de Gaulle who wanted to say 'No' and had not the slightest difficulty in imposing his will.

The Treaty of Rome had been settled some time before, creating the Community of the Six. For various reasons British Governments had not been able to recommend Britain's membership, though we would have been welcome. The main reasons were the remaining tradition of Commonwealth preference and our close and special links with the United States.

We were still basically a maritime power, unlike the members of the Six, and our choice emotionally was bound to be, as Churchill put it, 'the open sea'. But the European Governments were anxious that we should be part of a European system. The basic purpose of the Community had not been economic so much as political. Europe had been torn asunder twice within a generation by wars between the European nations, our European civilization had virtually been exhausted. It was in Europe's interest, and in America's too, to prevent this happening again, and the most important means of doing so appeared to be the creation of a European political unity in which German ambitions and energies could be deeply enmeshed. In order to ensure that this system was stable, and to counterbalance fears of the enormous potential strength of a resurgent Germany, a British presence seemed highly desirable. So it had been explicitly agreed by the heads of the French and German Governments that as soon as possible after the signature of the Treaty of Rome, negotiations should take place to bring Britain and the other Western European nations into a system of European free trade, which, while not demanding the political unification of the Community, would provide a lasting European unity.

This was the remit of the so-called Maudling Committee, for, as Britain's representative, I took the Chair. For many weary months we endeavoured to find solutions until finally we foundered on the rock of General de Gaulle. How this came about is still highly relevant to European unity.

The real objections to the scheme were twofold. There was the particular French objection to British entry into European trade on what they believed to be specially favourable terms – they thought that if we had free trade with Europe, while retaining our Commonwealth position, we should be specially favoured. They felt too, I think, that the political influence and status they hoped to gain for France as part of the Community would be diminished if it had to be shared with Britain. There were also those staunch supporters of the Monnet doctrine of the United States of Europe, who feared that the young Community could be drowned in a wider and looser association and so fail to develop its essential identity. Finally, as always, there was the agricultural problem. The British desire was to have a free-trade area confined to industrial goods, a proposal which naturally seemed to France and Italy in particular, as potential agricultural exporters, a very unfair bargain.

We had a number of allies in the negotiation. Our staunchest friend was Ludwig Erhard, who was then German Minister for Economic Affairs and an immense believer by temperament in the maximum freedom of trade, and, I suspected, a considerable sceptic about the more institutional side of the Community. He was an admirable man to deal with, frank, warm and human, and despite his academic background he was always ready to brush aside the niceties of argument in favour of the importance of commonsense. When the final crunch came, and the French decided to kill the negotiations, de Gaulle went to Chancellor Adenauer for his support, which was given. I have always believed that this was against the advice and wishes of Erhard, and that Adenauer overruled him entirely on political grounds, because of his deep commitment to the concept of Franco-German alliance. All the way through our long, and sometimes difficult, talks, Erhard was a staunch friend. There was only one thing about him that I found disconcerting, and this was his habit of wearing a wristwatch

DAILY MAIL — NOVEMBER 18, 1958.

'*The light that failed.*'

with a rather strident alarm incorporated in it, presumably intended to warn him when his next appointment was due. It was never very easy, when discussion of a fairly intricate economic problem was rudely interrupted by the sudden ring of the bell upon Erhard's left wrist.

The Italians were allies too, despite the genuine complaint they had about the exclusion of agricultural products. Their representative, Dr Guido Carli, is one of the most able men I have had the fortune to encounter, and his services to his country, and to Europe over many years, have been great and distinguished. He even tried to solve the vexed question of certificates of origin by producing the famous Carli plan, which for some time held the floor in our discussions. Alas, I fear, it proved in practice unworkable. His difficulty, of course, was that the Italian customs regime was one of the least likely to be able to operate it in practice.

The other members of the original European Community, the Benelux countries, were in favour of British entry on broad political grounds and did their best to help, but there were some doubts amongst them. Ernst van der Beugel, who spoke for the Netherlands, has always been a great friend of Britain, and a proponent of the maximum freedom of trade, but on the other hand, he was, I think, one of those most concerned that the Community would be over-diluted by the admission of more members and that much of its original concept of political unity might be thereby undermined.

The other member countries of the O.E.E.C. were broadly in favour of the free-trade concept. The Scandinavians certainly were enthusiastic. The Swedes in particular welcomed a system of establishing a free market for industrial goods in a Western Europe which would not involve them in the political commitments of the Community, which their diplomatic stance could not accept. The same was true of the Austrians and Swiss. The Danes were faced with the problem that their important agricultural exports were divided between Germany and the United Kingdom. Agreement in this field was therefore very important for them. The Greeks, after an initial attempt to delay the negotiations on tactical grounds, lent their support. The Portuguese were strong supporters.

There remained the European Commissioners themselves, who were, of course, a party to the discussions. I recognized that they were in a difficult position. They had the immense and complex responsibility of building up a new international organization enmeshed as they were in the rival and competing interests of differing national Governments. Their job was going to be hard enough anyway with only six Governments to deal with, and the prospect of a total of up to seventeen naturally filled them with some dismay. I am afraid, looking back on it, I have to admit I should have paid more attention than I did to their concern. Perhaps I never got on as close terms with them as I did with all the Governments involved. Their president was Professor Walter Hallstein, an eminent and distinguished academic with a total commitment to the cause of the Treaty of Rome.

It was my practice, as Chairman of the Committee, to give a series of lunch meetings for each delegation, and I remember well the time when I was entertaining Professor Hallstein and his colleagues. At one stage he said to me, 'Mr Maudling, I have a request to make. Sometimes when you call upon me to speak you address me as Professor Hallstein, on other occasions you address me as Dr Hallstein. I should explain that in Germany there are many thousands of doctors, but only a few hundred professors, and I should be grateful if you would refer to me on all occasions as Professor.' It was, I suppose, a reasonable request, but it did make me feel there was a certain gap of temperament between us.

So the discussions ploughed their weary way. I think we made quite a lot of progress, but the basic issue remained. The land-mine was bound to explode at some time. The French argument basically was that the British wanted to take everything and give nothing, that we were not truly *communautaire,* that our eyes were still turned across the broad Atlantic, that we would be the Trojan horse for American interests, that our Commonwealth gave us an advantage over European countries in the acquisition of raw materials. They had a lot of arguments, and many of them good ones I have to admit, but it is also true that for every solution they could find a new problem.

I remember at one such meeting the French were pressing that we should accept the idea of majority voting, which the British Cabinet were not at all keen to do. However, I managed to persuade my colleagues that it was necessary and I went back to our next meeting of the Committee to announce the glad tidings. Alas, success was denied us. The French representative in response to my remarks took note with interest that the British had now accepted the principle of majority voting, but he regretted to have to say that the French did not.

I have found French foreign policy, and in particular its relationship to the Community, absolutely fascinating over the years. Their policy has always been based, and who can blame them, upon the interests of France. In the 1950s they demonstrated with brilliance the technique of exploiting, as a negotiating factor, the combination of a weak economy and a strong Communist Party.

French antipathy to the modern American influence in their country, of which I could quote vivid examples, has been a dividing factor in their policies and, despite our ancient friendship, we have suffered the backlash of this. I think part of the trouble is that the Americans and the British talk languages that have a certain resemblance to one another. English and French have always been the official languages of diplomacy, but, with the emergence of America as a superpower, the need to talk American has become constantly greater. This has tipped the balance against French, and if they resent it who can blame them? We certainly would if the boot was on the other foot.

I have no doubt that it was to a considerable extent Britain's special link with the United States that made de Gaulle determined to destroy the free-trade area and destroy it he did very effectively by obvious tactics. He went straight to Adenauer and said, in essence, 'Whatever has been said in the past, we cannot support this free-trade area. The new-found intimacy of France and Germany is essential to us both. We must exercise hegemony over Western Europe. If the British come in that is bad enough in itself, but what is far worse is that if they do, they will bring the Americans with them.' Adenauer listened and agreed, for reasons which I have never fully understood, and that was the effective end of the free-trade area and the Maudling Committee.

I now begin to wonder whether it was really the end of the free-trade area concept. It was put to sleep for many years, but when one looks at the Community now there is a certain case for arguing that it seems to be developing much more on the lines of the free-trade area than of the Treaty of Rome. There are many new members, and others to come. The common agricultural policy is proving in its present form a nonsense. The concept of political coherence through institutions is giving way to the concept of political cooperation between individual Governments, which was the essence of the free-trade area plan.

Is it possible still that what Erhard and Carli and I were arguing for twenty years ago may now prove to be the effective development of Western Europe if under another name?

Well, we had to decide what to do next. We had to pick up the bits.
It was quite a setback for Europe, politically and economically. Three
things were required. First, if freedom of trade in industrial products
could not be expanded over the whole of Western Europe then it
should be expanded as widely as possible. Second, there was a need for
the European countries that were not members of the Community to
organize themselves, because, otherwise, the superior bargaining power
of the Community would enable Brussels to pick them off one by one.
Third, any organization which was to be formed had to be of a
character which would not serve to perpetuate the division of Western
Europe, but which would rather provide a useful basis for future
negotiations to achieve a wider European settlement.

I think all these ideas were in the minds of European Governments
outside the Community. The idea which emerged, that of the European Free Trade Association (E.F.T.A.), was really based on these
three principles, and in practice served them well. If we could not
have free trade with all our European neighbours, at least we could
have free trade with some, Scandinavia as a particular example. If we
could come to arrangements with, for example, the Danes then we
could prevent them being pulled into the Brussels orbit, and if we
could have a united policy then our chances of an effective negotiation
in the future would be all the greater. Clearly, the position of Britain
was crucial in this. Ours was by far the strongest economy and our
market, particularly for agricultural produce, was essential to a number
of our colleagues. Yet, on the other hand, there were clear political
disadvantages if the initiative appeared to be a purely British one. One
can see how easily some members of the Community would say, 'Ah,
this is just sour grapes, this is the British trying to retaliate, trying to
save something from the wreck of their hopes.' And, indeed, there
were those who were inclined to say this sort of thing. Fortunately, the
initiative was taken by the Swedish and Norwegian Governments.
They came to us at the beginning and we warmly supported the ideas
they were developing. Much of the subsequent impetus for the negotiations came from them, particularly from Mr Hubert de Besche of
Sweden, and Mr Søren Sommerfelt of Norway. They did the initial
spadework on the setting up of E.F.T.A. and they are entitled to a
great deal of the credit for the establishment of what became an
effective organization, and one that certainly served the purposes I
have described, above all combining the maximum freedom of trade
that could be achieved with the political and economic unity of Europe

on an individual basis that would be generally acceptable to European countries.

I will not go into the details of the negotiations; that is for the historians. Suffice to say that they were serious, open, and friendly. Personally, I enjoyed them very much. They involved so many agreeable personalities and charming occasions. There were the Austrians, Leopold Figl, the Foreign Secretary, and Julius Raab, the Chancellor. My wife and I well remember Figl's splendid hospitality at the Viennese Jägerball. I remember too going to call on Chancellor Raab in his palatial office. As I walked up the marble staircase I could hear in the distance an Austrian band going 'oompha, oompha'. I talked with the Chancellor for about fifteen minutes, by the end of which we had done all the business we had to do, because there were few differences between us, and then he said, and the time was shortly after noon, 'Mr Maudling, do you like sausages and beer?' to which I replied 'Yes'.

'Well,' he said, 'you may have heard some music. There is a band from a village in my constituency visiting Vienna today, and we are having a party down the corridor. Would you care to join us?' I must say it was a splendid party. My only wish is that I could envisage the same sort of thing happening occasionally at 10 Downing Street.

The other story I must recount, though no doubt I shall be accused of frivolity, is the final stage of the E.F.T.A. negotiations in Stockholm. Everything had been settled, even the vexed and vital question of the tariff on Norwegian fish fingers. Of all the great issues of state only one remained, the customs duty to be charged on Danish men's overcoats in the British market. It was a matter of grave crisis. Gunnar Lange, the then Swedish Minister of Commerce and Chairman of our negotiations, an old friend whose death I mourn, invited me and Otto Krag, then Foreign Minister of Denmark, out to dinner to settle the problem. We had a splendid Swedish dinner, which lasted late into the night. We reached total and happy agreement. The next day we returned to the conference hall. Gunnar Lange announced that agreement had been reached and we concurred; but then the problem arose. Krag said that we had reached agreement on the Danish proposal whereas I was convinced that we had reached agreement on mine. There was only one solution, to allow Gunnar to adjudicate, which he did, and the E.F.T.A. bandwagon rolled ahead in stately fashion.

6

President of the Board of Trade

1959–1961

T H E Board of Trade, to which I went in 1959 after the election, had not then been absorbed in the mammoth new Department of Trade and Industry. I think there are many who still regret the process that has happened. Certainly there was attraction in being still officially President of the Committee of the Privy Council for Trade and Overseas Plantations, with a membership which formally still included, among others, the Archbishop of Canterbury. It is a rather sobering thought that the work then done by one Department with three Ministers, now requires three Departments with a dozen Ministers, the Department of Industry, the Department of Trade and the Department of Prices and Consumer Protection. All these various activities were the responsibility of my team. The range and diversity of problems was remarkable but I do not think we were overworked any more than any other Department, nor am I convinced that trade, industry or the consumer were better served in 1977 under Messrs Varley, Dell and Hattersley than they were in 1959.

I had a very strong team working for me. My leading political colleague, Freddy Erroll, was Minister of State, and concentrated his exuberant activities on promoting exports, which he did with great energy and effect. Freddy and I have always been good friends; our outlook on life is very similar, and our temperaments not all that far apart. We claimed to be the heaviest Ministerial team in the Government, weighing some thirty-five stones between us, and when we played tennis together, as we occasionally did in Cadogan Gardens, the earth shook as we trundled from side to side, and small children and animals using the garden were known to take fright and flee. (I also used to play tennis occasionally with Sandy Glen, who subsequently took over the Chair of the European Export Council, including one occasion in Namur, when we felt compelled to play a game of tennis on the hotel court, even though it was covered with weeds and lacking a net. The effect on all who watched these two Britishers pretending they were playing over a net and arguing from time to time as to whether a service had crossed it, must have convinced them of the insanity of our island race.)

When I arrived at the Board of Trade the Permanent Secretary was Sir Frank Lee, a very redoubtable man. He soon moved on to the Treasury, where I was very happy to find him on my arrival as Chancellor some years later. As a replacement Sir Richard Powell was proposed to me. I was not very happy about the idea : I had a great regard for his ability, but his experience had been mainly in Defence, and I had been particularly impressed by the Deputy Secretary of the Board of Trade, Herbert Andrew, by his knowledge of British industry and by the confidence that industrialists had in him. So I blithely suggested Herbert Andrew instead. Little did I know what kraken I was waking. The Secretary of the Cabinet, Sir Norman Brook, no less, immediately sought to see me. He explained in a most convincing manner how the whole pattern of future promotion of leading Civil Servants would be distorted if I had my choice and I beat a hasty retreat. However, I was happy in six months' time to be able to tell Norman that he had been quite right, and happy also when Herbert Andrew became Permanent Secretary in his own right at Education and Science. As my Private Secretary I first had William Barnes, a most agreeable and helpful man who was succeeded by Sir Peter Carey, now the highly regarded Permanent Secretary, who impressed me both by his penetrating mind and by his ability to carry his umbrella throughout a fortnight's trip round Russia without ever once losing it. This was almost in line with the legendary Nubar Gulbenkian, who was reputed on his first return to Russia to have succeeded in getting his customary orchid for his buttonhole delivered daily wherever he went in the Soviet Union.

There were many aspects of the work of the Board about which I could write : they certainly consumed a good deal of time. There were all the problems of company law, which I referred to a committee under Lord Jenkins. There was consumer protection, in which field we introduced a Weights and Measures Bill. We had to legislate on patents and designs. There was a Cinematograph Films Act 1960, amending the quota legislation. Insurance came under us, and safety at sea. The Export Credits Guarantee Department, a remarkable Department of which I formed the highest opinion, was responsible to the Board of Trade. Then there was the responsibility for the whole range of private industry, from heavy engineering through to fashion, in which latter responsibility I had the invaluable assistance of Beryl, who enjoyed it, and whose efforts I believe were welcomed by the industry. But these were the detailed matters. Very important as some of them were, the main problems with which I was concerned were commercial policy, export promotion and the distribution of industry in the U.K.

There was much to be done in the field of commercial policy. We successfully concluded the E.F.T.A. negotiations and the convention was initialled in Stockholm on 19 November 1959, but we clearly could not rest there. The purpose of E.F.T.A., as I have explained, was not only that it should be of value in itself, but that it should form a basis for negotiating a comprehensive European settlement. This still looked a long way off. The gap between the E.F.T.A. countries and the Six remained a wide one. The Commonwealth countries, who were reconciled to E.F.T.A., were far from being reconciled yet to our membership of the Community with all that could mean in changing the patterns of their trade. We held many lengthy discussions which culminated in the decision to apply for membership of the E.E.C., and that was announced to Parliament by Harold Macmillan on 31 July 1961. At the same time we had to continue the constant work of the G.A.T.T. and the further reductions of tariff barriers, and any new European settlement clearly had to be reconciled with this. On the whole the progress that was made was not unsatisfactory.

The need for a vigorous expansion of our exports was quite apparent. The problem was what the Government could do. The overwhelming proportion of our exports came from private industry. Export subsidies were strictly prohibited by international trade rules. E.C.G.D. was efficient and stood comparison with any similar Government organization among our competitors, and further extension of its activities was limited by the Berne Convention. It was very much the general view of the Western industrial powers at that time that there should be no artificial aids to exports for two good reasons which we fully accepted. The first was that history had shown that attempts to export one's problems to one's neighbours in the long run did not work, and the second was that any Government measures deliberately to sub-sidize exports would only lead to the sort of competition which in previous years had taken place in currency devaluations, a competition which is bound to be, in the long run, self-defeating. Of course there were constant complaints that other Governments were giving help to their exporters which we were not giving to ours. No doubt this did happen on occasion, and whenever we could detect it we took such action as was possible. But in general I think the complaints were exaggerated. They were all related to the basic assumption that an Englishman is never fairly beaten.

So what could the Government do to promote and encourage exports? Government usually works through subsidies or selective tax reductions, but these were ruled out. Direct instructions to companies to export a certain proportion of their products were clearly both impracticable and in principle undesirable. Was there nothing that Government could do beyond ensuring, so far as lay in their power, the health of the home economy, and what did health mean in this context? There were considerable arguments between those who believed, with Winston, that exports were just the steam on the kettle and that a buoyant home market was essential, and those who held the contrary view that tight restriction of home demand was necessary to squeeze businessmen into export markets.

As usual, there was some truth in both arguments. A vigorous home market reduces unit costs and provides financial support for export ventures. On the other hand, a vigorous home market is a temptation to businessmen to stay at home and forget the difficulties of the trade routes of the world.

What was rather baffling to us was that other countries, particularly Germany and Japan, were able to solve the problem. Various reasons were suggested. One was the comparison between the tax structures in the various countries. There certainly was a contrast between personal taxation in Britain and in some competing countries, and this was a factor, but taxation of companies did not appear to differ very much. Somehow it seemed that there was more determination, more vigour, more enthusiasm for exporting in some competing countries than we could muster here at home.

The reasons probably lay fairly deep. It was part of a general malaise that affected Britain in the postwar years, and it is significant that the countries most successful in competition were those who, having tasted the bitterness of defeat in war, were now enjoying the fruits of their recovery.

I and my colleagues felt that much could be done by way of effort, explanation, even exhortation. What was needed was a combined appeal to patriotism and to commonsense. We had to show that exporting was good not only for the country but for the individual business as well; the one without the other would have been useless. To exhort people to export against the interests of their companies, their shareholders and their employees was unlikely to bring a response, but merely to point to the financial benefits of exporting clearly was not enough either.

I know a number of people, Enoch Powell, for example, scorned this approach at the time, and no doubt others who believe in orthodox monetary economics would scorn it now. They would argue that if you get market conditions right and a proper valuation for your currency, the problem will solve itself. This is splendid in theory but manifest nonsense in practice, nor does it really accord with human life. Patriotism is still an important emotion, and equally important is the desire to feel a sense of purpose and achievement not measured solely in terms of personal financial benefit.

This was certainly appreciated by leading figures in industry and the Trade Unions, who willingly cooperated in our efforts. We had as a precedent the Dollar Export Board, headed by that remarkable man, Billy Rootes, which had undoubtedly stimulated the interest and success of British exporters in the U.S.A. I thought the time was right to set up a similar organization for Europe, because it was essential to grasp the export opportunities that would be arising there. Sir William MacFadzean was the first Chairman of the Export Council for Europe, and I was lucky to be able to assemble a strong team, including Sandy Glen, who later succeeded to the Chair. This group of men, businessmen and Trade Unionists, with some Government representatives, set about the task of encouraging a new enthusiasm for exports, based on an appreciation of the service this meant for the nation and a like appreciation of the value it could be for individual companies. Sir Cyril Kleinwort rendered similar service in the vast field of invisible

The new Chancellor arrives, 16 July 1962

The day I became
Chancellor in 1962,
walking in the grounds of a
friend's house

The family at home
Bedwell Lodge, in the early
sixties

Jamaica Independence Conference, February 1962. Left to right:
Sir Alexander Bustamante, Hugh Fraser, myself, Norman Manley

With Jomo Kenyatta and
Ronald Ngala, Government
House, Nairobi, 1962

Meeting the Deputy Leader
of the Opposition in Kenya,
1962

exports. At the same time Ministers embarked on a series of speeches. The Prime Minister himself led off at one famous gathering in Westminster. That was the time when he said, or is alleged to have said, 'Exports are fun'. In fact he did not say it. The truth is that it appeared in the draft speech which Freddy Erroll had prepared and I had sent on to him. It was also in the press handout, but when the time came he recoiled from using the words. But just because they were in the handout they were attributed to him for ever afterwards, sometimes, I fear, to his slight embarrassment.

The other great problem was the distribution of industry. Here again there was and still is a feeling among the more austere economists that things should be left to the market and businessmen should choose always for themselves, unimpeded, the location of their new investments. Again a splendid theory, but again it does not work in practice. A good analogy is that of a small boat; all those in her may rationally calculate that the seats in the stern are most attractive, but if they all rush simultaneously to get there, the result is disaster. In just the same way the rush of industry to the Midlands and the South-east was threatening the stability of our economy. It meant that shortage of labour was created in some areas, while there was very heavy unemployment in others, and the net effect of this is obvious. Either we had to run the economy too hard in order to make sure enough jobs were available in the North and Scotland, or we had to restrain growth in the South and Midlands at the cost of persistent unemployment and wasted resources in those other areas. The simple fact is that people are not movable like pieces on an economist's chess-board. Heaven forbid they should ever become so.

The Local Employment Act which was passed in 1960 brought up to date the powers we had for grappling with this problem. They were of two kinds, negative and positive, the power to prohibit development in the congested areas and the ability to give financial help to people setting up and creating jobs in the depressed areas. We made quite considerable progress in those years, mainly because it was a time of substantial industrial expansion. The motor-car industry, for example, were all expanding at the same time (one of the most frustrating features of British industry in its effect upon the work-load of the capital goods producers). It was possible to refuse them permission to expand in the South either altogether, or unless they were prepared to expand in the North as well. I myself negotiated extensively with the leading motor-car manufacturers, Pat Hennessy of Fords, George

Harriman of British Motors, and Pearson of Vauxhall, together, of course, with Billy Rootes of the then independent Rootes Group.

As a result there was a dramatic change in the pattern of the motor industry, and the pattern of its employment. Ford and Vauxhall went to Merseyside, British Motors to Scotland and Wales; Hillman went to Scotland too, and they were followed, to some extent, though less than we had hoped, by component manufacturers. Certainly the result was the creation of a great number of new jobs in those areas where they were badly needed. Critics can say that the story has not been altogether a happy one since, but I have no doubt in my own mind that if we had allowed the expansion of the motor industry at that time to take place in the already crowded circumstances of the Midlands and South-east, the state of the industry, particularly its labour relations, would be even worse than it has been in recent years, while the development areas of Scotland, Wales and Merseyside would have suffered severely. And what is true of the motor industry as an example, is true also of manufacturing industry generally.

The Board of Trade gave me considerable opportunities to travel and learn, which I seized with alacrity.

I first went to Russia in 1960 to open the British Trade Fair there. Trade between Britain and Russia was then very much in the news, and Russia seemed an important market for British goods. It was not so long before that my predecessor, Lord Eccles, had signed an important Trade Agreement with the Soviet Union. Their Minister of Foreign Trade, Mr Nikolai Patolichev (who, incidentally, I believe is still serving in that post), had visited London already, and I had come to know and like him. He had a considerable sense of humour. Once I had to tell him at the Board of Trade that we were very worried about the sales of Russian barley on the British market, because from the prices they were charging we thought they were dumping and undermining the position of the British farmer, so we wanted them to put their price up or we would have to put a ban on their imports. 'Tell me, Mr Maudling,' he said, 'have I got it right. The barley that we are happy to sell you at £19 a ton, you want us to charge you £22 a ton. You want, in fact, to pay us a higher price than we are asking. Is that really the position?' Regretfully I had to admit that that was precisely the position. 'Ah,' said Mr Patolichev thoughtfully, 'all right, but I never did understand capitalist economics.' I must say I did not feel inclined to try to explain them to him myself in that context.

He took me and my wife on a fairly extensive tour round Russia, including a performance of *Aïda* at the Opera House in Leningrad. As we settled in our seats and looked at the programme, he grunted sadly, and through the interpreter said, 'Regretfully, I am sorry to say, Mr Maudling, that tonight the part of Aïda is played by her mother; she is like a truck.' When the opera began we understood the force of his criticism.

The Trade Fair iself was a considerable success. British industry, with the support of the Board of Trade, had produced an imposing system of buildings and a very wide range of British products, both capital and consumer goods. The opening was rather a strange affair. Patolichev and I were due to make speeches from the rostrum installed in front of the Exhibition building, which was fairly small, but on which there appeared to be a surprising number of vacant seats. He himself seemed rather restless, till suddenly, just before the opening ceremony was due to commence, he seized me by the arm and led me round the corner of the building, saying, 'Mr Maudling, you must meet our Leaders.' There, wholly unannounced, and unexpected by any British, we saw advancing on us the better part of the entire Praesidium, led by Khrushchev himself, moving in a tight phalanx, and all apparently wearing identical raincoats and carrying identical hats, apart from the only woman member, Furtseva, who was bringing up the rear. It was, to put it mildly, a bit of a shock, but they all took the vacant chairs on the platform and applauded our mutual platitudes in a kind manner, and then spent a long time visiting the Exhibition and examining the stalls in great detail. I had the task of taking Khrushchev round, and I was fascinated by the speed of his reactions and his considerable sense of humour. He had with him Mikoyan, who was his deputy, and who acted as fall guy for most of his humour, which, on the whole, was pretty good. We were at one stage walking up the ramp leading to the first floor of the building, at the top of which there was a large stand of multi-coloured corsets installed by the Gossard Line of Beauty Company on very slim and non-Russian models. Khrushchev on seeing them turned to me and said, 'Mr Maudling, is this the secret weapon with which you intend to terrorize our Russian women?' It was hard to dislike a man who talked like that, and hard to believe that he was totally remote from the feelings of ordinary people.

The Russians at that time were extremely well briefed about the only argument we had on trade matters, which was about the import of Russian oil, which we were not allowing. I had a long talk about this with Mikoyan in his office in the Kremlin, and tried to explain to him that while we had then no oil produced in Britain, there was in fact a surfeit of sterling oil throughout the world, and that on the whole it suited Britain to have a high price structure for oil. To import cheaper Russian oil was, therefore, contrary to our national interest. 'You are not telling me the truth, Mr Maudling,' said Mikoyan. 'Look what your own capitalist magazine has to say,' and from a drawer in his desk he produced a clearly well-read and heavily underlined copy of *The Statist*, then a most distinguished British economic journal, which was taking exactly the opposite line from mine. I must say it was rather disconcerting, though, perhaps, it was not as disconcerting as the time in India when, as Economic Secretary, I was attending the Colombo Plan meeting, and I went to call on T. T. Krishnamachari, then Minister of Trade and Commerce, to complain about the restrictions the Indian Government were placing on the import of Lancashire textiles. 'I quite agree with you,' said T.T.K., 'I think our policy is inexcusable, but what can you do with a Prime Minister like Nehru?' and from his desk he produced a letter signed by Nehru himself, insisting that a ban should be maintained on the import of British textiles. One can only say, in the words of *Punch*, 'Collapse of stout party', but it certainly was a lesson in the techniques of commercial diplomacy. A similar technique was adopted by President Charles Helou of the Lebanon, when I visited him after the 1967 War. The Lebanese then were maintaining a blockade of British goods, which really was quite unjustifiable. He did not attempt to defend that policy, rather he said this, 'Mr Maudling, I agree, the Lebanese Government are behaving very badly, on this there can be no dispute. You have two courses open to you, either you can criticize us, blame us, possibly retaliate against us, or, alternatively, and I suggest this may be the course of wisdom, you could say to yourself, "Our Lebanese friends are behaving very badly, now is the time when they need our help most." ' You know it is awfully difficult to argue with people who say that sort of thing.

I had the opportunity of one long talk with Mikoyan when he came to a dinner at the British Embassy, given by Sir Frank Roberts, the then Ambassador. It was a pleasant occasion, only disturbed by the moment when, at the end of dinner, a group of Scots pipers, wholly unannounced by our host, entered the room and paraded round the table playing as lustily as only Scots pipers can play. The reaction in our guest was immediate: he paled and appeared for a moment determined to seek refuge under the table. I was, in fact, told later that he had only escaped being shot by the British on a previous occasion, during the abortive White Revolution, by throwing himself under a stationary tram, so, perhaps, his reflex was conditioned. However, after dinner he had recovered sufficiently to tell us much about Soviet policy. At that time they were particularly hostile in their attitude to Western Germany, and I asked him why they feared the Germans so much when Soviet military power was so great that they could crush the West Germans with a single massive blow. 'You do not understand,' was his answer. 'The Germans are in a position to bring in the Americans.' Russian thinking was then dominated by fear of America. It was a genuine fear, however ill-founded.

The Russian authorities were very hospitable to Beryl and myself. They showed us a great deal of Moscow. Indeed, I remember one senior Russian official on a later occasion saying, 'In Moscow, Mr Maudling, all doors are open to you.' We have, between us, a lot of memories, both of Moscow and of provincial Russia. There were the fascinating crowds in the Kremlin Museum, people on holiday from the remote peasant areas of Russia wandering round that splendid collection of Imperial treasures gaping at a past that they but dimly yet instinctively understood. They reminded me of Rupert Brooke's words :

> So a poor ghost, beside his misty streams,
> Is haunted by strange doubts, evasive dreams.

There was the charming Uzbek girl student who was detailed to show us round a great exhibition in Moscow. She took us to the main hall of the exhibition building which was surrounded by vast photographs. 'Here,' she said, 'you will see photographs of people demonstrating against the atom bomb in many capitals of the world – London, New York, Paris, Rome.' 'Ah,' we said, 'very interesting, but where is the photo of people demonstrating against the atom bomb in Moscow?' 'Oh,' she replied, 'demonstrations are not allowed in Moscow.' I do not think she ever understood why we laughed.

There was the Foreign Office official who very kindly took us out for an evening to a restaurant in one of the inland-waterway ports of the river. He promised us a feast of lobsters. When we arrived there were none to be seen, but he and his colleague left us happily drinking vodka while they made a tour of the various food-selling kiosks in the neighbourhood, returning with a large paper bag full of rather dubious-looking crayfish.

We were able to see a good deal of provincial Russia. I suppose the overall impression is of the space and the emptiness and, certainly in large areas of western Russia, the dreariness of the landscape. The villages still lacked any sort of modern roads, the housing in many cases seemed pathetic, but practically every house in practically every village had its television mast, indicating how well the rulers of Russia understood the political importance of a state television service. We stayed in Sochi on the Black Sea, in a miners' rest-home, which was most comfortable and very impressive, though I did work out that on the average a Russian miner would be very lucky to spend a week there in the course of his entire working life. We travelled by train from Sochi to Tbilisi, noting with interest the sentries posted at either end of the tunnels and bridges, presumably to prevent the Turks stealing them, and the intense precautions which meant we had to close the blinds of the compartment with the train in pitch darkness in the middle of nowhere when it happened to be a security area. In Tbilisi we were impressed both by the industrial development and by the large crowds still attending Church. Hospitality was warm, and Georgian wines are very good. Beryl and I were expected at dinner to stand with linked arms and each down a large drinking horn of the local red. We succeeded in doing so, and still preserve the drinking horns as a souvenir of this achievement. I also managed to play a trick I had wanted to do for years : I had seen it in a film. I made a very faint pencil mark across two adjoining loose sheets of paper on the top of my suitcase, so that I could see when I returned, by the position of the pencil mark, whether the contents of the case had been examined. They had been. I suppose after all there is no objection to that; as capitalists we were a security risk.

From Tbilisi we flew to Leningrad, that superb city where there are so many things to see of both Imperial and Soviet history. The great palaces so well preserved, the Hermitage Museum, the cruiser *Aurora*, where the Revolution started. But most clearly of all, we remember the Palace of Weddings on the bank of the River Neva, a superb old three-storey building, providing all facilities needed for weddings. On the ground floor were the offices where the necessary formalities could be completed. On the first floor there were shops where wedding presents could be purchased. On the second floor there were two large rooms, one the official room where the ceremony was performed, the other across the way a reception room for the subsequent festivities.

We were invited to attend the wedding of a young couple, which we did with intense interest. The fascinating thing was that it was as closely akin to a Christian ceremony as could be achieved, and this whole system, mark you, we were told had been brought about solely and explicitly by popular demand. There were the seats for the congregation, the friends of the bride and bridegroom. There was something very closely resembling an altar, but instead of a crucifix there was a bust of Lenin. The young couple walked up the aisle and paid their respects to the presiding officer, who duly and ceremonially married them. The only difference here was that instead of being a priest, the presiding officer was a rather grim-faced lady with a high-necked dress, who, I must irreverently say, reminded me of the Madame in one of Toulouse-Lautrec's paintings of a brothel scene in Paris. However, the young couple were evidently extremely happy and I have no doubt this provided for them a better start to their married life than would have been obtained in some doctrinal Marxist registry office.

As a considerable contrast I visited West Africa for the meeting of Commonwealth Finance Ministers in Accra, where Selwyn Lloyd as Chancellor led the delegation. The Finance Minister of Ghana was Mr Goka, who had succeeded Mr Gbedemah, a cheerful extrovert who delighted us at the end of the Commonwealth Finance Ministers' meeting in Montreal, presided over before the television cameras by Don Fleming, the Canadian Finance Minister, a renowned teetotaller, by declaring his appreciation of the Canadian hospitality. The first night, he said, there was a full bottle of whisky in his chalet; he had not drunk it all, but lo! and behold! the next day it was replaced by another full bottle, a sentiment that did not go down all that well with his host. It was on the same occasion that Morarji Desai paid his own tribute to the Canadian hospitality by saying that he had often been the guest of Her Majesty in the past but never in such comfortable circumstances.

The financial problems of Ghana, though difficult, were not all that complicated : everything depended on the price of cocoa and the progress of the swollen-shoot disease. The whole economy of the country, from the fruit and vegetable markets to the inland transport system, seemed to be in the hand of the Mammies, a truly remarkable race of buxom smiling women, with whom any man would dare to compete only at his peril. It seemed a happy country despite the problems they had gone through.

So far as I recall nothing much was achieved at the meeting of Ministers, but, quite frankly, not a great deal was expected on such occasions. The meetings of Commonwealth Finance Ministers before the World Bank gatherings had taken on a fairly ritual form, but we all, I am sure, enjoyed the company.

The renowned Krobo-Edusei who achieved fame largely because of the story of his wife and the golden bed was then Minister of Transport. He gave a party for the British delegation, headed by Selwyn Lloyd and the Duke of Devonshire, at one of the local Highlife nightclubs, where the fashion was to dance the local equivalent of the 'Lambeth Walk' under the open sky. It certainly was a splendid party, with lavish supplies of champagne, and because he was, in his Ministerial capacity, head of Ghana Airways, he had arranged for their stewardesses to come as our partners. I still treasure the recollection of Selwyn and my other distinguished colleagues dancing until the early hours; I only wish I had been able to obtain a photograph.

7

Colonial Secretary

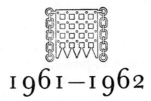

1961–1962

IN October 1961 I was in America when I received a cable from Harold Macmillan, asking if I would take on the Colonial Office. This I readily accepted. It was a total contrast to the economic Departments, and the problems involved were as fascinating as they were dangerous.

My predecessor, Iain Macleod, had come under a great deal of wholly unjustified criticism from the Right Wing of the Party. The Government's policy of progressively granting independence to Colonial territories was as wise as it was inevitable. It could be argued that in many cases independence came too soon, but the penalty for avoiding premature action would have been a very grave one. Nevertheless, there was a considerable resentment among the Conservative Right Wing, and among the European residents of the Colonial territories involved, at the speed of change, and this tended to focus upon Iain Macleod. It was thought that he was deliberately and unnecessarily accelerating the pace of independence. His good relations with a number of African Leaders such as Dr Hastings Banda inevitably caused some resentment, and a particularly unfair remark by Lord Salisbury, that Iain had been 'too clever by half', acted as a focus for the discontent. The truth is that Iain was a man of integrity and vision whose only fault might have been that he was a little ahead of what the Right Wing thought should have been his time.

The main task of the Colonial Secretary at that time was to supervise the move of Colonial territories to independence, which broadly speaking took the form of presiding over an initial Conference to settle a form of self-government under residual British sovereignty, and a subsequent Conference to confirm total independence.

The problems that arose were fascinating, but they seldom, if ever, arose from a conflict of interest between the Colonial power and the people in the Colonial territories. The real problems concerned either struggles between the indigenous peoples themselves, or, and this could coexist, the continuing role of people of British stock in the life of the newly independent territory.

There were many and varied problems. In Trinidad, for example, there was the conflict between those of African and of Asian stock. The same thing was true to an even greater extent in Zanzibar. In Kenya there was the combined problem of the conflict between the Kikuyu and the other tribes, particularly the Kalenjin, and the future of the very large landholdings of the British population and the memories of the Mau Mau. In Uganda we had the problem of Buganda and of the lost counties of the Bunyoro. Then there were the growing and urgent problems of the federations that the British had tried to set up, in the Caribbean, where it was creaking very loudly, and in central Africa, where clearly it could not last very long.

The basic problem was to provide a constitution on independence which would enable the various races to live together in harmony and which would preserve the British concept of freedom before the law and impartial Courts of Justice. The practical difficulty was, however, that there was no understanding of the British concept of Government and of Opposition. The Westminster style of democracy was not an easy concept, and we had not pursued in our African territories, for example, the policy which the French had pursued in theirs of making leading Africans think of themselves as Frenchmen and successors to the French tradition of culture and of constitutional Government. To put it simply, there were two practical problems. First, every constitution must make some provision for special powers in an emergency, and how can you prevent the Government in power at any given time from abusing such special powers? Second was the simple fact that it is no safeguard to anyone to write into a constitution a condition that it shall be unlawful to break this constitution. What we were dealing with was not words written on paper, but human emotions and human understanding. This is what made the task so fascinating.

The role of the British in each particular Conference was best conducted by exercising the maximum of patience, and by waiting until the disputing factions had exhausted their arguing capacity, and then coming up in a situation of deadlock with an impartial solution that might be acceptable.

Jamaica was the first of these Conferences over which I had to preside, in February 1962, and it was a success, largely because of the work that Iain Macleod and the Colonial Office had already done. The Jamaicans were charming people to deal with – in particular, Sir Alexander Bustamente, who always appeared to me a most engaging man, part Jamaican, part Irish and part Spanish. I never forget the occasion when he came to see me in the Colonial Office after independence and said in the most ingenuous manner, 'But, Reggie, you surely don't mean that just because we have become independent you intend to reduce the amount of British financial aid to our economy.'

The other problems of the Caribbean were mainly the future of the Federation and the constitution of Trinidad. More and more one learns from experience that federations cannot easily be imposed and must grow naturally. There was a considerable argument, on political and economic grounds, for the establishment of a Caribbean Federation. But the facts of geography and of human nature were against it. The islands were too far apart in terms of miles and in terms of personality, and it became obvious that the Federation was not going to work and that, therefore, it was wiser to wind it up, which was done finally at the end of May 1962.

Trinidad was one of the most difficult problems. The Government Leader, Eric Williams, was a man of remarkable intellectual calibre and great strength of purpose. On the other hand, and probably inevitably in a divided society, he had many enemies among the minority community, who were of Indian origin. The Conference in Marlborough House in May-June 1962 was a real cliff-hanger. For day after day it appeared that no solution as between the African and Asian racial parties could be achieved. Then suddenly one afternoon we came back to a new session of the Conference and I found that they had resolved the problems between themselves. Quite how they did it I shall never know, but the relief was intense. On the whole it confirmed the view that the role of an impartial Chairman should always be exercised with the maximum of patience, and that you should not try to advance your own solution until the compulsion of sitting, talking and living together has worked upon the various parties to produce theirs.

The Caribbean also had some problems on a smaller scale. There had been an inquiry into the activities of a Premier of one of the islands. It had produced a very adverse report, so it was clearly necessary that he should go. I was visiting the area and staying with Lord Hailes, the Governor-General, and we asked the Premier to appear and meet us. It was a strange occasion. I had to say to him, 'I am very sorry, Premier, but you must go.' He was, not unnaturally, somewhat upset – for that I had been prepared. What did surprise me were the tears that poured down his cheeks. The table round which we were sitting was covered with green baize and I remember so well how his tears fell in a pool on the table covering and how the darker green spread across the table before us. It was a sad occasion, but it did not break my heart, and he was back again as Premier not many years later. There was another Premier who turned up at a reception at the Governor-General's house and left his briefcase in the cloakroom. The attendants were somewhat surprised when it happened to fall open disclosing a loaded revolver. But that was the nature of life in the Caribbean in those days.

The greatest problem of all was Kenya. I inherited from Iain Macleod a strong emotional involvement in this country, which was, and I think still remains, the outstanding example of British influence in Africa. At the time when I took over the problem was a difficult one. There were deep suspicions and fears. The African nationalists were divided between K.A.N.U. and K.A.D.U. The Asian community, though relatively small, were fearful of the possibilities. The European population were deeply alarmed at the prospect of independence. It was only fairly recently that the horror of Mau Mau had come to an end. People genuinely feared, as I knew from letters I received, that independence and African rule would lead to atrocities on a large scale against the whites. More real was the danger of struggles between the various tribes, and the possibility that this battle would be fought over the farms and bodies of the European settlers. But difficult and daunting as the problem was, it was essential to grapple with it. Independence for Kenya could not long be delayed.

We arranged a constitutional conference which met at Lancaster House from 14 February to 6 April 1962, with the purpose of settling an agreed constitution for self-government, which would in the normal course of events be followed shortly after by full independence. It was a long and weary conference, but in the end it was successful. The two main forces represented were those of K.A.N.U., represented by Jomo Kenyatta and Tom Mboya, the forces of K.A.D.U., by Ronald Ngala, and the Europeans, whose natural leader was Michael Blundell. The underlying problem really was tribal antipathy. The smaller tribes feared that the Kikuyu, with their substantial numbers and great ability, would dominate an independent Kenya. The K.A.D.U. Party for this reason favoured a system of regionalism. Incidentally, I remember on my tour of Kenya visiting a K.A.D.U. area where I was faced with placards demanding 'Regionalism', the only trouble with them that, unknown to their holders, they were written upside down!

The Conference was long and hard. It was certainly not helped by Mr Oginga Odinga, the Vice-President of K.A.N.U., the only man I have ever seen actually froth at the mouth in a moment of excitement, and his moments of excitement were many. It certainly was helped by Tom Mboya, a man of outstanding ability and sophistication, whose murder was a terrible loss to Kenya. He and Bruce McKenzie used to come and see me often after meetings of the conference, to assess how it was going, and to chart the way in which success might be achieved.

The only possible tactic, which is one Iain Macleod had adopted on previous occasions, was to let the participants talk themselves to a standstill and then produce a British solution in the hopes that they would accept it. Timing was the essential element. On this occasion, fortunately, it worked and we reached agreement on a constitution for a self-governing Kenya, with Kenyatta and Ngala as joint Premiers, which would pave the way for independence.

My relief at this result was profound, and I was deeply indebted both to my advisers in the Colonial Office and to Michael Blundell, who had been a tower of strength throughout. One problem remained, namely Oginga Odinga. On the Saturday when the Conference was due to end, I invited Kenyatta to come to see me in my office in Lancaster House in the morning. I told him how glad I was that he was going to be a joint Premier of Kenya and that he was entitled to pick his own team for his share of the Government. I had only one reservation. I was not prepared, for reasons which I think were good, to accept Oginga Odinga as a member of any Government under the British Crown. Kenyatta took this hard. He said, 'You are asking me to desert my oldest friend'; tears even came to his eyes, but there it was,

and so he left me. That was the morning. In the afternoon we were
due to sign the new agreement under the glare of the television lights.
I did not see Kenyatta after he left me. I know he sat some while on
the balcony of Lancaster House. Where he went thereafter to lunch
I do not know, but I remember vividly our meeting in the afternoon,
when the agreement was taken formally for him to sign, wondering
whether he was in fact going to sign it. It was a tense moment. Fortunately he did sign, and on the whole I think subsequent experience led
him to believe that my judgement about his old friend had not been all
that wrong.

But of course this agreement, welcome as it was, was only another
stage on the hard road to satisfactory independence. Old enmities and
old suspicions would not die that easily and the two sides, though
formally combined in a coalition Government, tended to place their
own interpretation on what had been agreed at Lancaster House. This,
in fact, is what I had expected and hoped for. I am a great believer in
the habit of working together as a means of solving problems. As *The
Times* said on Thursday, 12 July 1962, 'Fortunately Mr Maudling's
prescription for developing the habit of thinking nationally in Kenya –
Cabinet teamwork by K.A.N.U. and K.A.D.U. Ministers with departmental responsibilities – is taking effect, day-to-day Government goes
on and teaches Ministers salutary lessons in realism, some of which
even leak into Ministerial speeches.' A number of years later I tried to
apply the same principles in Northern Ireland, where it seemed to me
that the practice of working together in a power-sharing executive
might be a salutary one. But I am afraid Northern Ireland has proved
more intractable than Kenya.

On a visit to Nairobi in July 1962 I was able after a number of
discussions to announce new proposals for the distribution of powers
between the central and regional Governments in a new Kenya constitution. Admittedly we had not answered all the problems but there
had been progress. There was a need to proceed to elections as soon as
possible, and I made it clear that if agreement could not be reached
between the parties in Kenya themselves the British Government would
have to take the necessary decision; this seemed the most likely method
in practice of making progress.

At the same time I was able to announce the tripling of the Land
Settlement Scheme. This gave the prospect of settling some 70,000
landless African families on a million acres of White Highlands. It was
designed to avoid the danger of tribal warfare over these lands and

possible bloodshed – African and European alike – on a large scale, while at the same time giving fair compensation to the European farmers who had gone there in good faith, and often on British Government encouragement. It was a high price to ask the British taxpayer to pay, but it seemed very much worthwhile, and so it proved in practice.

This was my last direct connection with Kenya. On my return to Britain I was made Chancellor of the Exchequer and turned to other matters. My tenure of the Colonial Office had been a brief one but I had enjoyed it enormously because the challenge of the human problems involved was immediate and apparent. In some, no doubt, we made mistakes, but in others I think we made progress. Certainly Kenya seemed to be set on a course that might not have seemed possible a bare year or eighteen months before. Kenya eventually came to independence in an atmosphere of which Britain could be proud. Of all the countries we have governed in Africa I think Kenya in many ways has been closest to the British heart, and the British tradition. This was as I have said Iain Macleod's strongly held view, and in it I agreed with him. It was a great privilege to have been able to make some contribution to progress there, and to the maintenance of what was best in the British traditions of Government. What a change there had been, and in what a short time !

When I first went to Nairobi in 1961 Kenyatta was regarded almost universally by the European population in Kenya and by many of my colleagues in the Government as an evil and dangerous man, a leader, as was said, 'to darkness and death'. Such was the antipathy to him that I avoided at that time being photographed shaking his hand, for to do so would have made my task infinitely more difficult. Yet he became leader of his country, and the horrors that had been predicted, both for the Europeans and for the minority African tribes and parties, did not materialize. He proved a wise and tolerant leader of his people, and one moreover who valued his contacts with Britain and the West, and the traditional Western concepts of democracy. Would there had been more like him.

But what I think pointed to me the contrast most clearly was when I returned to Kenya briefly in a private capacity in 1965 and attended an agricultural show. At the dinner of the farmers, a great occasion for the European community of Kenya, the first toast proposed, and enthusiastically received, was not that of the Queen, but of Mzee, the grand old man. On a lighter note, I sat beside Kenyatta at the gymkhana which by tradition took place at the show. In a splendid show-ring, reminiscent of Cheltenham, young ladies in immaculate jodhpurs on well groomed ponies competed with one another in a bending race. At the end of it a gracious lady in a grey two-piece suit with a generous string of pearls presented the rosettes and the prizes. The only difference was that she was not English but Kikuyu, not the wife of some distinguished settler, but the wife of Kenyatta himself. This seemed to me to set the seal on the handover of power.

The other great problem at the Colonial Office was the Central African Federation, where the situation I inherited from Iain Macleod was, as he himself readily admitted, not an easy one. The racial tensions within the Federation were considerable. While the concept had been a noble one and while the economic arguments for it remained very strong, the political strains were growing and it was difficult to see how the Federation could hold together. In Malawi (then known as Nyasaland) Dr Banda had taken charge, and clearly would demand separation. In Zambia (then known as Northern Rhodesia) Kenneth Kaunda was coming near to power, and he and his followers too would clearly not support the continuation of the Federation. Even in Southern Rhodesia, which, though effectively self-governing since 1923, had become part of the Federation, the signs of strain, of disillusion with the Federation and of conflict between territorial and federal Governments were apparent. In each country there were strong personalities leading their own forces and above all there brooded the powerful figure of Sir Roy Welensky, whose dedication to the cause of Federation was great and totally sincere.

In London our problem was complicated by divided Cabinet responsibility. As Colonial Secretary I succeeded Iain Macleod in the responsibility for the two dependent territories of Malawi and Zambia. Duncan Sandys, as Commonwealth Secretary, was responsible for Southern Rhodesia and for the Federation. This system did not make agreement any easier, and Harold Macmillan was very wise when he entrusted Rab with overall responsibility for the problem. There had been too a legacy of dissent between Iain and those who thought like him on the one side, and Roy Welensky and his supporters on the other. The feeling between the two men was bitter. Once Welensky went so far as to describe an attack on him by Iain as like being bitten by a sheep. Those were not happy terms between statesmen, and the pity of it was that they had so much in common; both were intelligent, pugnacious, dedicated. Both could at times be devious, though always in the pursuit of what they thought a proper objective. Both, frankly, I liked and was happy to count as friends.

The immediate problem I was facing was the necessary reform of the constitution of Northern Rhodesia. The issues were quite clear. Kaunda and his supporters wanted control of the territory and independence from the Federation. Welensky's side wished to prevent both. The job was to devise a constitution which would give adequate recognition to the just claims of each side. The problem was not made any easier by the serious outbreak of violence that had taken place within the country and in which Kaunda's supporters had been involved, nor was it exactly eased from my point of view by Welensky's habit of appealing round the British Government to the Conservative Party in Parliament, for whom he exercised a great attraction. I had, therefore, to tread a delicate path between the dangers of renewed bloodshed in Northern Rhodesia and loss of support within the Conservative Party which would make any useful progress to a peaceful solution virtually impossible.

Fairly soon after my appointment I visited the territories to try to assess the situation for myself. Dr Banda I found, when he met me at the Governor's house, an engaging man. He has often been criticized since, and there can be little doubt that his critics have more than once been justified in what they have said. But it did seem to me that he was fundamentally anxious to be friendly with Britain and the West. I remember asking him at lunch why this was so, and he told me that he had been trained and had practised as a doctor in Britain and America, and that in both countries he had been received without discrimination and allowed to develop and deploy his medical skills. This treatment he felt made him a friend of the Anglo-Saxons and a friend I believe he has remained.

Incidentally, it is interesting how sometimes what seem relatively small things can by their human content influence quite large events. When we were negotiating the free trade area, and subsequently the E.F.T.A., an important Swiss Minister was a Mr Wahlen. He was always most helpful, though, of course, like a good Swiss he never in any way sacrificed any interest of the Swiss people without ensuring full compensation, and he seemed to have a special sympathy for the British point of view. I asked him once, 'Why are you such a good friend of ours?' He said, 'It is quite simple. When I was a young student I came to Birmingham and arrived late at night by the last train, with nowhere to go. I saw a policeman and asked his advice, he

M.—D

gave me an address and told me how to get there, and said I should tell the lady that he had sent me. She received me in a most charming way, I had a very comfortable night, and when I came down the next morning for breakfast, there was the policeman. It was in fact his own house. Does it surprise you that when I think of the British thereafter I think of them as my friends?'

I left Zomba for Lusaka in a tiny twin-engined aircraft, and as we flew down the river we got constant reports of the demonstrations that were developing at Lusaka Airport. I must confess that they put the wind up me, as the numbers grew thousand by thousand and the mounted police were called in to control the mob. In fact all was well, no violence took place and the most awful ordeal we had to endure was when the crowd, as apparently was their wont in expressing their disapproval, pushed before them into our gaze the ugliest and oldest woman of their tribe, totally naked. In fact, despite the violence that had taken place, it was extraordinary to note how little real animosity there was.

Several incidents come back to me. I drove from the Governor's house in the early morning to catch my plane to Salisbury. There were a certain number of local Africans along the roadside, including apparently several dozen plain-clothes policemen, who proceeded to blow their cover entirely by coming smartly to attention and saluting when the Governor's car passed by. On another occasion, when visiting the Copper Belt, a number of demonstrators one after another threw themselves in front of the wheels of our car. The driver was firmly ordered by the Governor's A.D.C. not to stop, and I think that was wise, but his skill in avoiding the fallen bodies was remarkable, and I felt deeply grateful to him for it. When we came to the mine that we were visiting, there were vast crowds of African workers bearing large placards with slogans about me in particular and the British Government in general, of a distinctly unflattering character reflecting both on my ancestry and my future prospects. Yet, in fact, there was no violence, and I noticed among the crowd, on more than one street, small groups of European children of school age, all mingling happily with the African crowds apparently totally unaware of any animosity or danger. This was heartening.

I came back from central Africa with some proposals for the new constitution for Northern Rhodesia. These were designed to improve the position of the Africans in the forthcoming elections, inevitably at the expense of the Europeans, though they were still designed on the basic principle of trying to avoid a runaway victory for either side, and trying to ensure that members could not be elected without being able to show some support from both communities. I think on the whole my proposals were logical, though in situations like that logic is not always a good guide. They certainly did not go with a swing, but I was consoled by the reflection that both sides seemed to disapprove of them. The most vehement on the whole were the Europeans led by Roy Welensky. Within the Cabinet there was a great deal of controversy, with Duncan Sandys, speaking quite rightly from his responsibility for the Federation, taking an opposite view from my own. Several of my colleagues were rather shocked that I appeared to be going even further than my predecessor. As Harold Macmillan says in his memoirs, 'However, had I thought that there would be some relief in the pressure from the Colonial Office, I was doomed to disappointment – I soon found that Maudling was quite as "progressive" as Macleod. Indeed, in some respects he seemed *"plus royaliste que le roi"* ' (*At the End of the Day*, Macmillan, 1973, p. 318). I do not think this was quite fair. I had applied my mind, as Iain had done, independently and freshly. If in some ways what I had proposed went further than he had done it was because events had marched on since the summer. There had been the outbreak of violence which I did not think could be ignored, though, of course, this made me liable to face the charge of giving way to violence. But that was not really the issue; the problem was to avoid that degree and form of violence which would make a solution satisfactory to both races virtually impossible to obtain.

So the battle went on and Roy Welensky thundered away. Just before my announcement he arrived in London breathing fire and smoke, and causing a fair amount of alarm, which I think in fact was probably counter-productive from his own point of view. We had quite an important Cabinet meeting and it was rumoured at the time that it was likely to result in my resignation. Harold Macmillan records in his book what happened, though not quite accurately. In my recollection what I said, after much discussion, was that while I disagreed still with my colleagues I would be prepared to accept their decision because I felt that an act of resignation and an open breach in the British Government could have grave effects on the prospects in Africa and stir up just the kind of bloodshed which I was most anxious to avoid. So we reached agreement. I had not obtained all I wanted but I had made progress, and everyone was relieved, Harold in particular, who immediately asked me to lunch with him to celebrate. Bucks Club, I think. It was an agreeable lunch.

In fact it did not work at all badly. I announced the decision in the House of Commons on 28 February and it was, as *The Times* records, well received. As for Roy, the only protest he made was less violent than had been expected. I think he was a little taken aback by the way the Press portrayed, and possibly exaggerated, the threats he had been uttering; in any case, he acquiesced. Who was the victor and who was the vanquished? It is hard to say – I do not think that one should look on it in those terms. Certainly Roy Welensky remained a friend of mine and has been so ever since, and I do not think our views on Africa or on the world as a whole are temperamentally all that different. My admiration for him has steadily increased.

I did have one decision to make as Colonial Secretary which in many ways was the most difficult I have ever faced. There was some sudden upheaval in the province of Communist China that adjoined Hong Kong. The local Governor, or whatever his title was, decided suddenly that any of the people of the province who wanted to leave and go to Hong Kong could do so. Not surprisingly a very large number did. Large processions of civilians formed up on the road to Hong Kong, mainly women and children, and pressed their way forward. There were several lines of defence for Hong Kong. They were designed to meet a military attack; what should be done in these circumstances? It was absolutely clear that if this human tide were allowed to sweep forward unimpeded it would engulf the whole colony, such was the scale of the movement, and yet how to stop them? The Foreign Office were trying all they could to contact the Chinese authorities and enlist their cooperation. Meanwhile, the defences of Hong Kong were being breached one by one by the sheer pressure of unarmed human beings. It came to the point when the last barriers were threatened and I was advised by the Governor that the movement could only be stopped by force and this would involve firing on unarmed civilians, including women and children. He asked for my decision on what course he should take. I consulted the Prime Minister and other colleagues involved, and gave him the authority to order the use of force. Thank heavens at the last moment the Foreign Office efforts succeeded and the Chinese authorities themselves put a stop to the movement. So the tragedy never took place, and I doubt if the damage that it might have done has ever been widely known. But I quote it as an example of the kind of responsibilities that Ministers sometimes have to take. When people, as is fashionable, deride and decry politicians or Ministers, and proclaim that they do little to earn the living the country gives them, I sometimes wonder how much they would have enjoyed being in my shoes at a moment like that?

One other thing I did just before leaving the Colonial Office was to publish the first of a series of letters to my constituents, which I have produced from time to time since. It attracted a good deal of attention at the time partly because it was a new technique of expression which gave one a wider coverage than either a speech on the one hand, or an individual newspaper article on the other, partly because it did represent some new ideas in political thinking. I reproduce the text in Appendix 2.

8

Chancellor of the Exchequer

1962–1964

I WAS delighted when in July 1962 Harold Macmillan asked me to take on the Treasury. I had had a good deal of experience there, first as Economic Secretary and subsequently as Paymaster-General. What was even more important, I felt I had a close accord with Harold on economic policy, and there were a number of things I could do under his guidance and with his support.

I always found it a joy to work for Harold Macmillan. There was little in common in our respective backgrounds, but I think a great deal in our outlooks. He had a sense of style, a feeling for history, and a sensitivity that I have not known in any of the other Prime Ministers I have served. In many ways he is a strange mixture, deeply proud of his Scottish crofting ancestry (I seem to remember he kept a photograph of the humble croft always in his office) and equally proud of his connection by marriage with the great ducal family of Cavendish. He is a scholar and a man of wit, with a splendid turn of phrase. Many people would call him a snob, and maybe there would be some justice in that. To me he seemed the greatest actor/manager of the century;

the way he set and staged his scenes was quite brilliant. Yet with it all he had a common touch, a real appreciation of what the ordinary men and women of Stockton, in particular, and Britain in general thought, wanted, hoped for, and dreamed about.

There could not be a better man to work for, always ready to listen to his Ministers' problems, quick as a flash to understand what they were all about, totally reliable as a friend and supporter in times of difficulty. He also had a wonderful way of putting his Ministers in their places. He gave one dinner at No. 10 when I was Chancellor and I turned up wearing a light-blue dinner-jacket which I had recently acquired and of which I was rather proud. Harold met me at the entrance to the drawing-room. 'Ah, Reggie,' he said, 'playing the drums at the 400 Club again tonight, I see.' I did not wear it again. It is still in my wardrobe but its main function since then has been to provide food for moths.

Two problems were worrying him. Both of them related to his experiences in Stockton which so moulded his subsequent approach to economic affairs. He believed that the purpose of economic policy was to expand output, thereby making people better off, not so much as an end in itself, but as a fundamental condition of enabling people to live better and happier lives. He believed also that the economic orthodoxy of previous decades had held back possible progress and had created difficulties and caused waste of resources of a kind that was both unnecessary and unjustifiable.

So his broad directive to me was twofold. First, he was worried about a contraction of international trade and a general growth of depression, which would arise from a shortage of international liquidity. I remember him describing it quite clearly in an analogy, which I still think is a pretty good one. If a lot of people are playing a game of cards and using cowrie shells for money, the game can progress so long as all the participants have some shells to spend, but if the whole supply of shells is collared by one or two participants, then the game will come to an end. No doubt it was a crude analogy, but it was a pretty effective one, and his desire, which I fully shared, was to see that the supply of internationally acceptable cowrie shells was sufficient enough in total and adequately distributed in particular, to ensure that the game could continue.

His second concern was with the British economy, which had been going through a cycle of what was then popularly called stop-go. In other words, whenever we set the economy on a reasonable course of expansion, within a short time various factors made it necessary for the Government to change course, or to order an abrupt stop. The basic causes were twofold, first, the precarious position of sterling, with our heavy overseas indebtedness, and the simple fact that any economic expansion put the balance of payments under stress, because you have to pay for the raw materials and components you import before you get paid for the exports which you make out of them. The other problem, already in those days, was the problem of incomes policy, though then we were thinking in terms of three or four per cent rather than the current monstrous figures. Already it had become apparent that in the absence of some central Government guidance any expansionary phase was likely to lead to a growth of incomes more rapid than the economy could stand, and, therefore, to problems of domestic inflation, and of a further strain on the international value of sterling.

No task could have been to me more congenial. This was just the sort of thing I had for so many years wanted to do, to try to use my efforts to expand prosperity, both of my own country and of the international community. I cannot easily think of a better objective. I know it is fashionable nowadays in some quarters to deride economic growth and to say that it is a false idol. I suspect that the people who take this view are not those who suffer from the deprivations that come from inadequate economic growth, not the people who are poor, or disabled, or elderly, or under-educated, who are longing for the things that could come to them from their own efforts, if only the full potential economic growth made possible by modern science and technology could be achieved. World trade was in danger of being compressed by the shortage of finance. Contrary to the view of some bankers, I have always believed that the purpose of money is to serve the human race and not the opposite, and that financial systems should be designed to enable wealth to be produced on the maximum scale, and distributed as equitably as possible. The international monetary system then in operation had on the whole served the world well in the years since the end of the War, but it clearly had outrun its usefulness and new developments were required. Equally, it seemed absurd that the simple purpose of encouraging British industry or British commerce to maximize the benefit available to the British public should be hampered by technical considerations of the financial system. So we launched ourselves on new initiatives.

Mind you, there was some need for caution, and Harold particularly stressed this. Selwyn Lloyd, my predecessor, had established, rightly, a considerable reputation in the international financial community, and there was some concern that the change of Chancellor might be designed to herald an untimely dash to a new inflationary policy. It was important to stress continuity, and to make it clear that while there would be changes of policy, time would be taken about them, and they would be evolutionary rather than revolutionary. We put out a statement to this effect, which was well received, and there was time then for several weeks to review the details of the action we intended to take.

At the World Bank meeting in Washington that October, I put forward a new scheme which had been devised by the Bank of England and the Treasury. It was known as the Maudling Plan but, as usual, in fact it had been worked out by the experts of those two institutions, and my task basically was to promote it and to obtain international agreement. The fundamental principle was simple and sound. The difficulty was that the availability of money to finance international trade rested upon the two reserve currencies, the dollar and the pound. A very high proportion of the world's trade was conducted in these currencies, and it could not continue to expand unless they were available in adequate quantities. But, of course, the problem is that you cannot be a reserve currency unless you are in debt, because if you are not in debt no one holds your currency. A pound in the hands of a German, or a dollar in the hands of a Swede, represented an indebtedness of Britain or America to them. This was a perfectly sensible system so long as it was not pushed too far, but the trouble was that the indebtedness of the two major currencies, in particular sterling, was already at a very high level, and to expand it any further would have been dangerous.

Some other countries used to complain, particularly the French I recall, at the privilege that America and Britain had in possessing a reserve currency. It never seemed a great privilege to me. I would have been delighted to share such privilege as it was with our European friends, but one had to point out to them that if they wished to become possessors of a reserve currency, they must also become possessors of substantial international indebtedness, and this was not an idea that seemed to appeal to them very much. In fact, I remember that on one occasion when I was Chancellor and Giscard d'Estaing – now President of France – was Finance Minister, saying to him, 'Now look, you are sitting on a pile of dollars that you do not seem to like very much while I am very short of them. How about lending us a large supply of dollars on a medium-term basis?' His answer was that he did not think the Bank of France would be awfully keen to lose their ability to dispose freely of the dollars they possessed.

The basic idea of the scheme we put forward was to stamp, as it were, a lot of the internationally held sterling and dollars with the imprint of the International Monetary Fund, in other words, to transfer part of the international reserve liability to the main international institution. The idea itself did not get a very good reception at the first meeting of the Fund. There were a lot of arguments going on then about international liquidity, and the Americans in particular were nervous about anything that might appear to reflect upon the acceptability of the dollar. But it was a start, and it proved to be quite a useful start, because out of it was born the idea of the Special Drawing Rights, which have come to take such an important place in the general scheme of international liquidity.

The main protagonists in all these matters were Douglas Dillon, the U.S. Secretary of the Treasury, Giscard d'Estaing and myself, with, on the whole, the British and the Americans ranged on one side, which one might call the expansionist side, and the French leading a fairly determined European resistance based on more conservative banking principles. I do not think that on the whole it worked out too badly looking back on it. We made a start, largely thanks to Harold Macmillan's inspiration at the right time and on the right lines. Certainly I enjoyed enormously my opportunity to participate in these discussions, and the chance of working with Dillon and Giscard d'Estaing. As a matter of frivolity, I remember one breakfast I had with them, with Giscard as host in his office in the Louvre before an O.E.C.D. meeting. I was asked what I would have for breakfast, and said that on the whole, when in Paris, I preferred black coffee and a small glass of cognac. The others were more buoyant, and enjoyed their bacon and eggs. Doug, a true American, had soused his bacon and eggs with tomato ketchup, whereupon Giscard, as a true Frenchman, seized the marmalade jar and poured a large helping on his. I must confess, on looking at them, I reached for another cup of black coffee!

I well remember that my next breakfast with Doug Dillon was in a Tokyo hotel on the occasion of the 1964 I.M.F. Conference. He had kindly remembered my weakness for black coffee and cognac and I have a vague recollection that he had even succumbed, however gently, to it himself.

That visit to Tokyo in 1964 was fascinating for me. I went out via Malaysia and Hong Kong. Beryl and my daughter Caroline came with

me to Tokyo, Caroline financing herself by writing some articles for
the *Daily Mail*, as their 'Travelling Teenager'. We planned to return
via China and Russia, but unfortunately the General Election inter-
vened, and I had to fly straight back from Tokyo to London. Meanwhile, Beryl and Caroline proceeded on the route we had intended,
via Hong Kong to Peking, where they were very hospitably received
and performed the now much applauded feat of climbing the Great
Wall of China. They also, I think, learnt a good deal about the
Chinese, and I was able to profit by their experience. From Peking
they went to Irkutsk and thence via the Trans-Siberian Railway to
Moscow, and so home.

I was sorry to miss it; I had always wanted to travel on the Trans-
Siberian Railway, which seemed to me to combine the glamour of the
Orient Express and the Golden Journey to Sararkand. I was probably
lucky to miss it and so preserve my illusions intact, as I gather that
three days and nights across the steppes of Russia outweigh in dis-
comfort what they might contribute in glamour. The next year, 1965,
I wanted to go to China myself, and I asked the permission of their
Government but they told me that I would not be welcome. The
reason was never given, but it was up to them, so I did not go and
I have not been since.

I had seen little of the Far East. As Colonial Secretary I had been in
charge of Hong Kong and visited there at the time. It is an extraordinary place. The experience of flying in over the blackness of
Communist China, to the sudden dramatic lighting of a vista like
Manhattan Island, is quite remarkable. I suppose Hong Kong at that
time, and probably now, cannot be regarded as the ideal democracy,
but a very large number of people were enabled by British rule to live
a happy life there. What struck me mainly I think on my brief visit
were the happy faces of the children, who were quite enchanting, the
extraordinary ability of the Hong Kong families to live in relative
comfort while faced with appalling overcrowding, and the remarkable
ingenuity and flexibility of Hong Kong industry. I was taken to one of
the countless small factories. The first thing I noticed was an abacus
which the girl behind the desk was still using as the most efficient
method of computation. The second was the nature of their product
which was equipment and clothing for winter sports. No one in the
place so far as I could make out had ever seen snow, let alone taken
part in any winter sports; how did they manage to produce and export
this equipment? It was quite simple, the man said, one of the partners

went to London and New York once a year, bought the latest garments there and brought them back to be copied in Hong Kong at only a fraction of the price.

Talking of an abacus reminds me of an extraordinary example I once encountered of how the doers of good can sometimes trip up. There was a problem of birth control in Ceylon, where it appeared that mechanical methods were not practicable, and the pill had not then been thought of. So a splendid bunch of people in London, led by a distinguished Liberal Peer, decided that they would help with the problem by providing free to the wives of Ceylon a vast number of abaci. It was explained to them that the number of beads on each abacus represented the number of days in the month. If they moved one each day they could be sure that by the established rhythm method they could avoid becoming pregnant simply by counting. It was a splendid idea, but, alas, it was doomed to failure because the good ladies, all too full of faith in the magic of European Liberalism, merely moved four or five beads ahead instead of one when they felt in the mood, and the net result was not fewer pregnancies but more!

We held a meeting of Commonwealth Finance Ministers, the normal prelude to an I.M.F. meeting, in Kuala Lumpur. It was a routine occasion save when we were dramatically informed that invading Indonesian patrols had landed in Malaysia not far from where we were meeting. This was a time of considerable tension between Indonesia and Malaysia. Harold Holt, then Finance Minister of Australia, and later Prime Minister, an old and valued personal friend whose death in a swimming accident I deeply mourned, in company with so many people in both our countries, proposed at once that the Conference should record its whole-hearted support for our Malaysian colleagues. I seconded. It was a matter of surprise and concern for us both that we could not get immediate and unanimous support from our Commonwealth colleagues. Some had to 'seek instructions'. So one lives and learns.

The I.M.F. meeting was in Tokyo where I was able to spend several days though, to my regret, I had no time to see anywhere else in Japan. The same alas was true of my visit in January 1977 for the meeting of the Trilateral Commission. I wish I could have been more often. Indeed I feel that British politicians have tended very much to neglect the importance of Japan. There are some outstanding exceptions, Julian Ridsdale, for example, but in general I do not believe that we have recognized their immense importance in the modern world.

They are a country of over a hundred millions, their economic efficiency is prodigious, and they happen to be on our side. If Japan were to be wrested from the West and encompassed in the Communist camp our loss would be great indeed. Fortunately this seems unlikely to happen, but nothing can be taken for granted. We have tended of recent years to be biased against the Japanese for a number of reasons. First, of course, their culture is so different from ours as to be virtually incomprehensible. Second, we have the memories of what the Japanese did to us during the last War. It always seems to me strange how the British people, who tend rightly to pride themselves on their tolerance, have nurtured resentment against their enemies of the Second World War longer and more deeply than other peoples who suffered more acutely than we did. Thirdly, of course, there is the Japanese competition in the world trade. Everyone suffers from this, the Americans, for example, to a very large extent, and everyone feels some resentment at the way Japanese efficiency can defeat us in competition; but I think the British have had special reasons underlying their resentment.

First, we have had greater problems than other countries with our balance of payments, and have so felt more acutely the blast of their competition. Second, we felt early on the initial impact of Japanese competition in the textile markets of the world, where traditionally we had been dominant. Third, there was also our special position in Commonwealth markets such as Australia, where the Japanese penetration has been especially severe. So there are reasons for the particularly strong British reaction. I have no doubt also that there was justification in our claims for many years that the Japanese did not produce their own ideas but merely copied those of other countries, particularly Britain, and produced imitations at lower prices based on much lower wage rates. This was true in the past, but it has not been true for some years now. The quality of Japanese products based on their own research and development from textiles to optics, steel and shipbuilding, has become pre-eminent.

There is in fact taking place a major technological revolution in the world with a switch of leadership from West to East. Japan has taken the lead, others will follow. Korea is a particular example of this. Before I went there I had been told that when they decided to build large tankers it took them little more than two years from the date they cut the first sod for the shipyard to the delivery of the first tanker. But I was not even then prepared when the Minister of Industry told me that they were worried about British import controls, and when I asked him on what products, thinking he would say textiles and footwear, he replied, 'Not at all, it is special steels that I am thinking of.' No one should underestimate the spectacular economic and technological growth that is taking place in Asia.

But visiting Japan is not all solemnity. I was delighted as Chancellor, when given the inevitable name-badge to wear at the I.M.F. functions, to see that my office was translated into Japanese as 'Lord of the Great Warehouse'. They gave a lunch for me to taste Japanese whisky. It was good but not quite Scotch. I said, in all innocence, 'Very good. Rather like Irish whiskey.' The reaction was catastrophic. No one had ever heard of Irish whiskey. Clearly I was indulging in a typically British insulting joke! It took many glasses to sort it all out.

I cannot claim that Tokyo is an attractive city; it sometimes seemed to me to combine the worst features of London, Manchester and Newcastle, and, alas, I have never had the opportunity of seeing what, I understand, is the great beauty and freshness of the Japanese countryside. Certainly the Japanese have always been most hospitable, though sometimes their hospitality is a little surprising. During the World Bank meeting in 1964 I was invited, together with Maurice Macmillan, then my colleague at the Treasury, and some of our senior Treasury officials, to a party at a geisha house. It was a most decorous affair; indeed, Maurice said it reminded him of a party given by Young Conservatives in Halifax. We sat on the floor and drank saki, and we played various parlour games such as pencil and paper and passing the orange. The highlights of the evening were two. The first was when the Permanent Secretary of the Japanese Treasury did a splendid song and dance act. The second was when we were enticed into a competition with the largest geisha of all. Each guest in turn had to stand on the little stage back to back to her, and on the command, one, two, three, we bumped bottoms until one or the other fell over. I have to recall that the Europeans were invariably defeated!

I also was taken to a *sumo* wrestling contest, which was quite fascinating. The enthusiasm of the Japanese public for these vast figures outstrips even the adulation given in Britain to footballers or pop stars. They are remarkable men of remarkable size, and their contests, brief and highly ritualized in a very small ring, are dramatic if difficult for Europeans to understand. I remember very well the journalist who was my host saying at one stage, 'Mr Maudling, you will observe that our wrestlers push and pull one another; they never punch, for if they were to punch one another they might draw blood. And we Japanese cannot stand the sight of blood.' The same man on the way to the arena had shown me with some pride the historic place at which a number of senior Japanese officers in wartime had committed hara-kiri in public after a great defeat. I found the two things a little difficult to reconcile.

The Domestic Economy

The real problem of the domestic economy was how to achieve a steady and adequate rate of growth without inflation. This problem had baffled successive Chancellors in the past, as it has done ever since. We had done a lot of work on establishing the National Economic Development Council (N.E.D.C.) and we had begun the establishment of the National Incomes Commission (N.I.C.). The idea behind these institutions was that Government, management and the unions all had a part to play in establishing steady economic growth; they were interdependent and without cooperation between them the nation could not prosper. The Government's basic responsibility was to find a policy for demand management which would ensure the full use of resources without generating fresh domestic inflation and without diverting resources from exports and thus undermining the balance of payments.

We agreed at N.E.D.C. on a target growth rate of four per cent, which we thought could be sustained, being based on a combination of a 3.2 per cent rate of productivity growth, which historical data led us to think was practicable, as indeed it was; and a 0.8 per cent growth of the available labour force. One of the major tasks of N.E.D.C. was to eliminate obstacles to such a rate of growth and our conclusions were published in an official paper.

I have no doubt that the work of N.E.D.C. was extremely valuable. One of the great advantages was the cordial relations that were established with the Trade Union representatives on the Council, particularly George Woodcock, Harry Douglass and Sidney Greene. The frankness of our discussions and the genuine spirit of mutually seeking national advance were of great value. Of course there were occasions when we had our difficulties. I remember George Woodcock once saying, 'Well, Reggie, I have come to the conclusion that if achieving greater productivity means getting up half an hour earlier in the morning, I am against it.' Could there have been a better encapsulation of the views of the English people at that time? There was another occasion when George was rather cross with me because the Treasury had published an important White Paper about public expenditure without consulting the Council beforehand. 'If we are really to do our task,' he argued, 'the Council must have this information.' I was contrite. I agreed that in future it would happen. 'But,' I said, 'the Government's agreement to this course of action is on condition that the Trade Unions also inform the Council before announcing any major wage claim which, by its nature, could have as great an effect on the economy as any item of public expenditure.'

Sidney Greene's face was a study. His jaw dropped. 'Chancellor,' he said, 'you must be joking.' But of course I was not; I was just forlornly hoping.

This was the basis of my Budget of 1963, which was designed on an ambitious scale, to range beyond the normal circumstances of revenue gathering and revenue dispensing to encouraging a rate of development of the economy which could be sustained. We had been going through a difficult time, unemployment had been very high, and the case for expansion was strong and was argued not only by the Trade Unions but by the employers as well. I had produced an interim Budget, in effect, in the autumn of 1962, which had been designed largely through a drastic reduction in purchase tax on the motor-car to expand activities in the heartland of British industry, namely the motor-car industry, and all associated with it.

The 1963 Budget went further. I was in the happy position of being able to make substantial reductions in taxation, and I concentrated these reductions on income tax, particularly by increasing personal allowances and making improvements in the reduced rate bands. This was to some extent criticized by the City, who wished to see greater reductions at the higher end of the incomes scale, but I felt then, as I feel now, that incentives operate all the way down. It is, incidentally, a fascinating comparison of economic history that it cost Denis Healey in 1977 £2 billion to relieve 850,000 people of income-tax liability, whereas in my Budget of 1963 a reduction of £269 million provided similar exemption for $3\frac{3}{4}$ million people. There was a wide range of other measures, depletion allowances to encourage industrial invest-

Mr Macmillan in
1963

Working on the 1963
Budget in our Chester
Street home

THE LEADERSHIP BATTLE 1963:

Above: following Iain Macleod from No. 10

Opposite top: The winner and one of the losers, both in good humour

Opposite bottom: The three unsuccessful candidates for the Tory Leadership—myself, Lord Hailsham and R. A. Butler at the Conservative Party Conference, 10 October 1963

Beryl and Edward entering No. 11 in October 1963 on Edward's ninth birthday

ment, for example, and a specific allocation of £10 million for industrial retraining – perhaps the first time that any Chancellor had proposed an increase in public expenditure in the course of his Budget speech.

Another idea we introduced was that of free depreciation, not exactly a favourite with the Inland Revenue. I remember how in Rab's day they had violently opposed the introduction of investment allowances, but then when the Chancellor of the Exchequer had made his decision they had loyally produced a very effective working scheme. Precisely the same happened with free depreciation.

We also decided to allow people to brew beer at home without having to pay for the expensive excise licence that had hitherto been required. Fourteen years later, in October 1977, I was very gratified to receive the following kind letter from Bolton :

> Since you seem to have had more kicks than ha'pence for some time of late, it struck me that a bit of a boost may not come amiss.
>
> I am just about to blow the top off my thousandth pint of 'home brew' and on behalf of the rest of the million of us, please be assured that we have not forgotten the kindly and thoughtful chap who made it possible for us to afford it.
>
> Yours gratefully
> Reginald V. Brown

The concept of the 1963 Budget was to stimulate output on a basis that could be continued, both in terms of domestic inflationary pressures and the balance of payments. It was, on the whole, well received, not least by those who came subsequently to criticize it. I well remember a summing up by *The Economist* in a leading article, 'Damn the torpedoes, half speed ahead'.

The dangers clearly were two. First, the danger that there would be a cost inflation. Spare capacity in the economy was adequate to sustain a very large expansion of output, and as unit costs of production fall when output increases from the same equipment, this should have been helpful in terms of unit costs and prices, a factor somewhat overlooked by modern monetary economists. But all this would have been nullified if the rate of wage increases rose excessively. Under Harold Macmillan's guidance, Selwyn Lloyd had started, and I had continued, the development of the National Incomes Commission. This was an important concept. In those days we were thinking solely in terms of a voluntary incomes policy.

Our belief was that within N.E.D.C. we could get broad agreement on the general level of wage increases that could be absorbed by the economy without further inflation, and in this proposition we were not unsuccessful. But, of course, the problem as always was the special case. There are many factors that determine the level of wage claims from the key Unions. Expectation is one, the desire to protect living standards is another, but the comparison with other people is undoubtedly a very important factor. In practice exceptions had to be made in certain cases, particularly where there was a just claim from people who did not possess the industrial muscle to impose their will on the nation. We sought a system whereby exceptions could be identified, and the reasons why they could be treated as exceptions clearly defined. So we hoped they would be able to remain exceptions and would not, by exciting the emotions involved in comparability, accelerate the whole pace of wage advance.

It was a good idea. It was what Harold Macmillan described as the 'open-air cure'. Short of a statutory control of incomes no one has so far produced a better one. But I am afraid it was frustrated very largely by the Trade Unions. It got off initially on the wrong foot, because a lot of the work was done with Vic Feather, then George Woodcock's deputy, when George himself was not available. When he returned it was with an obvious feeling of antipathy to the whole concept, and for this and other reasons the Trade Union movement not only refused to cooperate with the N.I.C., but tried to persuade independent people not to do so either. This was a pity. Under the Chairmanship of Sir Geoffrey Lawrence, the Commission did a lot of valuable work. But it was never the force that it could and should have been, and it was never allowed to make the contribution to our national problem which it could so undoubtedly have done.

The second danger was the balance of payments. The British economy had always shown since the War a very high propensity to import manufactured goods and semi-manufactures, and we would feel the strain of this, for, as I have said earlier, it is quite obvious that you bring in your raw materials and your components and have to pay for them before you can get the expansion of exports from their use, which provides you with the revenue. But our calculation was that any strain on the balance of payments would be temporary and that we had adequate borrowing facilities to tide over any short-term difficulties. Of course attitudes to international borrowing had not at that time progressed to the point which they have reached today. It was still regarded as something rather unorthodox, to say the least, to plan deliberately to cover the current-account deficit from overseas credit facilities, but it seemed to me that those facilities existed to be used and the time their use could be justified was precisely when they could act as a cushion against the inevitable short-term difficulties which would precede a stronger long-term balance. I made it quite clear that this was the policy we had in mind, and the reasons why I considered it justified.

Britain had until then been held in a strait-jacket when it came to expansion, and this was neither good for us nor good for the rest of the world. Part of the problem was the system of fixed exchange rates which then was the order of the day. I had always myself been a supporter of flexible rates, and I was delighted when Rab had adopted the concept of a floating rate for sterling as part of his general approach when he was Chancellor, and an integral feature of the plan for returning to sterling convertibility. Alas, however, he had been forced off this by the weight of orthodox establishment opinion at the I.M.F. meeting in the autumn of 1955, and some years had to pass and many crises be endured before the concept of floating rates came to be internationally acceptable.

But this problem was not unique to Britain. What was unique was the position of sterling as an international currency and the large sterling holdings which had accumulated during and since the War. It was always a little difficult to explain the sterling balances and the advantages or disadvantages of the special position of sterling. No doubt a good deal of prestige was involved, no doubt also it was of some help to the City of London, though it is quite remarkable how the City has adapted itself to the change in the position of sterling, and how rapidly they have developed their outstanding facilities for dealing in other currencies, particularly, of course, the Euro-currencies. On the other hand there were very considerable disadvantages involved because all the sterling balances could be withdrawn virtually on demand and large movements of money could always take place with very little notice. The balances held by Commonwealth Governments were on the whole fairly stable, and they recognized their own interest in maintaining the strength of sterling, but there were other large balances to which the same considerations did not apply, and this meant that, with the international transfer of capital on a short-term basis, coupled with the so-called leads and lags in the financing of trade, so much of which was conducted in sterling, sterling could come under pressure very swiftly. Confidence factors, hard to sense, hard even to define, could play a decisive part, and, of course, our interest-rate structure was very largely determined by the need to maintain a differential against other countries, a differential which had to widen at times if there were any suspicions about our domestic economy.

I tried to find ways and means of loosening these shackles. Floating rates were clearly unacceptable at that time. I had a study made by the Treasury and the Bank of the possibility of a two-tier interest-rate structure, one internal and one external, which would give us more freedom of manoeuvre in our own domestic economic management. Unhappily the unanimous advice of the experts was that in the peculiar circumstances of the City of London and the sterling area this would not be practicable. Then there was the possibility of funding the sterling balances, but at that time such a possibility was not really open to us. Most of the holders of sterling treasured it for its availability and its liquidity. Some Governments no doubt would have been prepared to give some sort of undertaking about a proportion of their holdings, but that would probably be no more than what in practice they would hold in sterling anyway, come what may. Finally, we worked continuously to expand the international credit facilities available on lines which I have already described. While we made progress, it was useful rather than decisive.

So we went for expansion, quite deliberately, with our eyes open, recognizing the dangers. The prize to be obtained, the prospect of expansion without inflation, the end of stop-go and a break-out from the constrictions of the past, was a glittering one. My policy has been described as a 'dash for freedom'. I think that is ascribing to me, rather unusually, an excess of energy and enthusiasm. In fact the whole policy was deliberate, calculated and coherent. No one could guarantee success, but the chances were high, and the alternatives were drab and depressing.

On the whole the reactions of the economy to the 1963 Budget were much as I had anticipated, and I was able to inform the House of this in my Budget speech of 1964. There had been a sharp expansion of output, there was growing confidence all round, investment was improving, unemployment had fallen, prices had risen over the year by something like two per cent, which was certainly not more than anticipated, and of course fantastically modest in comparison with today's figures. Output overall had been rising at a rate of something like six per cent. We had, however, reached a very important stage in our policy. That six per cent rate of growth was to a considerable extent derived from bringing back into use capacity that had previously been unemployed. This process could not continue. We had to reduce our rate of advance to something more like the four per cent long-term growth rate, which all parties on N.E.D.C. considered was sustainable. There was growing pressure on the balance of payments, as anticipated. Stock-building was likely to continue at a high level, together with imports of raw materials and semi-manufactures. Exports were doing well, but not quite as well as we had hoped. Confidence in sterling remained high. We had now to steer a narrow course; we had to take some of the prospective demand out of the economy in order to slow it down, but if we went too far and appeared to be slamming on the brakes, the whole policy would be undermined and we should be back once again in the frustrations of stop-go.

It was not an easy calculation to make. It would not have been easy even if the financial forecasts available had been as accurate as we thought they would be. Experience has taught us so much in subsequent years about the fallibility of all forecasts be they from Government or private sources, and to try and fine-tune the economy, however desirable it then seemed, really was something of an illusion. On the whole it might have been better to have produced no Budget at all in 1964, but that was impossible, so wedded were we to what Aneurin Bevan once called the annual rituals of a pastoral society. There had to be a Budget, there had to be a Budget judgement, I had to fix the rate of taxes for the forthcoming year. I decided to make an increase overall of some £100 million, which today may seem puny, but which by the standards of 1964 was considerable (compare the Budget of 1963 which though dramatic only involved a tax reduction of some £269 million). I put all the weight of the new taxation on alcohol and tobacco, on the simple principle that if you want to encourage expansion and give incentive you should tax people at the point at which they spend money and not at the point at which they earn it – a principle which, I fear, has been rather neglected in recent times. It was certainly not a dramatic Budget on this occasion. I remember Harold Wilson's comment. I met him in the corridor afterwards, and asked him what he thought of my Budget and his reply was brief and to the point : 'What Budget?' However, I made it clear that there was to be more flexibility in taxation policy. We had increased the possibilities of varying tax rates more frequently, which seemed to me immensely important in such an uncertain situation, and I made it quite clear in my Budget speech that I would be prepared to make substantial changes in either direction if, at a later date, they appeared necessary.

I also stressed the availability of international borrowing resources and made it absolutely clear that I intended as a matter of policy to use them to tide over any temporary difficulties that might occur on the balance of payments. At that time it so happened we were not expecting any serious problem. There would be temporary strain for the reasons I have described, but this we were confident would soon disappear. The Chancellor was provided every quarter with official estimates of the future balance-of-payments prospects. The one I received at the time of the Budget of 1964 did not predict any deficit at all, and it was on that basis that I then acted. Subsequently in the latter part of the year the picture changed and the forecasts for later quarters deteriorated though they always lagged behind what in fact happened. The deficit accelerated more than we had expected in the latter part of the year, both on current account and on capital account. We had for reasons set out in the Budget speech expected an unusual outflow of capital, but the trade figures in the summer and early autumn were obstinately refusing to move as we hoped they would. We knew the move would come sometime, but we could not predict exactly the timing, and timing is of the essence in economic problems.

This is when the imminence of the election becomes a problem. As I explain in a subsequent chapter, I pressed Alec very hard to hold the election much earlier in the year. Chancellors always prefer early elections because of the difficulties of uncertainty, but in this case there was the particular problem that the course upon which we were set and which had been publicly proclaimed was likely to produce at some stage temporary difficulties for the balance of payments, and it would be peculiarly difficult if they should coincide, as in the event they did, with a General Election, when the normal combination of uncertainty about the result and wild exaggeration of argument para- lyses economic management and is liable to give foreign opinion fits of the vapours. Neither I nor my advisers believed there was any need to change our policy. We were convinced that we were on course, but clearly we could be wrong, and I thought it my duty to instruct the Treasury to provide, to be available for the incoming Government of which ever Party, schemes for temporary action on the balance of payments if they thought them to be necessary. We did not contemplate devaluation as a possibility, because there did not appear to be any economic argument for it. What the Treasury examined and set out at length were the possibilities of direct action on the balance of payments, either by import quotas or by import surcharges. Both schemes had their disadvantages. Neither, in my opinion, was desirable or necessary, but I thought it right that the possibilities should be examined in advance.

The worst trade figures of all coincided with the election. Despite what was commonly thought, the figures were not available from the Board of Trade until the very last moment before publication. The Chancellor had rarely more than a few hours' advantage over the public and the Press in this matter. I returned on the night of the election from my final day's campaigning to find at No. 11, in my red official box, the trade figures for September; they were extremely disappointing. They became public next day, and they were the figures upon which the incoming Government had to make their decisions.

I believe all the evidence is that they made a profoundly wrong decision. They immediately declared that the situation was disastrous, and that they had to take action. Thereby they magnified Britain's difficulties dramatically, and virtually ruined the prospects of the policy of expansion without inflation on which we were set. Foreign opinion, naturally, took them at their word. If a British Government decries the prospects of the British economy, how can anyone else be expected to think otherwise? For it is a sad irony that Governments are always believed to be speaking the truth when they are saying unhappy things.

I will not go into detail about the actions taken by Mr Wilson and his colleagues. They chose to use the method of the import surcharge, which, as I have said, had been prepared for them as a possibility. I do not think they were right to do so. The facts seem to me to speak for themselves. Whatever the deficit, there were, in Mr Wilson's own words, reserves and facilities more than adequate to cover it. The trade position was already dramatically on the mend. The figures of the current balance quarter by quarter speak for themselves, second quarter 1964 minus £63 million, third quarter minus £192 million, fourth quarter minus £101 million; first quarter 1965 minus £35 million, second quarter minus £8 million. The trend was definite, and as we had predicted. It could not in practical terms owe anything to the Labour Party's decision to impose the import surcharge. The pattern we had predicted proved justified. The improvement had come a few months later than we had hoped, and the peak in September had been rather higher, but the general argument had been fully justified.

Between December 1963 and December 1964 unemployment had fallen from 459,000 to 348,000, production had increased vigorously. The total increase in prices, either wholesale or retail, in the period had been under five per cent. Investment had risen. Confidence in sterling until Mr Wilson took charge of it had remained high. A great opportunity for Britain which the Conservative Government had created had been destroyed by Labour's loss of nerve. Such an opportunity has not recurred since. And we did not have any North Sea oil then.

11 Downing Street had been a splendid address, but as a place in which to live, particularly with a family, it had its drawbacks. Though, on the whole, I must say, we enjoyed it very much.

For the children it created some problems, and I suspect we created some problems for the Downing Street security authorities as well. My oldest son, Martin, then at Oxford, spent his vacations with us. At one time he was earning some money working on a building site in Battersea. I think the guardians of Downing Street were slightly surprised to see him emerging in his navvy's costume at six o'clock in the morning, and even more surprised to see him returning in the same costume with all the stains of a day's hard work about six o'clock in the evening. Though no doubt this was less perturbing for them than the time he arrived with some friends after a fancy-dress party at about four a.m. all dressed in ancient Roman outfits. But they were all very tolerant to us, particularly the police on duty on the doors. I am afraid they were not always repaid with kindness.

On one occasion my two youngest sons, Edward and William, were talking to the policeman on duty at No. 10, who, with great tolerance but some indiscretion, lent them his police whistle, whereupon, to my shame, they rushed through from No. 10 to No. 11 into our first-floor bathroom, where they proceeded to blow blasts on his whistle from the open window. All the massive security machinery for the protection of Downing Street was immediately mobilized and the Maudling family were in the doghouse for some time afterwards.

The same thing, I am afraid, applied when Alec Douglas-Home was making a recorded television broadcast. His advisers recommended that the dining-room at No. 11 would be an ideal setting, and he borrowed it for that purpose. The proceedings went ahead, many versions were taken and rejected for technical reasons, finally all was going perfectly and the recording was faultless until at the last moment

Edward and William burst through the dining-room door engaged in a vigorous game of cowboys and Indians. But, perhaps, the best recollection is my wife's at the time when the Conservative Leadership battle of 1963 was at its height. She was looking out of the kitchen window which overlooked Downing Street and saw Edward, then aged nine, leaning against the lamp-post holding an impromptu press conference, in which he apparently was telling the Press, 'Oh no, my father will not be Prime Minister, he is much too young. My godfather, Rab Butler, is the man. You should plump for him.'

Life in an official Government residence has its advantages and its drawbacks. It is, of course, of great value to have accommodation in London rent free. On the other hand, you are not provided with any staff and you have to do it yourself, or pay out of your own pocket, and some of the regulations are really very quaint. I remember at an early stage, when a lot of electric-light bulbs had failed, asking the Ministry of Works if they could send me over a dozen spare bulbs. I was told this was quite impossible. I could not myself replace an official bulb, but if at any time of day or night an official bulb should fail, I had only to phone the emergency number at the Ministry of Works and a qualified engineer would be sent to replace it. It is hard to believe that such things could happen, but believe me they do. Like the time when we had some electrical work to be done in the dining-room and the sideboard had to be moved to get at it. I came back to find the sideboard moved out obliquely from the wall and I said to Mr Class, who was then working for us, 'Why doesn't someone put it back?'

'Chancellor, it is very difficult,' he said. 'The electricians say that they cannot move furniture, it is against Union rules.'

'Well,' I said, 'why don't you and I put it back?'

'Ah,' he said, 'I am told if we do there may be an industrial dispute.'

However, we did and there wasn't.

Mr Class was a splendid man and a great friend of the family. We wanted someone to help us around the house generally and he had answered the advertisement. He was, in fact, a retired and very jovial fishmonger from Hull, and he came to us in the style and title of butler (he was everything else as well, because we had no other help). His wife had recently died, his family business had caused him difficulties, and he decided that he wanted somewhere congenial to live and work. It suited us very well. He was full of nautical tradition. It was never 'Yes, sir' but 'Aye, aye, sir'. If a taxi that had been ordered had arrived, it had 'come alongside', and the homely way he welcomed our guests was a delight to all but the pompous. We had a little brush with the security authorities about him once. I had a complaint that he had been seen bringing women back to No. 11 late at night. My response, knowing as I did that in fact it was his daughter, an airline hostess, and a friend of hers, was 'Why shouldn't he, and what was it to do with the security authorities anyway?' They took the whole matter very seriously, and when I refused to dismiss him, they insisted on having fresh bolts on the doors between No. 10 and No. 11, which seemed to solve the problem to everyone's satisfaction, though what the value of the operation was still baffles me. Anyway, he was a great friend of ours, and we were very sorry when we heard the news of his death some short time after I had left No. 11, and he moved on to another job.

Many people think that officials at the Treasury or the Revenue Departments are simply prosaic, calculating people. In fact this is to underestimate them. Let me quote one example. At one stage I was considering the possibility of imposing a tax on gaming in Britain and, as I understood that such taxes were operating in France and Germany, I suggested to the Customs and Excise that they should go and investigate. They were a little coy at first, but once they realized that I was in earnest, they agreed to do so. So we wrote off to the French and German Governments, asking if they could be so kind as to arrange suitable facilities. The French did not reply; no doubt they thought this was another Anglo-Saxon plot. The Germans were very forthcoming, and as a result a team from H.M. Customs and Excise went to Baden Baden, the site of one of the leading German casinos. They were gone for several days, no doubt impelled by their sense of thoroughness in the pursuit of their duties. When they got back, they came to report to me. Their report was short and simple and to the point: 'Chancellor,' they said, 'we are very sorry to say that having examined the whole system we can really find no satisfactory way of taxing gaming in this country, but,' they added, as an afterthought, 'we have discovered a very good system of winning at roulette.'

9

The Tory Leadership Contest

1963

IT was while I was at the Treasury that the leadership of the Tory Party and the Prime Ministership passed from Harold Macmillan to Alec Douglas-Home. I was deeply involved in this struggle. It was not the only such struggle that affected me. There was the later one with Ted Heath in 1965. The two were conducted on quite different lines. In 1963 the Party was still working on the old system of the right man 'emerging' from various rather arcane Party processes. I do not think many people felt that in 1963 the process really measured up to modern conditions, and that was why by 1965 the new system of a ballot among Members of Parliament had been instituted and was operated. I think on the whole the second system was the better one, and more suitable to the problems of the second half of the twentieth century. I am, I suppose, the only person who can say this manifestly without bias, as I managed to get beaten under both systems.

I remember when Anthony Eden resigned, discussing the prospects separately with Rab and Harold Macmillan, both of whom thought they would win. Harold, in fact, told me the night before the decision that he had his son Maurice's assurance that he would win, 'Because the Party think I am too old and too sick to last for very long'. That was a typical Harold Macmillan remark, not meant to be taken seriously. Yet I feel the truth probably is that Rab lost rather than Harold won. Rab's problem always was that while he had very widespread and heartfelt support in many parts of the Party, there were also a substantial number of important people who were implacably opposed to him. Much of this opposition seemed to derive from the time of Suez, when people felt that he had in some ways tried to dissociate himself from the Government's policy. This, I think, was unfair and certainly there would be no argument for saying that he was too moderate a Conservative compared with Harold, for if he was the originator of Butskellism, Harold had been the author of the Middle Way.

Whatever the reasons, Harold won the day, and he set about the difficult task of giving new life and leadership to a Party whose morale had been sadly dented by recent events. He served the Party well. It took him a little while to play himself in, and the public did not quite know what to make of this man with his deliberately old-fashioned mannerisms and rather unfamiliar style. But when his authority was established it was complete. People began to realize that he was a man of political genius, and when the cartoonists showed him as Supermac or Mr MacWonder, this was not wholly intended to be derisory, it reflected a genuine appreciation of a remarkable capacity for government and administration.

By 1963, however, his grip on the Party had begun to relax. Politicians, like ships, grow barnacles on their bottoms which slowly but surely weigh them down. There is clearly a limit to the length of time any politician in modern conditions can hope to maintain the complete support and loyalty of his followers: the sheer passage of time was bound to weaken his position. The abrupt changes he had made during the night of the long knives in July 1962, when so many Cabinet Ministers were removed, had not helped. There was a good deal of resentment in many quarters. In these circumstances the Profumo affair was bound to be very damaging to him, however unjustly, and he himself, I know, felt this bitterly. I remember him saying to me on one occasion in Admiralty House, which he was using while Downing Street was being repaired, that he never thought he could be 'brought down by two tarts'.

So during the spring and summer of 1963 the pressure on him continued to grow, and people began looking around for alternative leaders. There were several available. There was, of course, Rab, there was Quintin Hogg, and there was myself. The strength of my position was that I had been fortunate enough to inherit, as Chancellor of the Exchequer, a situation in which large tax reductions had been not only possible but desirable. My Budget of 1963 had undoubtedly been popular in the Party and in the country, which was a stroke of great good fortune. Someone, I was never quite sure who it was, started to organize a regular poll of Conservative M.P.s, which was published in the *Daily Telegraph,* stating who they would like to have as Leader, and in the summer of 1963 they all gave me a very large majority. In these circumstances I thought it right to go and see Harold, to assure him that while I should like to be his successor, I would play no part at all in any intrigues to get him to go. I remember well being ushered into his little sitting-room at Admiralty House. It was mid-afternoon, and he was sitting perfectly poised, or posed, in a wing-chair reading a small volume of Trollope. I do not recall the details of the interview, but I do remember that it was an entirely friendly one, and the understanding between us was open and sincere.

During the summer recess things appeared to change. For some reason I could not quite discern, my own position had weakened, and I could gauge this from the reactions of some of my Cabinet colleagues, which, while always cordial, were somewhat less enthusiastically cordial after the recess than they had been before. But still the question remained, would Harold go or would he stay on? As the Party Conference approached none of us really knew in the Cabinet what his decision was, and I am not entirely convinced that he knew himself. But then fate took a hand, in the shape of the affliction which he suffered early one morning in the week of the Party Conference. The Cabinet met later that morning before leaving for Blackpool to join the Conference and he informed us of the position. I remember that I was sitting opposite to him and it was apparent from his face that he was in considerable pain. He asked that the necessary processes to select a successor should begin. So the first question had been resolved in a manner that was decisive but to all of us who were his friends as deeply sad as it was sudden.

And so we all went to Blackpool with things very much in the melting-pot. It was clear to his colleagues that Harold was going to resign, though the exact timing of the announcement was not clear. It was also obvious that there were a number of potential successors. There was Rab who in experience and status had a position that no one else could really rival. There was Quintin Hogg, for whom the Party had an enormous and justifiable affection. Both of these candidates had strong support for them but both of them possessed the disadvantage of having pretty strong elements in the Party against them. Then there was myself, who had, as I said, been enjoying a remarkable summer of support from the Parliamentary Party, who were likely to be in substance if not in form the decisive element. Finally, there was Alec, who had declared to his colleagues in the Cabinet when Harold suffered his illness that he was in no circumstances a candidate himself. But no man can really say this, however sincerely he believes it, for if his Party wants him he must do their bidding.

The Blackpool Conference that year was, as you would expect, a turmoil. There were many people pressing the case for Quintin Hogg, including Randolph Churchill who went round with a large supply of rosettes with a great 'Q' on them, which he affixed freely; including on one occasion irreverently on the generous posterior of the Lord Chancellor, Lord Dilhorne. There was a group of people dedicated to the defeat of Rab in any circumstances whatsoever (I called them the 'Blue Blood and Thunder' Group), and fewer people, I am sorry to say, who were really dedicated to Rab's success. My own support had certainly dwindled over the summer. I remember meeting a Cabinet colleague in the lobby of the hotel on my arrival, who had written to me only a short time before, saying that he was convinced that Harold Macmillan must go and that I was the only person who could possibly succeed him. I knew that in the meantime he had switched his allegiance to Alec, so I had great pleasure in thanking him warmly for his charming and sincere letter to me.

A lot was bound to depend upon how the various candidates performed at the Conference. I think all their performances were predictable. Quintin was his warm, ebullient, emotional self, commanding the enthusiasm and loyalty of many, but arousing the doubts and apprehensions of many others. Rab was himself, neither more nor less. He had to deputize for Harold and give the final speech of the Conference, and he did this with great dignity, not trying to seize for himself the opportunity to advance his own ambitions. Alec presided with discretion and a certain aloofness. I had to make a speech myself fairly early in the proceedings as Chancellor. My friends told me that it was very important that I should get it right. I am afraid I did not.

I do not think I can give a better account than was given in the *Sunday Express* of 4 October 1973 by Wilfrid Sendall, one of the most shrewd of political observers, who wrote as follows :

Realization that, whatever else happened Butler would be blackballed, opened the way for another candidate, the man whom had I been a Tory kingmaker I would have picked.

I had known Reginald Maudling since before he entered the Commons, when he was one of the ablest of Butler's team in the Tory Research Department.

I knew that my own admiration for his talents was shared by a very large number of Tory M.P.s. I knew that, though he had critics, he had no enemies, and that he was equally respected on the Labour side, an attribute I thought no disadvantage.

But Maudling would not wish to frustrate or defeat Rab Butler. His loyalty to his old Research Department chief was too strong. He therefore had to be convinced that Butler had no chance anyway. As I was convinced of this I resolved to pass on to him my evidence, for what it was worth.

I sent him a message declaring my conviction that the Hailsham bid, spectacular as it was, would fail, as Randolph Churchill was overdoing the razzmatazz and producing a hostile reaction.

The line about the Old Leader's choice was being over-exploited. The Tories did not care for their leadership to be treated like a personal inheritance, which could be handed on at the will of the previous incumbent as if Harold Macmillan were the Aga Khan.

I pointed out that Maudling had the conference platform reserved for him next morning, when he was to reply as Chancellor to an important debate. I exhorted him to believe that this was his moment.

That evening Reggie had similar advice from a more impressive quarter – John Morrison, chairman of the 1922 Committee had seen the Chancellor, and had assured him that the leadership was within his grasp.

Soon after breakfast next morning I received a copy of the Maudling speech. It was a cracker. I have read innumerable political speeches in my life but never one which seemed so right for the occasion. It was eloquent, moving, wise. It merited the adjective statesmanlike. Even now, reading it again after ten years, I feel that given the delivery it deserved it would have brought the conference to its feet and swept Maudling to the front in the leadership race.

On the platform as Maudling rose to speak, Iain Macleod generously whispered to him : 'Go on, Reggie, this is your chance.'

This is what Maudling had written :

'As I sit at my desk in the Treasury, as I sit there with sheaves of papers, columns of figures, I never forget that behind them all lie the family in the overcrowded home, the school-leavers we heard about this morning, the retired couple struggling in a perplexing world, the young couple starting out on a new life together, the Indian peasant who is wringing a mere existence from the unrelenting soil.

'They are the realities of economic policy, and we should never forget it. My job as Chancellor is to increase the wealth of Britain. There are some who decry the value of material prosperity. I do not share their view. There is no grandeur in poverty and the human spirit is constricted, not liberated, by squalor and privation.'

So it moved on to a peroration which Churchill would not have disdained :

'There are great things to be done; meeting the passion for education, clearing up the pools of squalor that still disfigure some parts of our national life, bringing light and air and beauty to our cities, bringing aid and succour to the people of Asia and Africa who live at the edge of subsistence.

'These are the purposes which we disguise under the name of economic policy. They are noble purposes.'

Thus Reginald Maudling, at the critical moment of his career, declared his faith. If only the delivery could have matched the words.

But, alas, it fell abysmally below them.

Handed to Churchill, or to Macmillan or Macleod, this text would have produced a famous speech. Maudling himself wrecked it.

I do not think I would disagree with Wilfrid's diagnosis.

So we left Blackpool with the great issue unresolved. I ventured to suggest that back in London decisions would be taken by 'deliberation and not by the decibel meter'. The decision did not lie in the hands of the Conference but in the rather mysterious channels of communication within the Party. What perhaps I had not realized was how closely those channels had been listening to the decibel meter.

And so the voices were collected. The traditional yet mysterious process continued. I am not quite sure to this day what happened. Reggie Dilhorne collected the voices of the Cabinet, and I remember our conversation very well. He asked me who I was voting for. I said myself of course, but as a second choice, Rab. The views of the Parliamentary Party, their Lordships, and the Party in the country were collected and sifted and presented under the guidance of the Chief Whip, Lord Redmayne, to Harold Macmillan, whose fundamental duty it was to advise the Queen. It became slowly realized by some, again mysterious, process that the advice was that she should send for Alec.

This did give rise to considerable concern and apprehension. There were many of us who felt that Alec, with all his qualities, suffered from a disability in political terms in being the fourteenth Earl of Home. Many of us, particularly those who knew Rab well, felt he would be a better choice, and we thought we were entitled to make this known. After all, we were a fairly important element in the Cabinet, especially Iain, Enoch and myself, and we had an entitlement to express our view. There followed the famous meeting in Enoch Powell's house that Thursday evening. I had been dining with the Governor of the Bank of England, and when I got home to my flat I was told of what was happening, that several people were deeply concerned, and I was invited to go to a meeting at Enoch Powell's house round the corner. The *Daily Express* found out about it with supreme efficiency, and when we broke up, were waiting for us on the pavement, led by that very great political journalist, Derek Marks. I think it was probably my fault that they found out. Someone from the *Express* phoned my home to ask to talk to me, and was told that I had gone round to a meeting at Enoch's. So simply do these things happen. Anyway, we met there, Enoch, Iain, Freddie Erroll, myself and Toby Aldington. Rab did not come, though we were in touch with him by telephone. The Chief Whip came round to join us. We made it clear that in our view the choice was a mistake from the Party point of view. I know Harold Macmillan has said that in his view there was something rather unseemly about our behaviour, but for once I cannot agree with him. We all had a strong and genuine feeling : we all thought a mistake was being made. It was not only our right but our duty to say this in the most effective way we could.

So Friday dawned, the decisive day. Alec was summoned by the Queen and asked rather unusually by her not to be Prime Minister, but to see if he could form an administration. He returned to Downing Street and immediately invited me to see him. He asked if I would be his Chancellor of the Exchequer. I said that I hoped he would withdraw that question because I would hate to say 'No' to him. Though I was happy to serve under him, I thought he was the wrong choice and Rab would be the right one. He said that I should realize that there was a deep underlying opposition to Rab in the Party, and that if I and Iain and Enoch prevented him becoming Leader, Rab would not get it because of the opposition to him and the choice would almost certainly devolve on me. I made it absolutely clear to him, and I have been grateful to him for his friendship ever since, that I was not trying to play that sort of game at all. My position was that I would serve under either Rab or himself, but, as I said to him, quite frankly I thought Rab would be the better choice. And so we left his invitation to me in abeyance.

There was much toing and froing thereafter, and many accounts have been given. It is a long time ago now and hard to recollect details with clarity and exactitude. There was a quadripartite meeting : Alec,

M.—E

Rab, Quintin and myself. I kept a record of it, about the only detailed record I ever kept. Alas, I kept it in pencil and when I came to look at it a year or two later, it had faded beyond reading. Anyway, the details do not matter all that much. There were those who were urging Rab to seize the opportunity, and telling him that his power was such that he could demand the premiership. I am not sure that they were really right. The opposition to him was too strong; and I do not think Rab himself really believed that they were right either. Certainly he decided, and it is to his eternal credit that he did so decide, not to make any such move. And so the decision was taken. Alec formed an administration and as it was both the will of the Party and, on the whole, the logic of events that he should do so, the other three of us accepted his invitation to join him. Iain Macleod and Enoch Powell would not. They felt as a matter of principle that they should stand out against a choice which they believed to be wrong. I respected the sincerity of their motives, but I thought their judgement was wrong.

I enjoyed working for Alec. He is a man, as the world knows, of total integrity. It wasn't quite the same as working for Harold Macmillan, or Winston Churchill for that matter, but he was a man for whom one could feel respect and under whose leadership one could give one's full efforts. He inspired an extraordinary affection among the rank and file of the Tory Party who regarded him as the sort of man they would like to be themselves : a good athlete; not brilliant but intelligent; a man of charm, integrity and balance. I think it was a good choice. He might well have become a great Prime Minister if there had been time. He was good at taking advice, he delegated and I believe, though I am biased, he was pursuing the right economic policy.

The only arguments we had were two. The first was about the timing of the 1964 election. The second was about his resignation. I wanted to go early in 1964. All Chancellors always want to have early elections, because uncertainty is immensely damaging to the economy, and the longer things are drawn out, almost invariably the worse they become. In 1964 we were engaged in the experiment which I have described, of breaking out of the stop-go cycle into a new phase of steady expansion without inflation. There was bound to be a crunch period some time, no one could say when exactly, but the most likely time was the autumn when by tradition sterling always came under considerable pressure.

I wanted the election in the early part of the year, Alec could not agree. He had been advised by the Party professionals that we would be bound to lose, and he was too modest a man to pit his own personal judgement against that of the professionals so he turned down a February/March election. I hoped that we would get one in June, but it was not to be. It came in October, a very bad time from the Government's point of view, and particularly for the Chancellor's, and yet Alec very nearly won it. I think people tend to underestimate how remarkable was his achievement in that election. We had been in power then for thirteen years. Governments too like ships and Party Leaders grow barnacles on their bottoms with the passage of time, which drag them down, and it would have been a triumph indeed to have succeeded in 1964. Richly, in my view, he was entitled to that success.

There was only a cat's whisker in it at the end. On the Friday morning after the poll I was in No. 11 when Alec came on the phone and said he was asking any Ministers currently in London to come and have a drink with him before lunch and review the situation. We were sitting round in his drawing-room, just a few of us, in No. 10 about midday, discussing when exactly he should go to the Palace to hand in his resignation, when Elizabeth Home put her head round the door and said, 'Alec, come and look at the latest results on the television. You have not lost yet,' and indeed for an hour or so it was as close as that.

10

The Years of Opposition

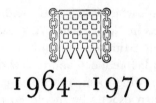

1964–1970

THERE are always considerable difficulties in getting adjusted to loss of office. The change is abrupt, the notice negligible. I can think of no other occupation where the procedure is so brutal. No Trade Union leader would tolerate it for a moment for his members. As soon as we knew we had been defeated in the election we had to leave our offices immediately, and in the case of those of us who had been fortunate enough to have official accommodation, our homes as well. I suppose it is inevitable, for the Queen's Government must be carried on, but it is sometimes slightly humiliating.

I remember our removal from No. 11. We had a van stationed by the back gate, through which we removed the remains of our domestic equipment, which, as you know, never look very dignified. I was struggling across the garden carrying a packing-case full of the usual debris of domestic life, such as ageing toys, and half-empty bottles of ketchup, when I happened to look up at the windows of No. 10, and there framed in the window next door to the Cabinet Room, with a wide grin, was none other than Lord Balogh, of whom it was said that he managed to get himself installed with telephone, secretary and even carpet in record time.

After you have departed from the corridors of power, you have the complicated business of restoring the facilities which you then enjoyed. Secretarial help is an obvious one; the use of a motor-car one misses perhaps even more. But perhaps all in all it is no bad thing, because to be absorbed in these minor distractions and irritations is a good anti-dote to the shock of political defeat.

I soon found myself involved in a bitter argument with Mr Wilson about the economic situation which he had inherited. This was only to be expected. Any incoming Government is liable to depict its inherit-ance in the gloomiest possible terms, thereby hoping to minimize its own initial mistakes and maximize its subsequent achievements. It is not a habit confined to any one Party. I remember a famous speech by Harry Crookshank in the House of Commons, describing the con-ditions we had inherited from the Attlee Government, when he said that it was not merely a matter of skeletons in the cupboard, 'They were hanging from the candelabra.'

But it is a custom that should be resisted, for it does no good to the country and, as I have already explained, the situation which the Labour Government inherited certainly had its difficulties, but these were made infinitely worse by its own actions. The battle about the Tory record and the Labour attack on what they called the thirteen wasted years continued throughout that period up to and into the election of March 1966. A good deal of my time was devoted to it. I summed up my attitude in an election platform article I wrote for the *Glasgow Herald*:

Mr Wilson has preferred to spend most of his time on the old, stale abuse about the past. He talks of the thirteen years of Conservative rule : but he does not give the true picture.

Those were years during which the living standards of people in this country rose more than they had in fifty years before. More than four million new homes were built; the number of owner-occupiers multiplied from four million to eight million. Taxes were reduced by the equivalent of £2,000 million. Pensions and other benefits were increased time and time again, fully implementing the Conservative promise that the pen-sioners would share in the rising prosperity of the country.

Expenditure on education rose from three per cent of the national income at the beginning of our period of office to five per cent of a vastly increased national income at the end. These are some of the facts about the thirteen years of Conservative government. Facts that Mr Wilson chooses conveniently to ignore.

His other theme is that he inherited a deficit of £800 million and that, in the course of 1965, he was able to halve it. The truth is that, of the 'deficit' of £750 million in 1964, nearly half was investment in mines, factories, and oil wells overseas : new, income-producing assets bringing strength to Britain.

What Mr Wilson inherited was not the problem of 1964 : 1964 was nearly over and the problem had been handled by the Conservatives without loss of confidence abroad.

What he inherited was the prospects of 1965 : rising production and an export boom based on orders received during the period of Conservative government.

In the meantime, of course, there had been the change of leadership. I do not think Alec was ever as happy in Opposition as he was in the Government, a sentiment which I myself much share. But I believe he underestimated his own achievement. As usually happens in the Conservative Party the old rules of public life applied, namely that there is no gratitude in politics, and you should never kick a man until he is down.

Criticisms began to develop. Harold Wilson, after his disastrous start, seemed to be catching some of the imagination of the public. There was grumbling within the Party at Westminster, and throughout the country, about Alec's leadership – grumbling which, incidentally, ceased the day he gave it up. He talked to me a little about it. My advice to him was strongly that he should stay. Apart from his patent integrity and the enormous affection he commanded in so many parts of the country, he had the supreme advantage of being a total contrast to Harold Wilson. In the two-Party system contrasts are immensely important. This asset, which Alec possessed, I thought he was seriously underrating, and so it turned out. I do not know exactly what happened, but I remember reading one morning in a national daily an account by some percipient political journalist, of a party which had taken place the night before, and the comment that those present felt that a new and fundamental change was taking place in the political situation of the Conservative Party. It was not difficult to guess what was meant by this, so I rang Alec that morning. He asked me to go round and talk to him, and then told me of the decision he had taken to resign, and the reasons for it. I could only repeat that while I disagreed with him I respected his reasons.

And so the next leadership battle began. The rules were different this time. It was no more a question of the magic circle, it was no more a procedure of a confidential and mysterious character whereby voices were collected and opinions expressed. There was to be a direct ballot among the Parliamentary Party for the leadership. There were three

"Fight over the leadership! What fight over the leadership?"

With every good wish from
Michael Cummings

candidates, Ted, Enoch, and myself. Clearly no one expected Enoch to get more than a handful of votes, though that handful in a divided Party could have been decisive. The main battle lay between Ted and myself and our respective supporters.

It went on for a fairly short time, amidst a great hullabaloo from the Press, while every move either of us made was portrayed across the front pages of the national dailies, or in the media. Ted had his friends and supporters and I had mine. I do not know what his team did, and I certainly had not the slightest reason to complain about anything.

I do not think there was any canvassing as such; there was certainly no argument, let alone acrimony. My supporters armed themselves with a list of all M.P.s and ran round asking them who were they going to vote for. Naturally a majority told them they were voting for me. I have no doubt that Ted's supporters got precisely the same reaction, in the nature of things. When it came to the day of the great vote in a committee room of the House of Commons, I turned up to record my vote for myself, and was told with great confidence by my supporters that the bandwagon had begun to roll. I omitted to question them as to the direction in which it was rolling. Certainly they had reason for confidence : an opinion poll in the *Daily Express* that morning had given me a very substantial lead.

I went out to lunch in the City at Kleinwort's while awaiting the result, and halfway through lunch I was telephoned by Robert Carr, who had been supporting me, to say that he had bad news, the figures were Ted 150, me 133, Enoch 15. That, it seemed to me, was that. The Party had spoken, and although there was a provision for a second ballot on such a narrow result, there was not much point in asking people to say the same thing over again. Ted commanded the support of just over half of the Parliamentary Party, and this I considered quite decisive. So I rang him up, conceded defeat and said I would be glad to serve under him in his capacity as Leader of the Party.

Looking back on it I think the Party were probably right. There is a strange instinct in British politics, both in the electorate as a whole and in the corporate membership of individual Parties, which leads people to the right conclusions. I will not deny that it was a bitter blow. I had been working for success for many years. I was looking forward to success and had reasonable grounds for expecting it. But there it was.

The only thing I resent at all is those people who since that day have occasionally written, like some of the more trendy political journalists, to say that Reggie did not get it because he was too lazy to work hard enough for it. How little do they understand human nature, these fervent scribes! The weight of responsibility that sits on a Prime Minister's shoulders is an awesome one. He can do more harm for his fellow citizens in one single act of folly than anyone else, and the opportunities for committing an act of folly are continuous and un-limited. While the contest was in progress, I could not help from time to time, particularly late at night, brooding on the responsibility that I was seeking to undertake. One thing to me was absolutely clear, if

the Party wanted me, I would be a happy and fulfilled man to undertake the responsibility. Then I could give of my best and make my own
decisions for better or for worse with a clear conscience, because I
would be responding to an invitation. Had I fought for the leadership
as a matter of personal ambition, had I seized it as a result of some
campaign or stratagem, the weight of subsequent responsibility would
have been infinitely multiplied. It is one thing to be leader of your
country because your own supporters wish you to do it. Then you can
sleep easy with your conscience if you know you have done your best
to fulfil your duty. It would be another thing to sleep easy with your
conscience in the dark and dangerous days that inevitably come if you
knew you had assumed the responsibility because you had wanted it,
fought for it, campaigned and contrived for it yourself.

Ted asked me to take on the job of Shadow Foreign Secretary,
which I did with great pleasure. It was a new field to me. Most of my
years had been spent in economic Departments but, of course, in
modern conditions there is a very large foreign aspect to economic
policy, and I had been able to acquire, through the various negotiations in which I had taken part, a fairly wide acquaintance with
leading figures in most of the main countries of the world. To put this
to use as Shadow Foreign Secretary was very enjoyable.

Early on I decided to make another visit to Russia. Experience had
taught me that fear is by far the most powerful and important of
human motives in political matters, and it is the existence of the fear
rather than its justification that gives it strength. This is one of the
reasons why the rational approach to political problems so often fails.

It is possible to take two views about Russian motives in their dealings with the West. You can believe, as many do, that their aim is
world domination, that they are determined to overthrow the capitalist
world and establish their hegemony over the continents, starting with
Europe. The other view is that basically what interests them is their
own country and all that they plan and do is really based upon their
desire to develop Mother Russia and the lives of the Russian peoples.
Their attitude, therefore, to the capitalist world is really defensive. Of
course, in many ways the results are the same whichever view you
take. If they are frightened of attack by the West, they will do all they
can to undermine the strength of the West, just as much as they would
if they were preparing an aggression of their own. So far as concerns
Western defence, therefore, the deductions to be drawn are the same
whichever view one takes of the basic motive. The West must keep up

'*Everyone likes the Prime Minister who never was.*'
Could any politician hope for more from a cartoon?

its guard. But if you look beyond the immediate future to the long-term problem of coexistence on a basis of mutual trust, which is the only satisfactory basis possible, then judgement of the Russian motive becomes of fundamental importance. The approach the West should make to the long-term problems of disarmament and coexistence must depend upon the judgement the West makes on the long-term Russian motive.

I have always myself taken the second view, and this has been strengthened by my contacts with the many Russian leaders I have met over the years. I think it was true of Khrushchev and Mikoyan, I think it is true also of Brezhnev and Kosygin.

It was on this trip to Russia that I saw most of Kosygin, who impressed me immensely. Humphrey Trevelyan was by then our Ambassador, and like his predecessor, Frank Roberts, an Ambassador of outstanding quality. When I was there he was shortly to retire under the Foreign Office rule of retirement at sixty, before he could complete even a third year as Ambassador. It seemed to me an outstanding example of the folly of this rigid rule, which, in effect, was to remove an Ambassador who had just achieved his maximum power and influence and knowledge in Moscow, and it was made to appear all the more foolish when he was subsequently recalled from retirement to sort out the problems of Aden.

Humphrey took us to a Grand Reception in the Kremlin, which was given for Tito, who was then visiting. Those receptions are remarkable affairs, and a trained diplomat can assess the importance attached to the particular visitor by the grade of food and drink provided. It was certainly lavish on this occasion, though while the British made straight for the caviare the most popular item among the Russian dignitaries themselves were the oranges, which they consumed with great gusto. This was one of the curious things about Moscow : if you went to the circus you would find people queuing up for caviare at the buffet in the interval, but you began to understand when you realized that the price of the caviare was considerably less than the price of the lemon which you squeezed over it. Incidentally, I still have in my mind's eye the scene at a football match we attended between the Moscow Dynamo and the Red Army, when a whole row of seats was occupied by a very distinguished group of Russian Generals, all wearing row after row of medals, and every one, without exception, sucking an ice-cream cornet.

My conversation with Tito was brief.

'Mr Maudling, I understand you support the American activity in Vietnam?'

'Yes.'

'Why do you support the Americans?'

'Because I think they are right.'

'Oh.'

It was not a very satisfactory conversation, but, at any rate, it was a friendly one, and I reminded Tito of it when I subsequently met him at a lunch that Ted Heath gave for him at Chequers.

Kosygin also dealt extensively with the position of America in Vietnam during the fairly length discussions we subsequently had. He asked me whether I did not agree that the Americans in Vietnam were acting like robbers, to which I felt bound to reply that a robber went into another man's house to take away his possessions, whereas the Americans had gone to Vietnam not to take anything away, but to leave their own blood and treasure there, in defence of what they thought to be right. Kosygin took no offence at this answer. He was a man with whom it was both easy and agreeable to have a rational argument. What, I think, struck me most about him was his great interest in all technological matters, and particularly in chemical engineering, which he had studied himself. He and his colleagues were genuinely absorbed in the need to bolster Russian technology, to enhance the living standards of their people, and there is no doubt they wanted to work with the West to this end. Mikoyan indeed, at one time, proposed to me that we should form an oil cartel, rather on the lines of the South African diamond cartel, because by reorganizing the distribution of sterling oil and rouble oil respectively considerable economies could possibly be made.

I wonder what their attitude would be now? The Conservative Party is not all that popular these days in Moscow. I was returning from a visit to Japan in January 1977, and planning to travel via Moscow. I asked the Soviet authorities if I could call again on Kosygin and Brezhnev, as I had in the past, but I am afraid the answer was that while anyone could come to Moscow, as a leading member of the Conservative Party I could not expect to have interviews of that kind. I pointed out to the Ambassador that this was a bit hard, as I had just been given the sack by Margaret Thatcher. He seemed to regard this as a great joke, though it made no difference to their decision. Nevertheless, I believe it is of enormous importance to try and establish some closer relations with the Russian leaders. Whatever there may be in their society that we dislike intensely, they are the men that matter, the men we shall have to live with, and you gain no advantage by shouting at one another across a void of mutual mistrust and misunderstanding.

After the 1966 Election we settled down to the long slog of Opposition, knowing that it would be several years before we were likely to have an opportunity of being in Government again. From time to time Ted asked me to do various jobs for him – Defence, Commonwealth Relations, Coordinating Opposition tactics in the House of Commons, Chairman of the Advisory Committee on Policy. All in all I was able, as a result, to familiarize myself and take responsibility, at one time or another, for most of the major elements of policy. Of course there were arguments within the Party at that time on a wide range of policy issues. A Party cannot progress save by thesis and antithesis (to quote Hegel again) and on the whole I think most of our arguments led to synthesis. I was generally regarded as the apostle of 'consensus' politics, and I had no objection to such a label. As I said in a newspaper article in 1968 in the *Sunday Times*, 'I for one do not object to the idea of consensus. I think it is better for a democracy to progress where possible by agreement. I know of no industrialist who prefers fighting the Trade Unions to working with them where this is possible. Disagreement and controversy are productive of new ideas, but sheer conflict produces nothing but damage; as Winston Churchill said, "Jaw jaw is better than war war".'

On the whole the balance swung to the Right during these years, culminating in the famous meeting at Selsdon Park. This was inevitable; Parties in Opposition always swing away from the centre though, ironically enough, if they wish to increase their chances of recapturing power they should do precisely the opposite and try to recapture the middle ground. It is one thing to please your own supporters, and certainly the more satisfied they are the more enthusiastic will be their support, but the basic rule of politics is that even your most enthusiastic supporter cannot vote twice over. The danger is that you are led to adopt policies simply because they are different from those of the other side. This process of opposition for opposition's sake has always seemed to me of dubious value. There are, of course, advantages in contrast, particularly in style of leadership and, as I have explained, this is one of the reasons why I urged Alec Douglas-Home not to resign when he did. But it is foolish to base your policies on sheer opposition of the other side, as I said in the *Sunday Times* article.

It cannot be sensible for any great party to set out to find a policy that is just the opposite of what its opponents are doing. The reasons for this are many. In the first place, of course, it gives the initiative to our opponents, creating a situation where we merely react to what they do instead of developing our own ideas. Secondly, it strains the credulity of the public. The electorate know perfectly well that no group of human beings can either be always right or always wrong, and the tactics of instant and automatic opposition carry no conviction.

Throughout this period there were constant rumours of arguments between Ted and myself. They really were not well founded. Our relations as Leader and Deputy Leader were not intimate. We seldom if ever had a meal alone together. Our temperaments were quite different, as were our interests, but there never was, to my recollection, any form of a row between us. We worked on a basis of mutual respect and confidence, and I have always been deeply grateful to Ted for that.

During those Opposition years I took up a number of appointments in industry, of which the first and principal one was as a part-time Executive Director of Kleinwort, Benson, Ltd., the merchant bankers. There is, from time to time, controversy about the question of Members of Parliament working in industry or commerce. I think a good deal of it is totally misguided.

There are some who sincerely believe that to be a Member of Parliament should be a full-time job, whether as Minister or Back-bencher, though this in itself is clearly self-contradictory. Either the Back-bencher would have too little to do or the Minister too much. I have never shared this point of view, nor has it ever been accepted as the collective view of the House of Commons. There are a number of reasons against it. The idea of a Parliament consisting entirely of whole-time politicians fills me with apprehension. In the first place it would mean subservience to the Party Whips and the Party Organization. If a man is to rely wholly upon his membership of Parliament to sustain himself and his family, it makes it far more difficult for him to adopt from time to time any independent point of view, if the consequences would be the abrupt termination of his career. Secondly, there is already danger enough of M.P.s being too remote from the ordinary industrial and commercial life of the country.

I have noticed this all the years I have been in Parliament. There are, on the Labour side, a number of Members with considerable practical experience of Trade Union matters. There are, on both sides, many professional men, lawyers in particular, lecturers and journalists, but the House of Commons, and particularly the Conservative Benches, have lacked people with practical experience of the problems of management, and this has been a considerable source of weakness. When I first went into Parliament there was a remarkable Back-bench Member on our side called Sir Peter Bennett, who was Chairman of the Lucas Company, and a very active executive Chairman too. He was able to come down to the House and describe exactly what had been happening that morning on the shopfloor in the Lucas factories in Birmingham. He was always listened to with great respect and attention on both sides of the House, and his contribution was very valuable. There have been few like him since.

There is too, quite frankly, the question of money. People do not go into politics in order to make money, or if they do, they are very misguided. But, on the other hand, they cannot reasonably be expected to neglect their interests and those of their families. The simple facts are these. An M.P. receives a modest salary and is entitled to a correspondingly modest pension; a Minister receives a substantial salary, which indicates that it is reasonable to expect to earn more money if you are doing a lot of work over and above being a constituency Member. But service as a Minister, unlike service as a Back-bencher, carries with it no pension rights whatsoever, save in one or two special cases. This means that all the years you are working as a Minister you are not accumulating the kind of pension rights from work which anyone in almost any other paid occupation expects as a matter of course. One of the ways in which you can offset this is by endeavouring to earn money in industry or commerce when out of office. It seems to me a perfectly reasonable system, and indeed a beneficial one to British industry, for which the advice of former Ministers should be of value. And there are many illustrious examples.

Working for Kleinwort Benson was an interesting and agreeable experience. I formed many new friendships which still exist. I learnt a great deal. Whether in practice I was able to make a really substantial contribution I cannot say. Certainly I was conscious from the start of the considerable gap in thinking between Whitehall and the City of London. Since then a number of former politicians and Civil Servants have moved into positions in the City and I think the gap has been narrowed if not closed entirely. But it was surprising to find, for example, what different interpretations would be placed upon the word 'liquidity' in the Treasury, on the one hand, or round the Board table of Kleinwort Benson on the other. I was fascinated too by our mutual reactions to the World Bank and the International Monetary Fund. It soon became quite clear to me that in bankers' eyes the International Monetary Fund was a bank, while the World Bank was in fact a fund.

I took on a number of other appointments as well. I was a Director of Dunlops, one of the great traditional British companies; I was on the Board of A.E.I. when we were taken over by G.E.C.; I was in Sydney, Australia, when I received a communication saying that as a result I was no longer a Director, the only communication which in fact I received. I became Chairman of a group called Shipping Industrial Holdings, a vigorous group of whom Sandy Glen was in fact the executive leader. They had a wide range of activities from shipbroking, in which they were world leaders, through shipowning and insurance, to the Clarkson Holiday Company, at that time the most vigorously expanding of the tour operators.

It was with S.I.H. that I learnt some of the difficulties of being a part-time director. The first example is this. It was proposed to the Board that we should buy two very large vessels in Japan, and I enquired where we should find the money to pay for them. This naive enquiry was greeted with derision. Did the Chairman not realize that the last thing you need when you want to buy a ship is money? What you need is credit. Most of it would come from the shipbuilder and the rest could be raised on the strength of the charters arranged for the ship. In fact it was a very good operation indeed from the British point of view. The money was raised from foreign sources and operations took place almost entirely overseas, carrying goods from Australia to Japan, for example. All that came to this country was the profit, forming part of the enormous contribution which the British shipping industry makes to the well-being of our country.

The other and more serious lesson was about the very difficult position occupied by any non-executive director. I have yet to see an answer to this problem. As a director he has to take responsibility, but as a non-executive he is not in a position to acquire with confidence and understanding the knowledge he needs to carry his responsibility. At the time when I was Chairman the Clarkson Board were assured by the executive, with, so far as I recall, the assent of the auditors, that we were making a profit of about £1 per head for every tourist we were carrying. This estimate was accepted by the Board, which included, apart from myself, several eminent men with great experience

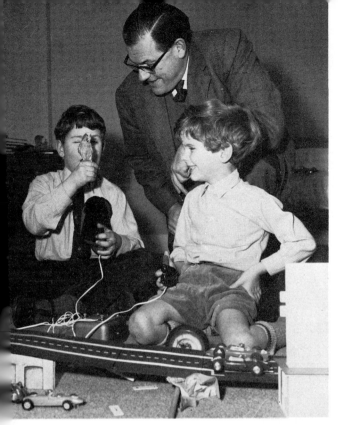

Life was not all serious in Downing Street

Is this where my father is working?

Edward Heath's Shadow Cabinet, 1965.

Left to right: Selwyn-Lloyd, Lord Dilhorne, myself,
Edward Heath, Alec Douglas-Home, Duncan Sandys,
Edward du Cann, Michael Fraser

Revisiting Professor Erhard in Bonn, June 1965

A family photograph, June 1965 — part of the hullaballoo of the leadership campaign

of commerce and banking, yet, in the event, it turned out that it was totally wrong.

After I left S.I.H. to return to the Government and my place had been taken by Mr Jocelyn Hambro, it was revealed to the Board that so far from making a profit of £1 per tourist, we had been making a loss of £3, so the more we had supported a policy of expansion, the more money we had been losing. I do not know how the non-executive members of the Board could possibly have discovered this, yet they were responsible.

I am sure that non-executive members of a Board are of great value. There are considerable disadvantages in a Board that is totally composed of executives. But unless some new solution can be found to this problem of responsibility without knowledge, I fear the problems of the proper organization of company Boards are not going to be satisfactorily resolved.

Other experiences I had in business, in particular with Mr Poulson and Mr Hoffman, were less happy. I deal with Mr Poulson in a later chapter. Mr Hoffman was introduced to me by Lord Brentford, then Senior Partner of the eminent firm of solicitors, Joynson Hicks & Co., who described him as a valued client of theirs, who was seeking some British directors for a new investment fund which he had established to collect funds overseas for the purchase of real estate in America. It was, on the face of it, a good idea; there was already more than one company operating with great success in a similar field. He had an imposing team of American directors drawn from business and former members of the U.S. administration. Brentford was joining the Board himself, so I agreed to do so. William Clarke, a distinguished financial journalist, who for some time now has been running the Committee on Invisible Exports, agreed to join at the same time.

Within the space of a few months we received disquieting news about Mr Hoffman, which had been unknown before to any of us and which reflected on his activities in the U.S.A. I made immediate enquiries in America. I was assured that the American directors and the Fund's professional advisers had no doubts about continuing. However, I decided myself that if there was any doubt I clearly could not continue, and William Clarke came to the same conclusion. I delayed my resignation for a short time while a successor was being found. He was a prominent American businessman, at the time President of the New York Board of Trade. Subsequently, Ambassador Wagner, the former Mayor of New York, took over the leadership of the company.

For some time after I had resigned the Fund seemed to prosper under their direction, but then it collapsed along with other funds operating in the same field.

One of the great advantages to me of my business appointments was that they made it possible for me to travel extensively. I think it is of very great value to this country and to the world generally, that both politicians and businessmen should be able to travel widely, and to meet one another. The problem, of course, is one of money. If I had not been a director of these various companies my ability to travel as a leading member of the Conservative Party would have been very much circumscribed and, as a result, the service I could render as a politician would have been much limited. I was able, in the course of business travel, to visit the Middle East extensively, to go to South Africa and learn much of what was happening there, to visit America and Australia, and to make acquaintance and have a meeting of minds with leading politicians in those countries, which otherwise would not have been possible. I have also been a member of two groups which comprise both businessmen and politicians, which have been designed to encourage mutual understanding among people in the Western world who have responsibility and influence in the affairs of their countries. These are the Bilderberg Group and the Trilateral Commission. They are both closely connected; indeed, the Trilateral Commission is in a sense the child of the Bilderberg Group. I have no doubt whatever that the concept has been an admirable one, and that the operations of these groups have been very much to the benefit of mutual understanding among the Western countries.

They have sometimes been subject to criticism, the Bilderberg Group in particular, because their proceedings have been strictly confidential, but this is precisely where their strength lies. The Bilderberg Group was founded on the initiative of Prince Bernhard of the Netherlands way back in the 1950s, and Hugh Gaitskell and I were the original British members of the Executive Committee. The purpose was a simple one : to improve mutual understanding between North America and Western Europe as a contribution to the enduring strength of the North Atlantic Alliance. Those who were asked to join the Group and to attend the meetings were people with a mixed background of politics, industry and information. They included politicians from all democratic parties, Trade Union leaders, academics, and people of political influence in the widest sense.

Our meetings were always confidential. They were attended at one time or another by most of the leading figures of influence in the Western world. The discussion was always frank and thorough. The contribution to mutual understanding was enormous. The Trilateral Commission was established very much on the initiative of David Rockefeller and a number of his associates, and was designed to extend the Bilderberg system, with any necessary adaptation, to include Japan, a country of rapidly growing importance in the democratic alliance. The discussions, once again, were confidential, though sometimes statements were issued. The importance of the organization can be judged from the way we were received by the Heads of Governments in all the countries in which we held meetings, and by the fact that President Carter and a number of his senior advisers were prominent in their attendance at the meetings before his election. The financing of these activities, which was not inconsiderable, was borne as it could only be borne, by industry and by foundations. It was, without doubt, a worthy purpose and continues to be one. International cooperation among the nations of the West is too important to be left entirely to the politicians; but, on the other hand, it cannot be divorced from them. The mixture of people assembled at these conferences has been a remarkable blend of the political and the non-political, of employers and Trade Unionists, of academics and men of business. Their long-term contribution to Western cooperation should not be underestimated.

As a director of Kleinwort Benson I paid particular attention to the Middle East, where I went with one of my fellow directors, Freddy Smith, to establish the business of the bank in the oil-rich countries there. This was both exciting and important. From Britain's point of view it was very important to secure as much as possible of the industrial and commercial business that was becoming available in the Middle East as a result of the growth of the oil royalties. This would offset the enormous burden on our balance of payments of imported oil at a time when North Sea oil was still not even a glimmer on the horizon. I was able to establish many friendships in the Middle East, including Rulers, Heads of Government, prominent Ministers and leading businessmen. I think this was of value not only to the bank but, more important, to Britain's interests both commercial and political.

In fact in 1967 after the Seven-day War between the Arabs and the Israelis, I was asked by George Brown, then Foreign Secretary, if I would make a visit to the Middle East and see if I could use my contacts and influence there to try to repair some fences between Britain and the Arab countries. This, naturally, I was only too happy to do, and I hope it was of some value. I certainly had maximum cooperation and assistance from British Embassies in the area. When I returned I ventured to put forward a five-point solution to the Arab–Israeli conflict on the 12 August 1967, which was as follows.

1. Withdrawal by Israel from the territories recently occupied.

2. In exchange for withdrawal, there should be effective guarantees against future aggression, and proper legal rights for Israel as a member state of the United Nations without being subject to any discrimination.

3. A resolute effort to solve the refugee problem permanently, with a lead from the World Bank.

4. Appropriate recognition of the unique religious status of Jerusalem.

5. Special attention to the serious and urgent needs of Jordan.

It was not very popular at the time. Few proposals for a compromise are ever popular, though in the long run they are normally inevitable. Certainly the Jewish community in this country were very angry with me. But I suspect that what I was proposing then, ten years ago, will not be all that far removed from the final solution when it comes.

For a number of reasons I paid special attention to the Middle East.

After my brief visit in 1937 I had not had the opportunity of returning again to the Middle East until the 1960s except for a visit in 1953, when I stopped for a short while in Baghdad on my way back from the Colombo Conference in Delhi. It was then the heyday of Anglo–Iraqi relations. Our beautiful Embassy, with its tinkling fountain in the main hall, dominated one bank of the river, and it was not for some years thereafter that it came to be burnt by a mob. The scars of wartime had largely healed. The King himself and his uncle, the Crown Prince, were extremely friendly.

Western influence was strong. I remember going to a night club on the bank of the river, which was wholly Western in its outlook, save for the fact that one girl in the second row of the chorus arrived very late for the performance with a large black eye, and that after the cabaret was over, a procession of three ducks waddled up from the river to the centre of the dance floor, where two proceeded to copulate while the other watched with intense interest. The only other remarkable feature of the evening was when Sir Leslie Rowan, then Head of the foreign side of the Treasury, who was sitting with me at the table, was kissed enthusiastically on both cheeks by a leading member of the cabaret, a hazard I imagine unusual for senior Treasury officials, but one which he accepted with complete aplomb.

But underneath it all somehow felt uneasy. The contrast between the Ruling Family and the rich merchants on the one hand, and the urban mob on the other, was too great. One could feel tension in the air, though there was general confidence that Nuri had the situation under control. The problem was, I believe, that the Ruling Dynasty had links with the West, and with England in particular, that were too close for comfort. The King had been educated at Harrow and retained a great affection for his old school. His uncle, the Crown Prince, who really ran the country, remarked to me in the course of our conversation, that he would be 'going home' that winter. This struck me as strange, as I had presumed he was in his own home, but it was an indication of how his family had become estranged from his own people.

I fear that the policy of encouraging the Rulers of Iraq, not after all a Colony by any means, to think of themselves as Englishmen was not a resounding success. The disaster, of course, came in 1958 with the overthrow of the Dynasty and the murder of Nuri. It was a great shock to the British Government, who had relied on Nuri's intelligence system for some forewarning of disaster that might impend. It made a profound change to the whole balance of matters in the Middle East, with the instability of one of the most important countries there, and the subsequent opportunity it gave for Russian penetration.

Since I started going to the Middle East again in 1965 when I was a director of Kleinworts, I have been a frequent and regular visitor, and my wife has often gone with me. It has been a source of immense pleasure, and we are happy to know that we have many good friends throughout the Arab world. They are not easy people to deal with, indeed, they are often infuriating. Seldom, for example, do they answer letters. Their ideas of punctuality are wholly different from our own. Indeed, I remember the first time I was in Saudi Arabia, discovering at the hotel that one had to order a morning call in three different times, Greenwich Mean Time plus three hours, Arab Suntime, and European Suntime; but it didn't matter very much, because you did not get the call anyway. They are slow and cautious about coming to the point, and, indeed, when you think how many people from all over the world have been trying to get the better of them in the last decade or so, who can blame them? The first words of Arabic I learnt were '*mish mumkin*' which means 'impossible'. It takes a long time to establish personal friendship and personal confidence but once you have established it, it is firm and absolutely reliable.

The countries of the Gulf were then developing fast and absolutely fascinating. Kuwait, of course, was pre-eminent by reason of its early oil strength and the sophistication of its merchant community. Qatar had long-standing ties with Britain, and had been an early arrival on the major oil scene. Bahrain was in many ways the most attractive to the British visitor, because the British connection there was strongest. The Political Resident for the Gulf, then the fabulous Bill Luce, later followed by Stewart Crawford, had his Headquarters there. The Ruler, Sheikh Isa, had very close ties indeed with Britain, and his sons were at school here. There were only two difficulties, first, that Bahrain had very little oil, and second, there was the dispute with the Shah of Iran, who at that time was claiming sovereignty, which made it necessary to have a separate passport for the two countries, as you could not visit Tehran if your passport had been stamped by the Bahrain authorities.

Incidentally, Bahrain is a good example of the capriciousness of the Almighty in distributing the oil deposits of the Middle East. Providence seems to have paid scant regard to population, and indeed the oil wealth of an individual country is often in exact contrast to the size and needs of the population. Egypt, one of the most populous countries and still culturally dominant throughout the area, had then virtually no oil resources at all. Abu Dhabi with a minuscule population had vast resources. The Shah had over 30 million people to feed and clothe and educate in Iran and felt this strongly. I remember him once describing to me what he called the 'monster Britain had created' in Abu Dhabi, whose oil we were buying when they didn't need the money, in preference to oil from his own country when he badly needed cash. He was not very impressed by my argument that we did so because the cost was much lower than that of Iranian oil.

Three of the most remarkable men I met were Sheikh Zaid of Abu Dhabi, Sheikh Rashid of Dubai, and King Faisal of Saudi Arabia. They all are, or were, in the case of King Faisal, men of outstanding quality and vision, and they had the ability to collect around them advisers and assistants of quality and education.

When I first went to Abu Dhabi it was in the days of the legendary Sheikh Shakhbut, of whom it was said (I do not know if this is true) that he distrusted banks and kept all his oil revenue in notes under his bed until they were eaten by termites. The airfield was a sandy strip marked out by empty oil drums, there was not a yard of asphalt road in the town, and the only buildings of any size were three large banks, the B.B.M.E., the Ottoman and the Asian, on what is now the waterfront, and the old Palace, an engaging Beau Geste style building in the centre of the city. Now when you go there, tarmac stretches for mile after mile, there is a Grand Corniche, a Hilton Hotel, with a fine swimming pool, and bankers can be counted by the dozen in every square kilometre.

Dubai is a contrast. Here the formidable Sheikh Rashid has held sway for many years. Commercially Dubai had long been way ahead of Abu Dhabi. The creek where the gold-smuggling dhows with powerful Leyland engines used to muster before their voyage to India is one of the most enchanting sights in the Middle East. There was, and still is, a sophistication about Dubai that is bound to cast its spell over any English visitor, and much of it derives from the personality of Sheikh Rashid himself. After all, how can you fail to like a man who says to you, as he once said to me in the course of an argument, through his interpreter, 'Mr Maudling, if you go on talking like that I shall join the Labour Party.' He adopted the wise policy of not building up large armed forces for he did not see whom he could successfully fight with them if he had to use them. As for the arguments about the price and supply of oil, he was always content, particularly as a fairly small producer, to go along with his Arab colleagues like a good Trade-Union member, in the knowledge that whatever they secured would automatically accrue to him as well.

But King Faisal was the most formidable of the Arab Rulers whom I met. Partly of course this was because of the position of his country, which dominated much of the Arab world, both because its oil reserves were by far the biggest of all and, no less important, because Mecca is in Saudi Arabia. He was a man of great presence and considerable authority, and the world was left much the poorer by his assassination. He had embarked on the task, which his successor is ably following, of moving a country forward a thousand years within the space of a generation. It is easy to understand the problems of poverty : mankind has known them since the dawn of history. But there are problems in affluence too. Suddenly to find yourself and your country endowed with unexpected wealth on a vast scale does present great problems. Change is essential, yet change for a society based fundamentally on tradition is very difficult to accomplish, and any country with a small population and vast resources is a target for many evil forces throughout the world.

I believe that the Saudis have made quite remarkable progress in recent years, and they deserve great admiration for the way they have developed their domestic policy, as they do for their enormously responsible use in international terms of their vast oil revenues. It is hard for a Western European to grasp the scale of the problem.

This was a country which, before the oil came in any quantity, had little in the way of popular education and only a very small ruling class. It was and remains basically an Islamic society with the old-fashioned hard-line religionists opposed to the sort of social changes which were bound to occur very rapidly with the influx of money, and particularly with the development of contacts between the ordinary people and the outside world, of which the transistor radio is the most formidable cause. One of the great problems facing the Saudis was their lack of administration in depth. They had in their top cadre a number of men of the highest ability, mainly Western educated, a lot of them in the University of California, some in the U.K., whose quality could compare with anyone in the world. But below them the general body of public servants, though honest and upright people, had neither the education nor the experience that could enable them to deal with the sort of problems of administration that new-found wealth was bound to bring. I found myself that the top people in Saudi Arabia were exceptionally able. On the finance side, the Governor of the Saudi Arabia Monetary Agency, their equivalent of a Central Bank, was a Pakistani, Mr Anwar Ali. He had a very grave responsibility indeed. The amount of petro-dollars coming into the Saudi coffers was enormous, and the way they used them could have crucial results upon the whole economy of the West. He was a man of great intelligence and perception, he served both his country and the Western interests well, and his death was a tragedy. But the traditions remain, and his successor, Al-Quaraishi, has worthily followed them. Moreover, S.A.M.A. have continued to show expertise of the highest order.

I met other outstanding men in their administration: Abu Kheil, The Minister of Finance, al-Ghosaibi, the Minister of Industry, Hishan Nasr, the Minister for Planning; all of them had knowledge, ability and a sophistication which could stand comparison with anything you could find in the developed financial and economic centres of the Western world.

The great merchant families are another source of strength to Saudi Arabia. There are several families who have earned by their ability and enterprise over the years a dominant position in the Saudi economy. One is the Ali Reza family, a fabulous name which you will meet all over the Middle East, not only as a source of commercial strength but as a source of worldly wisdom too. There are the Juffalis, in some ways perhaps the most successful of all the great commercial families. I and my wife came to know many of them, and it was an enormous pleasure to do so. It was not only that they were able men, it was not only that they were charming men, what always warmed one's heart was the genuine affection they had for Britain and the British. Two ties were particularly strong, education and medicine; so many of the children of these great families were sent to British schools, and it is perhaps remarkable that they not only survived but actually enjoyed the experience, so totally different from anything they would find in their own country. As for medicine, I think it is still the case that when a Saudi needs treatment that he cannot obtain in his own country, he looks always first to London. I find this immensely reassuring for the future of Britain, that the two things our friends should value most in our British traditions are the education of their children and the health of their families – there is, after all, nothing more important than this.

Certainly the Saudi influence in international affairs has always been a beneficent one, and it is fortunate that they should be the richest in oil resources of all the Arab countries. They consistently recognize their responsibility as a supplier of the energy on which the Western world has developed. It has not been an easy situation. As Hishan Nasr said to me, 'We do not want to be responsible for other people's amenities.' The dependence of the West upon their oil resources has been in many ways an embarrassment to them. They have been, and are producing more oil than really suits their national interest. There is a limit to the amount they can spend in foreign exchange imposed by the physical and administrative limitations of their economy. It would suit them better to keep more of their oil in the ground. There is precious little advantage to them, from a purely national point of view, in producing more than they can spend, and accumulating a vast amount of paper money which slowly loses its purchasing power, while oil under the ground has been steadily gaining it, yet they have been far-sighted enough to recognize the needs of the anti-Communist world as a whole, and they have based their policy on the very judicious appreciation of the relative claims of the interests of Saudi Arabia, and of the interests of the Western world. In this, perhaps, Saudi Arabia can be contrasted with Iraq. I remember talking to a distinguished Iraqi about the deployment of their currency reserves; he said to me, 'We only produce enough oil to pay for our current requirements, why should we produce more in exchange for your depreciating Western paper money?'

What is more, he said, 'We should borrow all we can on the European markets, knowing that when we come to repay it the real cost will be less to us than the real value of what we have borrowed.' He was a shrewd man, but I rather doubt if his wisdom was equal to that of the Saudis.

11

Home Secretary

1970–1972

MY main recollection of the 1970 election is Ted Heath's robust and sustained confidence. Opinion Polls were bad, many of us had our doubts about the result. But never Ted. – And he was right. When he formed his Government he invited me to become Home Secretary.

The Home Office was a new experience. I had not been Shadow Home Secretary, but I welcomed the position, because there were a number of important and challenging matters to be dealt with. I was fortunate in my team. Richard Sharples was Minister of State, and he was a great loss when he went to his tragic mission in Bermuda. Mark Carlisle was always a tower of strength, both of experience and commonsense, in the law, in politics and in human nature. He had that instinctive talent for blending what is practicable and what is desirable that is one of the greatest assets of any politician. Later we had Mark Colville (Mark II as we called him) and David Lane. Mark Colville succeeded David Windlesham as spokesman in the House of Lords. Both our House of Lords spokesmen were effective, and it is very important for the Home Secretary to be well represented in the House of Lords, because so many Home Office issues arise there and it is inhabited by so many experts.

How about the Home Office itself, and the extent to which it was equipped to deal in modern conditions with the problems for which it was responsible? It is always a difficult Department, in the sense that it covers an immense range of different problems. In fact, one sometimes thinks that anything that no one else wants lands up with the Home Office. At that time, apart from the basic problems of law and order, and the Police, and immigration, we had the enormous problem of Northern Ireland to deal with. The range the Home Office spans is vast and heterogeneous. In fact I believe one division had responsibilities ranging from obscene publications to Royal ceremonial. What made it so fascinating was that in any one year well over one million letters came into the Home Office and any one of them might have meant trouble for the Home Secretary because what was involved was individual human cases, which always can produce the major explosions.

My impression of the Home Office was not the currently popular one, that it was an old-fashioned Department steeped in tradition and unresponsive to modern ideas. Of course there were old-fashioned features, from the coal fire in the Home Secretary's office to the immense care and detail which the Department applied to drafting every single letter for a Minister to send to a Member of Parliament – often consuming much time but usually ensuring justice. By the time I had arrived, the alcove in the Home Secretary's room no longer contained the traditional table with its list of criminals sentenced to death awaiting the Home Secretary's discretion whether to pardon them. Its place had been taken by a refrigerator containing soft drinks.

The quality of Home Office officials was high. I was very fortunate in having Sir Philip (now Lord) Allen as Permanent Secretary. We disagreed on a number of things, but they were usually of minor importance. I could never, for example, persuade him to consume anything but bitter lemon, but for his judgement otherwise I had the utmost respect.

Apart from the Departmental problems, I had to carry out the normal functions of Home Secretary, presiding over the Emergency and Home Affairs Committees of the Cabinet. This led me into a vast range of policy responsibilities and policy decisions affecting most aspects of our society and our economy. Moreover, while I was not officially Deputy Prime Minister, because no such post is formally known to our constitution, I was in fact number two to Mr Heath in the Cabinet ratings, and in practice I deputized for him automatically on any occasions, either in Cabinet or in the House of Commons, where the services of a Deputy were required. All in all, therefore, particularly with Northern Ireland, the volume of work involved was quite substantial, and I found it difficult sometimes to maintain my reputation for laziness, certainly in the eyes of my family.

The major problems then were immigration, law and order, and Northern Ireland. It is difficult to say in what order one would have put them. Immigration was urgent, because of the undertakings we had given during the election to legislate to further restrict the freedom of immigration then existing in this country. Northern Ireland was urgent, because the situation we had inherited was, through no fault of the previous Government, one of great danger, and because the play of passions in the Province was already producing the mounting tragedy we have seen in recent years. Law and order were, if not so urgent, of fundamental importance, because of the growing crime rate, because of the pressure on prison accommodation and prison services, and because many people saw a very real danger of an abuse of freedom becoming an occasion for the restriction of freedom.

There were other problems too. The Police were under strength and needed sustaining and helping. The argument about pornography and the permissive society was growing all the time. But these, on the whole important though they were, were more long term and less urgent than the major issues.

We started straight away on the question of immigration, and the drafting of a Bill to give effect to the main undertaking of the Conservative Party manifesto, which had been to restrict further the automatic right of immigrants from the Commonwealth to come and to remain in this country. It was an exceedingly difficult problem to tackle. I could sense how important it was; one only had to look at America to know what dangers could arise. Fortunately it had not been made a major emotional issue in the election, but it had been important, and action was clearly necessary.

The key to the problem seemed to me to be this. What mattered in this country above all was good relations between the races, and the real threat to such good relations arose from fear of the unknown and the unfamiliar. Immigrants had been pouring in to this country from the Commonwealth in large numbers. We had been forced to put on some control in the previous Conservative Government, in which I was Colonial Secretary. I myself had been very reluctant to agree to such control. I clung to the view, perhaps outmoded and sentimental, that subjects of the Queen should be allowed the right to come and live in the Mother Country; but it was not possible to sustain this view absolutely and indefinitely.

The truth was that the numbers were too great. There were too many who could come, and too many who exercised the right to come. They came too fast and they came in numbers that were too large to be assimilated, especially as they concentrated, for obvious reasons, in particular areas, so that the local population found the whole nature of a district or a community changing, with people who were wholly different in colour, religion and culture sometimes establishing a majority, not only in individual streets but, more sensitive still, in the schools. It is hard to say what people find most offensive in an influx of this kind. Sometimes I felt the smell of strange cooking probably had more effect in people's minds than almost anything else.

Certainly it was not the case that the immigrant community behaved badly or unlawfully; they were good citizens. They were new people and different people, and no one knew how many were going to follow. This is where the element of fear arose and particularly the fear of the unfamiliar. So it seemed to me quite clear that race relations could not be established on a satisfactory basis so long as fear of a possibly un- limited influx continued and, therefore, a stricter control of the number of new arrivals was desirable in the interests of race relations themselves.

In this principle I found that we had the support of the leaders of the immigrant communities who were wise enough to see the practical factors involved. There was no real opposition to some further control of immigration. The problem was what form it should take. There was one particular principle to which I attached great importance, namely that no action should be retrospective and that anyone who had been admitted to this country as an immigrant on the basis of certain accepted rights, including those for dependants, should not subse- quently have those rights taken away from him. The other problem obviously was that of colour. While one talked always and rightly about the need to avoid discrimination between black and white, it is a simple fact of human nature that for the British people there is a great difference between Australians and New Zealanders, for example, who come of British stock, and people from Africa, the Caribbean and the Indian subcontinent, who were equally subjects of the Queen and entitled to total equality before the law when established here, but who in appearance, habits, religion and culture, were totally different from us. The problem of balancing the moral principle of non-discrimination with the practical facts of human nature was not an easy one, and the dangers that could arise from mistakes of policy in this field were very real indeed.

The solution we found was the introduction of the new concept of patriality, which would give the right of abode. This was greeted by the Labour Party with considerable suspicion, if not open opposition, though one could not help noticing that when they took over from us they made no attempt to depart from it. Broadly speaking, the idea was to define those people who had the right to live in this country unchallenged and to go to and fro at will. The first category, of course, were people who had been born here, there was no question raised about this by anyone. To this we added those people who by reason of a parental connection could claim an equal right either through the paternal or maternal side, because it seemed time to do away with any discrimination in this matter between father and mother. Our first idea was to give the right of abode to all of those who could show that either a parent or grandparent had been born in this country. This definition was quite heavily criticized as going too far. Mr Enoch Powell, strangely enough, was particularly virulent in his criticism, likening our concept to that of Hitler's Nazis in dealing with the question of Jewish extraction. I can well remember his quoting in the House of Commons, '*Grossmutter nicht in Ordnung*' – 'A grandmother can disqualify'.

In the course of Committee stages of the Bill, we felt it necessary to limit the distinction to direct fathers and mothers. This is the way the law was enacted as it left the House of Commons. It seemed on the whole not a bad compromise between the notion of ancestry and the desire for non-discrimination. On the whole the general concept of the legislation has stood the test of time, the test being the effect upon race relations in this country. Whatever the difficulties, and they have been great at times in the past and will be great at times in the future, it has not been a bad performance for this country in the light of the vast number of immigrants involved, and the performances of other societies in the field of race relations.

The second big problem was that of law and order. The Police Forces were sadly below establishment, and the previous Labour administration had allowed things to go downhill. The Police did not feel they had been fairly treated in the matter of pay and conditions. I was determined, following the illustrious example of Rab, to ensure that the Police were given such conditions as were necessary to bring their establishment and recruitment to a satisfactory level, in the light of the needs of law and order.

There were two reasons for this point of view. First, the maintenance of law and order must have an overriding priority for any civilized society. Without order you cannot have freedom and it is essential to have a system which prevents individual citizens from so using their own freedom as to deny or restrict the freedom of others. As Pollock once declared, 'Before you can have justice, you must have security.' Civilization calls for both, but they have to be in that order. Secondly, the Police pay claim could not be treated on the same basis as every other claim put forward by a Trade Union or an Association, because the Police were in the special position that they had not the right to strike, and the Police Federation were not members of the T.U.C. This was a logical and necessary arrangement.

The idea of a Police strike, which some unhappy countries have seen from time to time, would appal the people of this country. There had been one after the First World War which had led to the 1919 Police Act which is the basis of the present situation. The idea of policemen struggling to restrain policemen against the background of an industrial dispute was frightening. Equally, the impartiality of the Police in political terms was of the greatest importance, and with the T.U.C. continually extending their activities into broader fields of political controversy it was hard to see how their political impartiality in the eyes of the public could be maintained if their Federation joined the T.U.C. So, because the Police were treated, and rightly treated, as a special case in the limitation upon the exercise of their power in pay bargaining compared with other industrial organizations, it seemed only fair to say that they should be treated as a special case when it came to determining their conditions of employment. I believe the great majority of the British public firmly supported this view.

Incidentally, some very difficult situations arose from time to time when the Police were called in to deal with picketing or other aspects of industrial disputes. My own impression is that they always acted with great wisdom and discretion in situations which were often extremely difficult. I remember when during the miners' strike pickets threatened to close the Birmingham Coal Depot, and, in fact, succeeded in doing so, the then Chief Constable of Birmingham assured me that only over his dead body would they so succeed. I felt constrained to ring him the next day after it happened to enquire after his health! I am sure the decision he took was a wise one, because the number of strikers involved was so great, and feelings were running so high, that any attempt by the relatively small body of Police who could be assembled to keep the Depot open by force could have led to very grave consequences. Some of my colleagues asked me afterwards, why I had not sent in troops to support the Police, and I remember asking them one simple question, 'If they had been sent in, should they have gone in with their rifles loaded or unloaded?' Either course could have been disastrous.

There was another rather bizarre and typically English episode when it appeared necessary to arrest a small group of Trade Union leaders in London's Dockland. Great preparations were made. All over the East End, anonymous pantechnicons full of Police were stationed, truncheons at the ready for action if necessary. I was in constant and direct communication with the Commissioner of Police of the Metropolis. Tension rose hour by hour. Yet all the while, unknown to me and to the Commissioner, a dignitary of whose existence I was totally unaware, called the Official Solicitor, was busy before the High Court sorting the whole thing out, which he did very satisfactorily. No one at the time believed that Ministers were unaware of his activities, but the truth is that they were. I doubt if it could have happened that way in any other country.

I had always been a supporter of the retention of capital punishment for wilful murder, and it seemed to me that much of the case against it was based not so much on the principle involved, as on the horrific details of the particular method of execution that was employed. The issue had in practice been decided before I came to the Home Office. Any attempt to distinguish between various degrees of wilful murder with the death penalty for some and not for others had proved in practice unavailing and the penalty had been abolished altogether. There seems little doubt that this was contrary to the wishes of the majority of the public, but Parliament had decided by a free vote, which was traditional in these matters. I remember discussing the problem with Sir Philip Allen, himself an abolitionist, who, I think, presented me with the conclusive argument when he said, 'All right, Home Secretary, you want to restore capital punishment. Tell me. Where shall we advertise for a new hangman, in *The Times* or the *Daily Telegraph*?'

But it was wrong to suppose that the burden on the Home Secretary of confirming a death sentence is an intolerable one. It is a heavy one indeed, as I have experienced myself in Colonial Office days, but it is even more difficult to decide whether to release a convicted murderer, for you cannot really pursue a rule that all of them should rot in jail for the rest of their natural lives. The Home Secretary decides on the best available advice when it is appropriate to release a convicted murderer, taking the ultimate responsibility, and if he is wrong, it is the innocent who will suffer. It was under my authority that Young was released. He had been detained in Broadmoor for many years after committing offences involving poison. He was released because according to the best possible psychiatric advice available he was no longer a danger. He proceeded to murder six other people, who would have been alive today but for the decision for which I was responsible. This seems to me a heavier burden to carry than that of confirming a death sentence after due trial before a Court of Law.

Two other measures of penal reform were enacted when I was Home Secretary, one was the Misuse of Drugs Act 1971, and the other, the Criminal Justice Act 1972. In both cases, one of the possibilities involved was the stiffening of the sentences available to the Courts, but I thought it right, at the same time, to emphasize some distinctions. There was a general and, it seemed to me, justified concern about the growing level of crime and a feeling that in some cases, at any rate, more severe penalties should be imposed. The difficulty, of course, is that while Parliament enacts maximum penalties, and in most cases of violence these are very heavy, it is always in the discretion of the Courts to decide the appropriate penalty in a particular case. This sometimes gives rise to misunderstandings, because the public do not understand that instructions cannot be given by the Home Office to magistrates about the level of sentences they impose, and because it is very difficult, from newspaper accounts alone, to understand fully all the considerations that were in the mind of the Court when reaching a decision. But it did seem right in some cases to increase the penalties available, in the hope that when Parliament approved this, the Courts generally would recognize that it was designed as an indication that, in the view of Parliament, not only should the maximum sentence be higher, but the general level of sentencing should be higher too.

In the field of drugs and of crime generally, I decided to emphasize certain distinctions. I held strongly the view that trafficking in drugs was a very grave offence, far more serious than the actual possession or use of them. So we widened the penalties laid down for the two categories of offence, increasing the penalty for those who made a profit out of the drug-taking of others. I did give some thought to the question of legalizing cannabis, and in this I was much helped by the Drugs division of the Home Office, whose technical competence was internationally recognized, and whose experience and wisdom were of the highest order. It seemed to me, as it had seemed to my predecessor, Mr Callaghan, that the arguments against legalizing cannabis were conclusive. There were three of them. First, while no one could establish a conclusive case that the use of soft drugs led on to the use of hard drugs, there was always that danger, and when you saw the graphic evidence available to the Police and the Home Office of the effect on human beings of the use of hard drugs, you realized how great was the danger and how unjustified a risk it would be to run. Secondly, the legalization of cannabis would greatly reduce the morale of the many devoted people who were working in various fields to combat the whole drug menace. Any apparent weakening of the Home Office, however well intentioned, could have undermined the whole campaign against addiction by the many voluntary agencies whose work was so important in this field. Thirdly, I reasoned that people had alcohol and tobacco, why did they need something else as well? If the knowledge currently available about the relationship between smoking and lung cancer had been available at the time when tobacco was first introduced, it might well have been banned then, but it was now so massive a feature of our national life that to ban its use would be unacceptable, but there did not seem to be any reason to legalize cannabis or other drugs whose consumption had not become a generally accepted social practice.

I do remember at about that time addressing a meeting of the London School of Economics Conservative Association, which, being an open meeting, was normally attended by a large number of extreme Left-wingers, and being questioned afterwards by a large bearded young man, who said quite simply, 'You obviously like whisky, whisky is addictive and in large doses can be fatal, yet you are free to consume as much as you can afford. Admittedly cannabis equally is addictive, and drugs can be fatal, but if I prefer cannabis to whisky, why should you be entitled to your drink when I cannot have my smoke?' I quoted to him the arguments I have set out above, but I am afraid they did not carry total conviction. However, there seems some reason to believe that time and experience are having their effect, and my guess would be that the problem of drug-taking amongst students has become less serious than it was, though the extent to which it has been replaced by alcohol is another matter.

The Criminal Justice Bill was concerned with crime more generally, and here the distinction which I was anxious to draw was between crimes involving violence and crimes which did not involve it. We increased the penalties for the carriage and use of firearms, which was at the time a growing menace, and for which the penalties available to the Courts seemed inadequate. I have no doubt that the protection of the public against the violent criminal is a priority matter, and that long terms of imprisonment are right in such cases. But it did not follow that the same was true in cases where no violence was involved and I was convinced by the arguments that non-custodial sentences might be more widely used in such cases. There was also the great problem of the overcrowding of the prisons, though this was only a secondary factor.

It seemed to me that the principles of punishment should include, as well as the protection of the public, and deterrence of other criminals, the question of rehabilitation and restitution, and I was particularly attracted by the idea of community service as an alternative punishment, which had been put forward by Lady Wootton's Committee. It appeared to make sense in every way that in the case of many non-violent crimes the offender should not be incarcerated in an already overcrowded prison, but obliged to render a stated amount of service to the community. It would help to relieve the prison problem; it could help, for example, in the maintenance of hospitals or old people's homes, and provide a useful addition to the social services generally.

It seemed, moreover, a strong possibility that such a period of service to the community might give to the individual himself a new pride in what he was doing, and that a new sense of responsibility and of worthwhile service could play a great part in his rehabilitation. There were difficulties, of course, and it had to be started experimentally. What were the appropriate jobs? Would the Trade Unions object? How could supervision be properly organized? Quite rightly, there were doubts expressed on all these matters. But the Bill, piloted through the House of Commons largely by Mark Carlisle, was approved, and the experiment began. I am happy to think that, due largely to the devotion of the Probation Services and the imaginative approach of judges and magistrates, it has developed into a considerable success. Our penal system has been improved by this innovation, and I hope it will continue from strength to strength.

There were other provisions in the Bill based on the same principles.

A Committee under Lord Justice Widgery had made a number of proposals to improve the powers of the Courts to order offenders to pay compensation or make restitution to their victims. These were implemented in the Bill, and I am glad to see that they have been used increasingly by the Courts to the benefit of many victims. We also took from the same report the concept of criminal bankruptcy which was designed to prevent some major criminals getting away with ill-gotten gains.

One case that aroused a great deal of attention was that of Rudi Dutschke. One of the hazards of a Home Secretary is that he is bound to bump into a certain amount of such cases, and the passions that arise are very considerable. One thinks of Henry Brooke with Chief Enaharo, or Merlyn Rees with Agee and Hosenball. It really is a good thing that this should be so. It does confirm that the British people still have strong feelings about the treatment of individuals. It is very hard to explain this sometimes to people from the other side of the political divide. I remember one highly intelligent Communist Ambassador once saying to me, 'I do not understand all this fuss in this country about capital punishment. After all, only a few people are involved each year.' This is another reflection of the difference of attitude between us and Eastern Europe, which is genuine and important, and which needs to be understood if our two civilizations are to live with and not destroy one another. It is rather like the passionate British interest in animal welfare, another thing which is always very difficult to explain to our foreign friends. As a Member of Parliament one knows it and understands it. In more than a quarter of a century as M.P. for Barnet I have had more letters about cruelty to animals than any other subject, and I cannot recall a single one about cruelty to children. It is, to the foreign eye, a quaint attitude to life, but it is both genuine and endearing. But it certainly does create problems of international relations. There was the time when the Russians sent a dog called Laika into space in one of their satellites as the first space dog. The protests from British animal lovers were violent. Long queues with banners formed and picketed the Soviet Embassy in Kensington Gardens. It was very difficult to persuade the Russians that this was not some deep-laid capitalist plot but a genuine spontaneous reaction. Just another example of the fundamental difficulty of foreign policy which is mutual misunderstanding.

However, to return to Rudi Dutschke, the position was this. He was well known for his extreme Left-wing views, and had been involved in a number of controversies in his own country, Germany. He had been wounded in the head by a bullet and asked to come to this country for treatment. He had been allowed to come here in December 1968 on the basis, which was a perfectly reasonable one, that once his treatment was complete he would leave. He had freely accepted this condition. It was brought to my attention, as Home Secretary, that some of his activities while here were such as to raise doubts as to whether his presence was in the national interest. Having studied the evidence with care, I came to the conclusion that he should leave when his treatment was complete. All I was saying that he should do was to fulfil on his side the condition upon which he had entered Britain, just as we had completely fulfilled ours. This did not seem an unreasonable request, but it certainly gave rise to a tremendous rumpus. I referred the matter to a Standing Advisory Committee of three distinguished men, who supported my conclusion, and so Mr Dutschke left for Denmark in February 1971. I have not heard of him since, but I have no reason to suppose that my decision to insist on his keeping his own word caused him any physical harm.

But whatever the Advisory Committee had said, I would have felt obliged to insist on his departure. There are difficult problems involved here, of the security of the State, of the protection of British sources of intelligence. The Home Secretary personally carries the responsibility. I do not see that it would be possible for the Home Secretary to continue in office if he were forced to acquiesce in the continued presence in Britain of some foreign subject whom he thought was a danger to this country's security. Equally, it is impossible for a Home Secretary to be put into a position where he cannot take a decision unless he is prepared to disclose sources of information, and so, effectively, destroy them.

One can well understand the widespread disquiet about the principles involved in these cases. It is well that there should be such disquiet. It is in accordance with our traditions of respect for individual rights. But it has always seemed to me that just because we are the most tolerant society in the world, just because we have this precious tradition of free admission of people to this country, so we are entitled on certain occasions to say 'Enough', either 'You must not come here' or 'You must go away'. There is always a certain danger that the opponents of freedom will use their freedom to undermine the freedom of others, and there must be occasions upon which any Government, however liberal, must take action.

There is, after all, a distinction between citizens of Britain and citizens of other countries. We welcome them here : but they have no *right* to come here. It is our policy, and I think we have been generous and liberal in the way we have conducted our affairs. I remember, for example, being telephoned in Wales by the Home Office when the ballerina Makarova arrived, and asked if she could be given asylum, to which I replied immediately, 'Yes' with enthusiasm. But if at any time it appears no longer in the interests of Britain, including the interest of Britain's respect for human liberty, that an individual should remain here, then he must go.

The argument always put forward is that the person concerned is not in these cases furnished with details of the charges or of the evidence against him. This argument is misconceived because it fails to notice the difference between a prosecution and an exclusion. If you prosecute someone you have to produce evidence to the Court. So far as a British subject is concerned, he has the right to live here. He cannot be removed anyway, and the only action that can be taken against him is either prosecution if a criminal offence is involved, or, short of that, if he is a public servant, action through the system of the three wise men upon which the Appeal Tribunal in deportation cases was based. A different judgement has to be made when the matter is brought before the Court. To what extent are you going to risk your sources of information in order to establish a case? And let there be no mistake about it, however much sometimes the Left Wing may protest, the information that reaches the Home Secretary in these cases often is of a character which cannot be disclosed without in effect disclosing the means by which it was obtained, and thereby blowing a hole in our Security Services.

Where a British subject is concerned, obviously a decision has to be taken and if necessary the risk has to be accepted. But it is different where the man involved is a foreign citizen who is here by your permission and on the basis of our rules and procedures. There is no reason why he should have the right to say that we cannot exclude him without undermining our own sources of information. The procedure that was adopted I described on the Second Reading of the Immigration Bill in 1971, and it was followed by Merlyn Rees in the case of Agee and Hosenball. I think it is the best procedure that can be devised. No doubt it is not fully satisfactory, but when you are dealing with this sort of problem fully satisfactory solutions are pretty hard to come by. In any case, I think the practice in this country is without any doubt whatever as liberal as that of any country in the world, and I would vehemently rebut any criticism of British standards in this matter.

The Home Secretary is responsible for the operations of the Security Service, but it is a broad responsibility. He has to have confidence in those who are directing this Service and must keep in regular touch with them on broad issues. My senior advisers in the Home Office were always in close touch with them over detailed matters. If any breach of security occurs the Home Secretary carries the responsibility for it even though he may not have been in any way involved himself in the lapse. It is his job to ensure that the same thing does not happen again.

Otherwise he has the responsibility of ensuring that the activities of the Security Service do not improperly impinge upon individual liberty. In my time, for example, the rule, based on the report of a Committee of Privy Councillors, which I believe has not been changed and which seems to me a sound one, was that telephones could only be tapped officially on the personal authority of the Home Secretary in specific individual cases. It can be deduced from this, of course, that the instances involved were not as numerous as is sometimes alleged. I followed the simple rule that if an application was made to me to tap a telephone on the grounds that by so doing the Authorities might have the opportunity to prevent a breach of security, to prevent a serious crime, or to apprehend violent criminals, and I was satisfied from the evidence given to me that a substantial case had been made, I agreed to the application. This seems to me simple commonsense, if the offences involved were serious and there was no alternative method of obtaining the necessary information while there was a good chance of obtaining it from telephone tapping. There is no reason why criminals or spies should be guaranteed immunity in the use of the telephone. But the whole system was kept under very tight control and I saw no evidence at any time of any attempt to abuse it.

I often think that there is a widespread failure now to appreciate the importance of Intelligence, military and political, and I link the two together, because the aggression we face from the Communist world is of both kinds. It is no exaggeration to say that an efficient Intelligence service is just as fundamental to the defence of the West as guns, tanks or warships. Armed forces and their equipment are useless if they are blind or deaf. If you do not know what your potential enemy is trying to do, you are groping in the dark for your own defence. The constant attacks on the American C.I.A., for example, have always seemed to me most misguided. No doubt they make mistakes from time to time. It may well be they have done some pretty rough things on some occasions, though I have no means of knowing. But I would suspect that what they have done is a pretty pallid copy of what the Russian K.G.B. have been up to. But the C.I.A. are as important to our freedom as the American nuclear bomb. Indeed, the occasion might well arise where their knowledge and efficiency could prevent the outbreak of a nuclear war itself. For the dangers of nuclear war lie not in deliberate decisions by Governments – for deliberate suicide is not a natural act – but in folly of choice and miscalculation. The constant niggling attacks on the C.I.A. in public, the absurd habit of attacking them across the globe, fill me with anger. The only consolation is that they must be pretty effective, otherwise the Communists would not spend so much effort in trying to undermine them.

Of course there is always the problem *quis custodiet?* Who is to guarantee that the Home Secretary will exercise his judgement with responsibility and discretion? I fear, having thought about it a great deal, that there is no guarantee of an absolute character, only the personal standing of the Home Secretary and the estimate that the House of Commons has formed of his integrity and his judgement. Looking at it over the space of many decades, this is probably as good a solution as you can find in human affairs.

Another problem that raised its head was that of censorship. There was a lot of talk about the permissive society. My predecessor, Roy Jenkins, had got himself into a good deal of hot water by saying that the permissive society is the civilized society. I could not go along with him the whole way, though I would have done if he had said that it *could* be the civilized society. Standards in these matters were changing very rapidly indeed. What could be printed in publications, what could be said or shown on the stage, changed in the most dramatic fashion in the course of a decade. If one looks for a starting point I suppose the *Lady Chatterley's Lover* case was the legal watershed. Certainly the attitude of the film censors was changing. John Trevelyan was then Secretary of the British Board of Film Censors and I discussed all these things with him often. He was a man of highly civilized and perceptive views, and he knew that his job was not to dictate public tastes and standards, but to protect them, and if standards were changing he had to change with them. The factors involved were sex and violence. I always felt that it was quite astonishing that these two so different aspects of human behaviour should be so connected. Of course there is an area of overlap, but it is only a particular area, and it has always seemed to me that to talk in the same breath about what is most sublime and what is most abominable in human nature is a strange distortion of values.

I think one must start with this proposition. If one adult wishes to write a book or produce a play and show it to other adults, and they wish to see it, what right has the State to intervene? It is from this point that one must draw the argument, and the following factors seem to me important. (1) What may be true of the adult is not clearly true of the child, but on what grounds do you draw the distinction, and what practical methods do you employ? (2) While people may be entitled to watch any scenes of violence that they want for some strange reason to see (I could never understand obsession with horror films) is there not a danger that by doing so they will be more inclined to act violently towards their fellow citizens? (3) While there may be a strong argument that people may be entitled, if they so wish, to see any erotic play or film, are the promoters of the performance entitled by blatant advertising to thrust their wares under the noses of passers-by, who may be offended?

There is no doubt that the law on obscenity is a muddle, but there is considerable doubt whether it can ever be anything other than a muddle. Newspaper reports said that when *Oh! Calcutta!* was first staged, the Attorney-General had to consider whether to prosecute, but decided it would be impractical to do so because, in order to succeed he would have to prove that those who went to see the play were likely to have been depraved or corrupted, when, in fact, it could be argued that anyone who went to see the play and sat through it must have been depraved and corrupted already. As for the use of strong language when one knows what language is used from the fourth form to the pub or the nineteenth tee, and used nowadays I suspect pretty frequently by both sexes, is it not really hypocritical to say that it cannot be used in publications or performances?

So the difficulties of dealing with the three factors that I have mentioned are considerable. Take the case of books, for example, or magazines: how can you possibly say that adults can use a bookstall but not children? Is it right by law to confine the contents of a bookstall solely to anything suitable for the youngest customer? Attempts made in America and here to divide bookshops into sections, with one part reserved for adults, have never seemed to me particularly satisfactory, and, indeed, once a book or magzine is in circulation the inquisitive young will always find a way to lay their hands on it.

Films and plays are on the whole a different matter, because people below a certain age can theoretically, at any rate, be excluded, and this is on the whole a system that should continue, though it has led at times, in Central London in particular, to a situation where is has been virtually impossible to find a cinema to which to take a child as almost everything has been X certificate.

It is the effect of scenes of violence that bothers me most, and this applies to the television probably even more than it does to the cinema and the theatre. The constant piping of violence into virtually every home in the country in graphic form must have some influence upon people's behaviour, though it is difficult to know exactly what. I suspect myself that there is a great deal of difference between the old-fashioned cowboy and Indian scenario and the modern film which displays violence in an every-day setting. I doubt if the sight of cowboys and Indians shooting and firing arrows at one another has ever really inspired anyone to personal violence, because it has been so remote from their ordinary life and experience. But violence over the kitchen sink is another matter altogether, because the kitchen sink is part of life, and the display of violence in this every-day context may have quite a different effect. But, here again, it is very difficult to know what line to lay down. The producers will argue that life is violent, that they are only portraying facts of life, however disproportionately, and that no one should be entitled to suppress them. The same is true of television news, particularly in its coverage of Northern Ireland at certain times. There seems little doubt that in these circumstances violence begets violence, and, indeed, the presence of television cameras can often stimulate people into actions which otherwise they would not take. It is hard to justify censorship and any attempt to impose it would be vehemently resisted. But one is left with the nagging feeling that something is wrong, that a solution must somehow be found. I must confess so far it has eluded me.

When I was Home Secretary I set in train measures which were brought forward by my successors to deal with bogus cinema clubs and, more important in my view, with offensive advertising. Here I think the case is absolutely clear. There is no justification for forcing upon people scenes of violence or even highly erotic scenes if they do not wish to see them. If they want to go into a cinema that is their business, but many people can be offended by outdoor advertising who have not the slightest intention of going into the cinema themselves, and I think that is a case where the public are entitled to some protection.

And there were many other problems to tackle at the Home Office, requiring decisions of one kind or another. Some of the most important were concerned with appointments. The Home Secretary is Police Authority for the Metropolis and he has to appoint the Commissioner of Police. When I was Home Secretary Sir John Waldron came to the end of a long and distinguished term of service as Commissioner, and I had to appoint his successor. It was fortunate indeed that there was an outstanding candidate available in Robert Mark, who was so well qualified by both experience and intellectual quality to be the successor. Then there was the Totalizator Board. The Tote was in a financial jam. I felt it had to be maintained as an alternative to the bookmakers in the interests both of racing and of the betting public; to see the Tote disappear would have been a great pity. In order to maintain it we had to introduce fresh legislation, which Mark Carlisle manfully carried through the House of Commons. I was fortunate in being able to persuade Stormont Mancroft to take over the Chairmanship.

It is always the habit of Ministers when in doubt to set up Committees of Enquiry, or Royal Commissions. I established two such bodies, to both of which I attached considerable importance. It seemed to me that the time had come for a thorough overhaul of the law relating to licensing hours and the sale of liquor. My own inclination, and this will come as no surprise to my friends, was to permit liquor to be sold just as freely as any other commodity. I did not believe that the residual and arbitrary restrictions of licensing hours served any useful social purpose whatsoever. So I asked Freddy Erroll, quite frankly because he was a congenial spirit, apart from being a distinguished national figure, if he would chair a committee, which he was good enough to do. We were able to provide him with a good team. I wanted it to be as representative as possible, and in particular I wanted a sporting figure, so I asked Graham Hill, the great racing driver, who was always a good friend and whom so many of us deeply miss. The report, when it came, was just what I had hoped for, full of commonsense and practical suggestions. Alas, it has not been acted on. I wish it had. But they always tell you in politics that the combination of the Bishops and the publicans is a strong one, and though there was a Bishop on the Committee, I am afraid the powers of inertia to any legislation in this possibly contentious field have so far proved victorious.

The other inquiry was to deal with a very difficult subject indeed, namely criminal responsibility. Here too I had felt for some while that the state of the law was due for some reconsideration. It was not necessarily wrong. The MacNaghten rules still made a great deal of sense. But so much had happened and so much was being said by the exponents of the developing practice of psycho-analysis. I was always worried by what the psycho-analysts had to say. Fairly early in my days at the Home Office I was presented with a long and serious report about a man who had murdered two schoolchildren in particularly revolting circumstances. The report by the learned psycho-analyst concluded by saying that having examined the man in great detail, he could find no sign of any mental abnormality. It seemed to me quite simply that anyone who had done what he had done must be a lunatic, but apparently in scientific terms I was wrong. I began to have doubts about the validity of those scientific terms. Then came the case of Young, the poisoner to whom I have already referred. We had to take immediate action to tighten things up, and in this I sought and obtained the good advice of Judge Aarvold and a distinguished committee. But there was also an opportunity here to establish a major new enquiry into the principles of criminal responsibility, and I was delighted when Rab, as a former Home Secretary and a man of great eminence, accepted my invitation to be Chairman. The basic question I put to them, or sought to put, was simply this : can you determine when a temptation becomes irresistible? What is the difference between a temptation that was irresistible and a temptation that just was not resisted? It seemed to me that the whole question of criminal responsibility must hinge on this simple question. If a man gives way to temptation and commits a crime, he must be guilty. If it can be shown that he had no option but to give way to the temptation, that is another matter, but on what evidence can such a proposition be tested? Rab and his distinguished colleagues produced for my successor a major report which is of lasting value, but I must confess I am not entirely convinced that they answered my fundamental question; nor in fact did I really expect them to do so in full. It is, however, a little disappointing that up till now no Government action has been taken about it.

Being appointed Home Secretary creates difficulties for one's private life, particularly if you have a family. This is mainly because of the requirements of security. Traditionally the Home Secretary has been one of the very few Ministers who has a permanent armed guard. His car comes not from the normal Ministerial pool, but is a Metropolitan Police car with a Police driver. These precautions were certainly necessary, and in the light of the growth of terrorism remain so, but they were a constant reminder of possible threat and danger, which did not exactly help with one's peaceful family life.

I received one death threat when I was Chancellor. It came from a foolish man who wrote it on a pad of notepaper not realizing he had written his home address on the preceding sheet of paper to another addressee, and that it could easily be read under a microscope on the sheet sent to me. I think he was pretty surprised when the Police called on him almost immediately. However, he turned out to be a harmless nut, and a severe warning was all that was called for.

I received several threats while I was Home Secretary, including one letter which enclosed a live round of ammunition. But these were fairly routine matters. The only bomb I had was after I left office. It came in the usual post when scrutiny of my mail had ceased, and I found it when Beryl and I arrived at our home in the country for the weekend, together with a pile of other mail. It looked like a typical paperback book in a brown envelope, of which one receives quite a number. I felt it carefully, and flexed it, but could detect nothing unusual. When I opened it and started to pull the book out, there was a loud bang. I turned to my wife, who was behind me, with the brilliant remark, 'Darling, I think we have had a bomb,' then counted my fingers, which were all still there, swallowed a quadruple Scotch and rang the Police. We had been lucky: the detonator had exploded but the gelignite with it fortunately did not. Even then, however, the force of the explosion had blown a hole through a solid oak table, and a corresponding hole in a rafter immediately above. The sender of the letter was subsequently convicted. He was a very young man. I could not help reflecting how appalling the incident might have been if my granddaughter had been with us standing beside me at the time. So one comes first hand against the meaning of terrorism.

My Police guard were most delightful men, combining an agreeable manner with great competence. As they were Special Branch officers, perhaps I should not give their names, but they know they have my thanks, as does Peter Halsey, the official Police driver, who looked after me so well. They all were particularly good with the children, though I am glad to say they resisted blandishments that they should teach my sons how to handle their automatic pistols.

In London we had an apartment in Admiralty House, and security there was a fairly easy matter. At our house in the country, where we had been living for many years, it was a little more difficult. The Special Branch men were so unobtrusive that they might have been some of my sons' friends paying us a visit. Frankly, I did not think this was the right technique. I remember the senior detective-sergeant telling me, not entirely in jest, that, as he had told my predecessor, Mr Callaghan, his job was to shoot the man who had just shot me. Deterrence always seems to me a better policy than retaliation, so I arranged with the Chief Constable of Hertfordshire to provide a guard of uniformed Police with very conspicuous revolvers in webbing holsters. This he kindly did, and it seemed to work well. I am afraid the Police concerned must have found it a very boring duty, but they were invariably courteous and effective. Though, perhaps, I might recall that during the period when I was Home Secretary we had our first breaking and entry, a wooden shed in the garden was burnt to the ground, and my second son, Edward, was correctly, I am afraid, nicked by one of the coppers on guard for driving a Land Rover down the lane without a driving licence.

The only other problem we had was with the physical precautions. The garden was surrounded by an electronic beam, which gave a warning when someone broke it. Unfortunately, it was very close to the ground and people had forgotten the existence of foxes and rabbits. We had a number of false alarms – the final one, illustrating the efficiency of the equipment, when repeated false alarms were finally traced to the steam rising from a warm pool in the garden on a chilly spring night.

I greatly enjoyed my time as Home Secretary. The volume of work, allied with my wider responsibilities, was, as I have explained, heavy, but this is one of the factors that makes the task of a Minister as enjoyable as it is rewarding.

Of course it is a hard job. You cannot do it in thirty-five hours a week. But how many worthwhile jobs can be done and responsibility dismissed in thirty-five hours a week? The sheer fascination of the work and the problems, the sense of responsibility, and sometimes of achievement, even the struggle to wrestle with errors and difficulties, are in themselves a source of inspiration, not of exhaustion. I do not think any Minister really faces a burden of work greater than he can manage. If he finds it that way, it is because he does not know how to organize his life sensibly.

It is true that few weekends are entirely free of work. The red boxes come down to your home by despatch rider, and they are often crammed with official papers. But all those papers are usually interesting, often challenging, and certainly worthwhile dealing with. I remember Hugh Massingham once saying of Winston Churchill after an indisposition, that he recovered his health when he returned to work and was faced with a nourishing pile of Cabinet papers.

Of course there are difficulties about dealing with official papers outside the office. When you travel by train, for example, the security authorities insist that you have a complete compartment to yourself, which, on a crowded train, is not always popular with fellow travellers who do not understand the reason. At home you have to have a special safe installed to protect the papers you are working on. But I must confess there is one hazard which took me unawares. I was sitting in an armchair in the drawing-room reading a file, with my red Government box open beside me on the floor. It was only too late that I saw that one of our white cats had decided to take up its position in the red box and was expressing its views of Government policy by the most direct and unpardonable treatment of my official papers!

Much has been written recently, particularly in the Crossman Diaries, about Ministerial life, and, in particular, relations between Ministers and Civil Servants. I think the Crossman Diaries are misleading; I certainly think they are in some ways unfortunate. I proceed on the simple principle that if you and I say something to one another on the mutual understanding, either explicit or implicit, that it is in confidence, in confidence it should remain, and if Civil Servants cannot advise their Ministers without fearing that what they say will be made public, then their advice may often be inhibited, and this would be a bad thing. My view in general, which may be old-fashioned, is that Civil Servants should not be accountable in public for their advice. The Minister should be accountable for accepting it. Just as he will take the credit if things go right, then if things go wrong all the blame must rest on him. I know I made many mistakes as a Minister. Some of them were not my fault but arose from bad advice;

Kenya revisited, 1966

With Edward Heath and William Whitelaw at Selsdon Park,
1 February 1970

Belfast, 2 July 1970, meeting the men who were doing the job

With
Major Chichester-Clarke,
the Ulster Prime Minister,
on the steps of Stormont,
July 1970

At the British Trade Fair in Moscow in 1971 with Khrushchev and the
British Ambassador, Sir Frank Roberts

yet I regarded the consequences of the mistakes as equally my responsibility whatever their origin.

It is nonsense to say that Ministers are bound to be dominated by
their Civil Servants, and anyone who is so dominated does not deserve
to be a Minister. Ministers should only be dominated by arguments.
If your Civil Service advisers produce arguments which convince you,
then you should accept them. Your advisers produce the facts and
knowledge is power, but knowledge is shared between you. Your
advisers then go on to express their objective view of the merits of the
various courses of action open to you. You should never accept any
view or argument unless you are convinced that it is right; to do otherwise is a total abnegation of responsibility. I remember once, in one of
my senior Ministerial positions, being told by a very distinguished
public servant, 'Minister, do you realize that you are going against
the advice of all your professional advisers?' I replied, 'Yes, I do; to
do that on certain occasions is precisely the purpose for which
Ministers exist.'

There is just one way in which I think the burden on Ministers
could be reduced, and that is by cutting back the number of speeches
they have to make outside Parliament. I always thought that Ministers
made far too many of these speeches, and I remember once telling
Derry Amory, when he was Chancellor, that in my view the difficulty
was simply that if you made so many speeches either you would go on
saying the same thing, which would become boring, or you would
start saying different things, which would become embarrassing. The
views and policies of the Government should be expressed in Parliament. I have a strong suspicion that the public interest would not be
gravely affected if there were a sharp reduction in the number of
speeches made by Ministers, and I suppose this must include Shadow
Ministers, up and down the country (and that goes for Party Political
broadcasts too). No doubt my colleagues would say that this view is
another example of Reggie's laziness, but I suspect it would command
a fairly wide measure of agreement among the general public.

12

Northern Ireland

1970–1972

THE situation in Northern Ireland on the change of Government in 1970 was already a very serious one. My predecessor, Mr Callaghan, had taken the decision to send British troops to the Province to support the Royal Ulster Constabulary. In this he was undoubtedly right, for the R.U.C. were a relatively small force within the entire Province. They were becoming exhausted and their struggle to contain the rioting between the Protestant and Catholic factions was beginning to exceed their means. They were a heavily armed Police Force by the standards of Great Britain, with automatic weapons and even armoured cars, but even with this their numbers were insufficient. The backing they had received from the B Specials had the profound disadvantage that this particular Force was regarded by the Catholic population as wholly antipathetic to them, and there is little doubt they had some justification for this feeling.

Northern Ireland is a very personal place; personalities matter enormously. After all, it is not very large; the population, I believe, is about the same as an English county. This brings its advantages and disadvantages. Everyone knows everyone else in politics, but it does not mean that everyone likes or understands everyone else. Political relations can be the more intimate by reason of the small size of the community, but they can also be the more violent for the same reason. There were, among the leading politicians of Northern Ireland, many people on both sides for whom I had great respect. Their problems were enormous. To lead the Unionist Party in Northern Ireland was a hazardous job, and the Party were very tough on their leaders: sometimes, I think, not only tough but very unfair.

I came to know, in turn, Terence O'Neill, James Chichester-Clark and Brian Faulkner, for all of whom I had great respect: each in his own way was a man of integrity. Terence on the whole seemed to me the more intellectual, the more withdrawn; Chichester-Clark the simpler, the more blunt; Faulkner, the more professional politician. They all had their strengths and their weaknesses but one thing they had in common was a sincere dedication to the cause of their country. On the other side there were men of integrity too – Gerry Fitt, in particular, with whom I often disagreed but who seemed to me to show in his political and personal life a very great degree of courage, which should not be underestimated. The same was true of John Hume. And there were many others one came to know, from the boisterous on the one hand, to the bigots on the other (and they were not all that far divided in practice in many ways). The most sensible and impressive people were the leaders of the local Trade Unions, whose advice I found to be both impartial and invaluable.

There were others, of whom I will not speak because I could not do so in a charitable frame of mind, but there was the Rev. Ian Paisley, one of the most difficult characters anyone could hope to deal with. I have always found his influence in that Province dangerous. I deeply dislike his approach to the politics of Ulster and the methods he has employed to try to get his own way. But it has to be admitted that in private he has great charm. He came to see me not very long after I had become Home Secretary, and we had a long talk about the situation in the Province, and what he saw as the legitimate claims and purposes of his own supporters. At the end of a long talk I said, 'I find you very hard to understand, Ian. So far as I can see, you and your supporters spend all your time getting drunk and marching all over the place.'

'Oh, Reggie,' he said, 'I have never got drunk, but I have sometimes marched.'

'That is funny,' I replied, 'I have sometimes got drunk but I have never marched.'

We have got on quite well since then, though I did hear recently from a Parliamentary colleague that he bumped into Ian Paisley in the park just after our interview, and Ian said that he had just been talking to 'the unmade bed'. I suppose it was a fair reference to my untidy appearance, and it seemed to me more of a compliment than an insult, because an unmade bed is normally a symbol of happy memories!

It is very hard for an Englishman to understand the feelings of those who live in Northern Ireland. The history of their struggles is a long one, and they tend to cherish every moment of hatred in it. The deep divide between Catholic and Protestant, which, incidentally, is more racial than religious, had been handed down faithfully from generation to generation. Leading Protestants looked upon Catholics as traitors, and indeed it was said that Lord Brookeborough, when Prime Minister, would not have a Catholic in his house. On the other hand, those Catholics who did consort with leading Protestants were regarded by the Republican Extremists as traitors and known as 'Castle Catholics'. On this bed of hatred the two I.R.A. factions, Official and Provisional, flourished. The Official, pro-Marxist, section were on the whole far less active than the Provisionals, who were the men of violence and were organizing the most severe of the troubles. They relied upon and received the support of the Catholic community in practice, partly, no doubt, because of intimidation, but very largely by reason of the deep sense of injustice felt by the Catholics that they had been treated as second-class citizens. Above all, there was the historic hatred, blind, unreasoning, unrelenting. I remember how shortly after I became Home Secretary I saw a television film of a young couple in a small house in Belfast, with their baby daughter. I cannot remember whether they were Protestants or Catholics, but it would have made no difference. Assuming they were Catholic, the interviewer asked the father, 'When this daughter of yours grows up, suppose she should marry a Protestant, what would you do about it?' His answer was direct, 'I would never speak to her again.' My blood ran cold when I heard it, and I realized the virtual hopelessness of any attempt by reason to bring peace and reconciliation to this suffering and tortured people.

But we had to try, and try as hard as we could. There were those who said, and are still saying, that if the people of Ulster insist on killing one another and killing our British soldiers in the process, then the soldiers should be withdrawn and they should be left to fight it out amongst themselves. It has always been a tempting argument, but it is

'Aggressor! How dare you stand between me and my destiny?'

not one to which we should ever yield. The withdrawal of British Forces from Northern Ireland, the abdication of the responsibility of the Crown, would lead to civil war on a scale that would make even the tragedies of the last five years dwindle in perspective, and as the Protestant majority gained the ascendancy, as they certainly would, the Irish Republic would be bound to intervene. The prospect is a hideous one. I often reflected on the story of the two American G.I.s who were supposed to leave Belfast on a troopship during the War. As they looked back they saw the city with the usual pall of smog hanging over it, and above it the barrage balloons with their steel cables attaching them to the ground. One G.I. turned and said to the other, 'You know, there is one thing I shall never understand, why don't they just cut those strings and let the darn place sink?' But this was not and cannot be a decision that would be taken by a responsible British Government. It is essential to struggle on.

In 1970 the main problem was rioting between the two communities on the streets. This the Army had to deal with, and they dealt with it pretty effectively, and for a time things got a little quieter. But this was only to lead to a new and even more dangerous stage of the tragedy. The Provisional I.R.A. turned to acts of individual violence and terrorism, the shooting of policemen and soldiers, and the planting of bombs which caused casualties to wholly un-involved civilians. This is a far more difficult problem to deal with. In a vast city like Belfast, or in the wide countryside of Northern Ireland, even 15,000 troops can easily be absorbed. The initiative lies not with them but with the men of violence, who can come and go at will and whose strikes are unpredictable.

It has become apparent in recent years in many countries that the defences of society against the urban guerrilla are inadequate. Basic-ally, law and order rest not upon the Police and the Army, but upon the conventions of society, and when those conventions begin to crumble the presence of a few thousand policemen or even several thousand soldiers is not an adequate defence.

Our policy involved a difficult balancing act. We had to be as tough as we could with the terrorists, and the directives given by the Govern-ment to the Security Forces were strong. Certainly, I do not remem-ber, despite stories often circulated to the contrary, that the Security Forces were asking for powers which the Government were unwilling to give to them. But the great difficulty in using those powers was that the terrorists were a small active minority in a substantial Catholic community. It was essential to do everything possible to isolate them, because so long as they had the tacit support of the Catholic community it was impossible to obtain the information which was vital to apprehend them. If action were taken, such as searching houses for arms, which would be fully justified on many grounds, it could be very easily regarded by the whole Catholic community as a victimization of them as Catholics and, therefore, would bolster the support that they gave to the Provisional I.R.A. If, on the other hand, these vigorous actions were not taken and, in particular, if it were alleged that the Security Forces would like to do these things but were being held back by the politicians, then there was always the danger of a violent Protestant reaction, and we had to remember all the time that the Protestants could be just as violent as the Catholics, and they were far more numerous.

So we continued to do what we could to contain violence in the Province, walking a real tightrope of difficulties. I was often lost in admiration for the performance of the British Army in circumstances which I do not believe any other army in the world would equally tolerate. These men had an appalling job to do, open to provocation on the street, the target of the murder bullet on any dark night, know-ing that if they over-reacted to any provocation the results could be disastrous. The bearing and performance of our young soldiers, and young they were, all of them, was quite remarkable. I was always fearful that the duties they had to undertake in Northern Ireland would be bad for the morale of the Army as a whole, and certainly would be bad for recruiting. It was a great source of comfort and of admiration to see that this in practice did not come about.

All the time, as was our duty, we were trying to find some form of political solution. The difficulty is that if you make some concessions in a situation like this they are almost always too little and too late, and merely result in claims for more. There was no doubt in my mind that the Catholic community had had less than their fair share in the governing of their own country, and that there was severe discrimination against them. Successive leaders of the Unionist Party to their credit recognized and accepted this, and wished to move in the direction of progress. But the more the violence that came from the Provisional I.R.A. the greater the difficulty of meeting the Catholic claims, for the natural human reason that the Protestants asked with indignation why concessions should be made to the men of violence at the expense of their own community which they claimed was a peaceable one. The answer is, of course, that it is always more easy to obey the law when it is on your side. Britain's experience of Colonial rule has proved this so often; but it has also often shown the difficulty that it poses.

The previous Government, in a White Paper of 1969, had set out proposals agreed between the British and Northern Ireland Governments designed to eliminate discrimination against the Catholic community. There is no doubt that they were sound proposals. There is equally little doubt that they were overdue, and this was one of the great problems. Just as progress was being made towards removing discrimination, so the desire grew among the Catholic community that they should not merely be free from discrimination against them but more than this they should be able to play a proper part in the governing of their own country. For, as they rightly pointed out, if it was their own country they should be able to play a proper part and if in practice Catholics were excluded from any share of the Government, how could they really regard it as their own country? And so we went on with the process of implementing the White Paper. While all the time as we seemed to make slow progress in that direction, we were really trying to walk up an escalator that was moving down.

The security situation became worse and more important, the

political effects of the security situation became all the time more menacing. I am not talking in terms of Party considerations. The point simply was that a Protestant backlash was the great danger we all feared, and it could so easily be sparked off by the argument that the more concessions you made to the Catholics, the less result you got for them. The Army did their best to contain the violence that was taking place, but it is exceedingly difficult for any army to contain men of violence when they have the support of a large community which offers them protection and secrecy.

So in 1971 we came to the question of internment without trial. It was a very difficult decision indeed to take; no one could be certain what would be the consequences. The effect upon the Catholic community, with all its memories, would be bound to be severe. Equally dangerous were the possible effects in the Republic, and it must never be forgotten how important is the collaboration of the Government of the Republic to any long-term solution of the problem of Ulster. Passions were bound to be aroused by the introduction of internment. And yet the question was simply this, what other measures could be taken in the face of the mounting campaign of violence?

The Police and the Army Intelligence systems had a great deal of information about the membership of the Provisional I.R.A., and, let us make no bones about it, the members of the I.R.A. were dedicated to murder and terrorism and should have been locked up. The decision on whether to lock them up without trial was formally in the hands of the Northern Ireland Government, and, of course, in particular, Mr Faulkner, but there was an understanding between us that it would not be exercised without the agreement of the British Government, for the simple reason that it would be the British Government and, above all, the British Army who would have to carry the can for whatever happened. I was myself deeply worried about this whole question. In particular I feared any retaliation that the Provisional I.R.A. might embark upon, for example, a campaign of kidnapping innocent people, possibly even children. There were very few signs of any limit to the barbarity of the tactics they might adopt.

But I was persuaded, as was Ted Heath, that of all the courses open to us in an exceedingly dangerous situation this seemed the least disadvantageous. Accordingly we went ahead, and internment was instituted, and a very large number of dangerous men were put in a place where, for the time being, they could do no harm. But the consequences, as we had foreseen, were serious. The resentment in the

Catholic community was extreme. While the security situation had been improved the political situation had been made far more dangerous. This was the problem to which we had then to address ourselves.

I embarked on a series of consultations with all the organizations in Northern Ireland who could make some contribution to finding a political solution. Needless to say their advice was very varied, though all of it was valuable. What I was aiming at was some means of providing the Catholic community with what had really become their objective, and a perfectly legitimate objective, which was no longer merely the avoidance of discrimination against them but a guarantee of an appropriate place in the governing of their own country. I was able to agree with Brian Faulkner a form of words to describe what we were seeking to establish. The formula was a 'Permanent and guaranteed role for the minority community as well as the majority in the life and public affairs of the Province'. The words were admirable. The problem was to interpret them and make them effective in practical terms. This became increasingly difficult. It was uphill work, and the progress, if progress at all took place, was exceedingly slow : too slow, in fact, if we were to obtain our objective of peace and reconciliation.

I was forced more and more to the conclusion that a new initiative was needed of a radical kind, and I began to have growing doubts about the possibility of maintaining, in its then current form, the Stormont system of Government. The system certainly measured up to the classic conditions of a democracy in that the Parliament of Northern Ireland was elected by universal franchise. But could these classic conditions of democracy really be said to operate in a community like Northern Ireland, where they produced a permanent Protestant majority, where, in the absence of any proportional system of representation, this meant permanent exclusion from Government of any Catholics, and where there was a deep-seated and not wholly unjustified feeling among the minority community that in practice they were being treated as second-class citizens?

After all, we had come to learn that the Westminster pattern of democracy, which suits us so well, is not easily exportable, and I had a growing feeling that it could not for ever satisfy the needs of Northern Ireland. The trouble was simply this : elections were fought and Governments were formed not on the basic political issues to which we are accustomed in Great Britain. All these were overridden by the simple communal argument, if you are a Protestant you vote

Protestant, if you are a Catholic you vote Catholic. There were exceptions, but they were few and not really significant. The prospects of a change of Government frankly were nil; the chances of a Catholic Government in the foreseeable future did not exist. In these circumstances the Westminster system of two parties competing with one another, and power moving from time to time from one to the other, did not operate.

Allied to this was the continuing tragedy of the security situation, which showed no signs of getting any better. It was bad enough that British soldiers were involved, and were being murdered, but what was more difficult was that the British soldiers were there to provide support for a Government to which they were not responsible, and in whose policies their own Government had no say. The Northern Ireland Government at Stormont made the laws and ran the administration; the British Army which was responsible not to Stormont but to the Westminster Parliament had to maintain law and order in appalling conditions on the basis of laws enacted and administration conducted on the authority of the Stormont Parliament. I became convinced that this was a situation that could not indefinitely endure.

So I set about producing some proposals that were based on three principles. The first was that the Parliament, to which the forces of law and order were responsible, must have responsibility for the law that they had to protect. The second was that there was no prospect whatever of a long-term solution to the political problem in Northern Ireland so long as the minds of the politicians and the politically conscious were wholly absorbed with the issue of the Border. The third was that a period of practical working together by Protestants and Catholics in a common power-sharing administration was the best chance of building up a real will to collaborate for the general good of all citizens.

What I recommended to my Cabinet colleagues in early 1972 was in effect this. The time had come to take a new initiative. The dangers I could see in any initiative were very great, but I had become convinced that the dangers of inaction were even greater. For decades the Government in Northern Ireland had been dominated by the majority community to the virtual exclusion of the minority. As a result of this and other developments, the estrangement between the two communities had become virtually complete. The political situation and the security situation alike were deteriorating. The Army had done extremely well, but there were definite limits to what they could do.

However successful and effective they were, there was no prospect of eliminating urban guerrillas and terrorists so long as a substantial element in the population was alienated from the forces of law and order. The only hope I could see for the future was the creation of a united community in Northern Ireland which the Republic would be prepared at least to let live. Of course any solution was bound to be difficult, because it involved reducing the political power of the Protestants who claimed to be the loyal community. But no lasting solution could be achieved without something of this kind taking place. So long as the majority of people in Northern Ireland wished to remain part of the United Kingdom there could be no possible question of their right to do so, but this must be on two conditions. First, that United Kingdom standards of political behaviour were accepted, and, secondly, that the overall authority of the Westminster Parliament was recognized as in the rest of the United Kingdom.

My proposals were as follows :

1. Responsibility for law and order should be transferred to Westminster. This was the first and fundamental condition of progress.

2. There should be a referendum immediately about the Border, and we should make it clear that while there would be others in the future, they would take place at intervals of not less than fifteen or twenty years.

3. There should be a proper representation of the minority community in Government as well as in Parliament. They should be involved not only in the making of the laws, but in carrying out the administration of the Province. This is what subsequently came to be called 'power-sharing'.

4. There should be a Secretary of State for Northern Ireland who would take over from me, the Home Secretary, responsibility for the Province, and he should be advised by a Northern Ireland Commission.

5. There should be progressive reduction of the numbers in internment until it was totally abolished.

It clearly had to be faced that these proposals would be unwelcome to Mr Faulkner and his colleagues, and so it transpired. In fact things broke down on the first issue of the transfer of law and order. Mr Faulkner was prepared to make some moves in our direction, but from our point of view they were nowhere near far enough to meeting the basic principle. He was adamant. He knew what he believed was right for his country, and he was wholly justified in standing by his point of view. He told me once, I remember, 'Reggie, I am not prepared to be the chairman of a county council.' One could not help reflecting that the people of Warwickshire were about as numerous as the people of Northern Ireland, and very much more happy. But there were generations of history and emotion behind Mr Faulkner's stand, and I would never seek to minimize his feelings in this matter. Though he disagreed, I am happy to think we remained personal friends, and I was, along with many others, deeply distressed by his tragic death.

When our discussions broke down the British Government had to act on the lines I had suggested. This involved in the circumstances a temporary period of direct rule, because there was no one else who could possibly have taken Mr Faulkner's place. Stormont was suspended on a temporary basis, not dissolved, because, as I had pointed out, it was an essential part of the precautions about the Border contained in the Ireland Act 1949, which provided that no change could be made without the approval of Stormont. With Ted Heath's authority I sounded out Willie Whitelaw about taking over Northern Ireland, and I was able to report to Ted that he would respond with enthusiasm to such an invitation. So Ted asked him to take over, and he did, and how manfully he served in wrestling with the appalling problems that immediately faced him.

It is difficult, I suppose, at this stage to reach any fair assessment of how far the initiative I proposed has succeeded in making any progress. It certainly represented a fundamentally new approach from which all subsequent developments have flowed; the consequences for good or ill rest on my shoulders. Things move very slowly in Northern Ireland. All I can say is that in my judgement the situation would now have been far worse if we had taken no such initiative, and it still remains the truth that Northern Ireland will never be at peace until the two communities learn to work together, until their political leaders turn aside from the Border problem, with all that it implies, and concentrate on the everyday happiness of their people, and until the political struggles of the Province are based, as they are in the rest of the United Kingdom, not on communal issues, but on the fundamental political issues which divide the Right wing from the Left over the whole range of our public life.

13

Mr Heath's No. 2

1970—1972

S O far I have been dealing with the specific responsibilities of the Home Secretary. Of course they always in practice extend beyond this because of the nature of the office, and in my case they were particularly widened because of my effective though not formal position as Deputy Prime Minister. This meant that not only did I have to preside over a fairly wide range of Cabinet Committees, and, where necessary, seek the guidance of the Cabinet on their behalf where problems could not otherwise be resolved. It also meant that I was personally engaged over the whole range of Government responsibility. Once again, the political journalists tried to create the impression that there were tensions and disputes between Ted Heath and myself.

This just was not true, any more than it had been in the years of Opposition. As I have said, our temperaments were different, and we were never intimate friends, but that was not necessary. We respected one another, we listened, and each could be persuaded by the other. We never had a row. One interesting example of the political journalists at work was an article written by that very distinguished member of his profession, Derek Marks, who was a close friend of mine. It was on 16 January 1972, and it was headed by the cartoon which I reproduce on the following page. The theme was that I was very unpopular in the

higher echelons of the Government, and that Ted wanted to shift me from the Home Office. The reason was apparently, in Derek's words, that 'It is the Prime Minister's wish to develop a new initiative in Northern Ireland, and it is said that this cannot be achieved without dividing the responsibility of Ulster from the Home Office, and that this can only be done by getting rid of Mr Maudling.' The simple fact was that, as I have explained, the setting up of a Northern Ireland Office separate from the Home Office, and the installation of a separate Secretary of State for Northern Ireland, was an integral part of the reforms which I myself was then urging on the Cabinet, and which, thanks largely to Ted Heath (who was the first to understand and agree with what I was proposing), they accepted.

Of course there were differences of view between us, it would have been surprising, and, indeed, disappointing, if there had not been, but they were resolved by discussion and persuasion.

The other argument then currently popular in political circles was to the effect that I was leading a Left-wing faction in the Cabinet against the Right-wing majority led by Ted Heath. It could be argued that there was something in this, but like all generalities it is totally misleading. Talk of Left wing or Righ wing really is wholly superficial. People cannot be placed in compartments. It may be that in some matters my views were what could be described as to the Left of Ted's, but, to take another example, I was always a strong supporter of capital punishment, which is held to be a Right-wing point of view, whereas Ted, I believe, has always been an abolitionist.

The major issue of domestic policy with which we were wrestling was the same as we had faced for decades and which persists today, and to which I have made much reference, because it is one of the greatest of national problems. It is simply how to contain wage inflation and how society is to come to terms with the newly conscious monopoly power of the Trade Unions. This absorbed much of our time and energies in the early years of the Heath Government, and I was deeply involved by reason of my position in the Government and because of the specific responsibilities of the Home Secretary, both for emergency policy and for guiding the discussions of Ministers at a Cabinet Committee level on the issues involved.

At that time we were pursuing what came to be known as the N–1 policy. The basic thesis was that the main cause of wage inflation arose from the demands in the public sector. If, therefore, public-sector demands could be adequately restrained, we should find a solution to our problem. There was a lot in this, though it was not entirely convincing, nor was it unfamiliar. I could remember previous occasions when Conservative Governments had tried to pursue a policy described in the graphic phrase 'making the public tail wag the private dog', but on this occasion it became increasingly difficult to sustain, because of its catch-as-catch-can nature. N–1 was based on effecting individual settlements, and trying to ensure that each succeeding individual settlement was a little lower than the last one. It is not easy to base a consistent policy upon actions in individual circumstances, yet a consistent policy was what was needed. Many anomalies arose. As a distinguished academic has recently pointed out, doctors were offered three times more than dustmen, railwaymen were singled out for compulsory ballot, electricians and miners were offered an independent enquiry, yet postmen and local-government workers were refused similar facilities. I became more and more convinced that this was not an acceptable way of proceeding, and that a single coherent policy was required. The miners' claim and the strike we had to face brought this graphically into perspective. I sought to put to the Cabinet as a whole my views which were of a fairly radical kind, in a memorandum. For once Ted Heath and I had a disagreement. He asked me not to circulate the memorandum as it would have created difficulties for him. So, of course, I withdrew it. But I did in fact publish it much later in *The Times* newspaper in September 1972, three months after I had resigned, as the document I would have sent to the Cabinet had I remained in the Government. It is reproduced in Appendix 3. I do not think it was far wrong. In any case it was the course that the Government proceeded to follow.

Leaving Admiralty House after my resignation in July 1972

With Henry Kissinger, 7 March 1975

14

The Poulson Affair

THE Poulson affair became a public issue in 1972 as a result of his examination in bankruptcy. It then became apparent that he had been dispensing large sums of money in bribes to public officials of one kind or another. Clearly criminal offences on a large scale were involved, and the job of investigation into so serious a matter had to be undertaken by the Metropolitan Police. As Home Secretary I was officially Police Authority for the Metropolis, and was responsible for the Metropolitan Police. It seemed to me quite clear that I could not continue to hold that responsibility while the Met. were investigating, with a view to possible prosecution, the activities of a man with whom I had had a business association. I had no option but to resign, which I did, and I wrote a letter of resignation to the Prime Minister, asking him to read it out to the House of Commons, which he was good enough to do.

Ted Heath acted like a true friend. He was sorry that I felt I had to resign as Home Secretary, but did not dispute my judgement on this matter. At the same time he was good enough to offer me an alternative position in his Cabinet, and he pressed me not to retire from politics altogether. That was my inclination at the time. As I said in my letter to him, I had held Front-bench responsibility on one side of the Commons or the other for very many years. I also resented very strongly the intrusion of the Press and the Media into the affairs of my family. Any politician is fair game. While even politicians are entitled to some private life of their own, they know what they are taking on when they go into modern politics. The same is not true of politicians' children. They do not ask to be born of political parents. They get, in practice, very little advantage from this accident of birth. It is to my mind repulsive the way that publicity pursues them in their private lives in a way that it does not pursue the children of other parents. I felt a deep and bitter resentment in the way, in particular, my daughter had been treated. I was, therefore, inclined to call it a day, but Ted was persuasive, and I therefore used in my letter to him the phrase 'a respite', without commitment as to whether this was to be permanent or only temporary. I subsequently received from Ted this letter, dated 18 July 1972, which I have cherished ever since.

> My dear Reggie,
>
> Thank you for the letter which you sent me earlier today.
>
> I understand and respect the reasons for your decision to leave the Government, though, as you know from our talks, it is only with the greatest reluctance that I have accepted it. It is not just as Home Secretary that your resignation will be felt: you have brought both wisdom, and the benefits of your varied experience in many high offices of state, to the counsels of the Government, and your loss is a bitter blow to us all.
>
> I am deeply grateful to you for the loyalty you have shown in helping and supporting me personally in these last seven years, and I much appreciate your promise of support in the future. I profoundly regret your going now, and I hope that it will not be long before you are able to resume your position in the public life of this country.
>
> Yours ever,
> Ted

One of the consolations of running into trouble is that you get to learn who your true friends are. Many people wrote to me then with sincere expressions of regret. Some wrote rather more tentatively. One or two showed distinct signs of 'lifting the skirt to avoid the dirt'. I remember one former business colleague, who must remain nameless, who told me that he clearly could not anticipate the result of any inquiry – but surely that is just what a friend should do! On the other hand, I remember receiving from Henry Kissinger, amidst all his problems, a letter from the White House in his own handwriting, of the most friendly character.

So, how did it all come about? I first heard about Mr Poulson in the summer of 1966 when I was approached in the House of Commons by Albert Roberts, Labour Member for Normanton, a Yorkshire constituency in which Mr Poulson's offices were situated. He said he had a constituent, a very remarkable man, who would like to meet me. Mr Poulson then had developed one of the largest architectural practices in the whole of Western Europe. He was very active indeed in promoting his business in export markets, and he controlled a company known as Construction Promotions, the Chairman of which had been Sir Herbert Butcher, a National Liberal M.P., whom I had known as a colleague for many years, and who had recently died. It became apparent that Mr Poulson wanted to suggest to me that I should take Sir Herbert's place as Chairman of Construction Promotions.

As a result of Mr Robert's introduction we had a number of meetings and Mr Poulson did indeed propose that I should succeed Herbert Butcher. Frankly it was not an easy decision for me to make. I had plenty to do already, and I was not particularly anxious to add to my commitments. On the other hand, the work of C.P. was 100 per cent export, which did interest me, and whatever there is on the minus side for Mr Poulson, there is no doubt that he was genuine in his desire to promote British professional services in export markets in competition with those of other countries. In the light of his success in building up his own practice it seemed likely that C.P. would prove a long-term success in overseas activities, and, therefore, it represented a long-term asset and an insurance against the dangers and uncertainties of a political career.

My wife was then the Chairman of the Appeals Committee for the Adeline Genée Theatre Trust, which was collecting money for the establishment of a small theatre in East Grinstead. The concept of the Theatre, which was closely linked to a distinguished ballet school in the area, was to try to establish for British ballet something equivalent to what Glyndebourne had done for British opera. It seemed an attractive idea and it certainly had very strong support, both nationally and locally. Trustees of the project asked my wife to head the Appeals Committee, because as a girl she had been a star pupil of Adeline Genée, and she seemed the ideal choice as Appeals Chairman. Indeed she was, and she set about the business of collecting money for the charity in her usual whole-hearted manner. It was of course uphill work, as all charitable appeals are. At the time I met Mr Poulson it was progressing, but more help was very welcome. He offered to make a substantial covenant of £5,000 a year to the Theatre charity, no doubt in the belief that this action on his part would influence my subsequent decision as to whether I should accept his offer to become Chairman of C.P. He was to all appearances a man of considerable means who distributed large funds to charity, and the covenant was a generous one.

I made every possible enquiry about Mr Poulson; none cast any doubt whatever upon him. I took out a reference from his bank. I consulted a leading credit agency. I spoke to Government Departments for which he was doing work. I consulted several leading businessmen with whom he had an association. None threw any doubt whatever upon his ability or his integrity. He was, moreover, Chairman of the Executive Committee of the National Liberal Party, his wife was a J.P. and Chairman of the Yorkshire Women Conservatives. He had himself been appointed a Commissioner of Taxes. These very extensive enquiries that I made, and I do not see that I could have made any more, satisfied me that he was a suitable person with whom to be associated in this particular venture. So I accepted his offer. Looking back, it is very hard to see where I went wrong. Perhaps one should have instinctive judgement about people's integrity, but anyone who possesses such an instinct is a very fortunate and a very rare man. If all the enquiries you make over a very wide range produce a satisfactory result and you do not then act on them, what is the point of making enquiries at all?

So I took over from Herbert Butcher as Chairman of C.P. and proceeded to send letters to clients and potential clients notifying them of the change, and hoping that we should be able to do business in the future. The opportunities were very extensive indeed, ranging from Latin America to Iran. Fairly soon afterwards Mr Poulson proposed a change. He had had some argument with Mr Pollard, who was the Chief Executive of C.P., and he proposed that C.P. should concentrate on the contracts they already had in South West Africa, and that a new company should be formed, of which I would be Chairman, to be called International Technical and Constructional Services, which would cover the rest of the world outside the U.K. My Deputy Chairman in both companies was Sir Bernard Kenyon, the retiring Clerk of the West Riding County Council. The arrangement we made was that while I remained for a time the nominal Chairman of C.P., Sir Bernard Kenyon would in effect exercise the executive functions, while I concentrated on I.T.C.S. This seemed a fairly sensible arrangement.

The concept itself was a sound one. Mr Poulson's dramatic rise in his own profession derived very largely from the novel system he had evolved of combining under one umbrella a number of professional skills : architect, town planner, quantity surveyor, mechanical engineer. This made it possible to provide for the customer a comprehensive service. I.T.C.S. as a company would have the Poulson organization as its consultants and have the added advantage of being able, where necessary, to provide financial facilities to possible customers. This was of immense importance. International competition in this field was intense, and the relative quality of the competitors not necessarily all that far apart. This meant that in many cases the contract would go to people who could provide finance to go along with it. The importance of these activities to British exports generally was great. It was not only the income that would flow in foreign exchange from the professional services rendered, though this would be large, it was also the advantages that would follow for the British construction industry and many other British suppliers as well. What we were seeking to do was very much in line with British Government policy, to promote exports, and we always worked closely with the Board of Trade and their overseas representatives, having a mutual interest to secure business for Britain.

It was of course slow going; contracts of this kind run into millions if not tens of millions of pounds, and they take several years to consolidate. In the long run they are profitable, but in the short term they take a great deal of financing. Mr Poulson was providing from his own resources the necessary working capital, which was a considerable burden. He had proposed at the first meeting of I.T.C.S. that as Chairman I should be paid a salary of £9,500 a year. This was certainly not out of line with salaries paid to Chairmen of substantial international companies, but as it became apparent to me that it would be some while before I.T.C.S. became as profitable as it should be, I decided to postpone my own fees and not to take any of them until the company was earning a healthy profit. But, alas, it never did earn a healthy profit, and I never got any fees. Our main projects were in the Middle East, Saudi Arabia, where Mr Poulson designed a very important hospital, and in places along the Persian Gulf. We had a great disappointment with a major hospital in Tehran, as we did with some attractive projects in Mexico and a major irrigation scheme in Peru. But in this sort of highly competitive international business disappointments are bound to be many.

Mr Poulson had been working in Malta for some while before I became associated with him, and at the first meeting of I.T.C.S. he told us that he had been appointed as architect for a new hospital on the island of Gozo, which, in fact, his staff did design. I.T.C.S., on becoming in effect the overseas side of his organization, were due to receive twenty per cent of his fees from the Gozo hospital as part of the general arrangement for financing our activities.

I still think I.T.C.S. was a good idea. I believe if the company had continued we could have won many substantial contracts abroad on the basis of the Poulson organization. This would have made us a profitable company and, at the same time, a substantial asset to Britain's exports. But the clouds soon began to gather. They came not from any inherent fault in the concept or conduct of I.T.C.S., but from the fundamental fault, of which I and my colleagues could have no knowledge, in Poulson's own finances and his own professional practice.

It was in the early summer of 1969 that I was told how grave Mr Poulson's financial position was, and that, in fact, it was likely that he was insolvent. I immediately took such steps as were in my power. I approached Sir Henry Benson, the Senior Partner of Cooper Brothers, a leading firm of accountants, and asked him if he would send someone from his staff to try to sort matters out, which he did immediately. I also took steps to ensure that there was no question about the solvency of I.T.C.S., of which I was Chairman. I reduced expenditure to an absolute minimum, closing the office and arranging for such work as was necessary to be done from my own premises. At the same time Mr Poulson had turned for help to Mr John King, the Chairman of Babcock & Wilcox, who was related to him by marriage. John King's late wife had been Mrs Poulson's sister, and for that reason he was anxious to help, which he did with great generosity to no personal gain to himself, and, indeed, to considerable disadvantage. He arranged for a new company to be formed, Inter-Planning and Design, which took over and preserved the whole of the Poulson practice, thus allowing it to continue as a viable concern. I believe they have been running successfully since.

This appeared to have solved the immediate problems, though clearly Mr Poulson himself was insolvent and would have to face the normal bankruptcy proceedings. No one had the slightest inkling of what would emerge from those proceedings. The tale of Mr Poulson's activities, which was then revealed, needs no repeating today. It is a very familiar one now and the consequences of course have been widespread and lasted in the form of one enquiry or another for all of five years. This was a long time.

As I have said, when the nature of his activities emerged from the bankruptcy hearings I felt it my duty to resign as Home Secretary. I had hoped that at the most a year or two would have been necessary to bring matters to a conclusion, but I was disappointed in this, and it seemed to hang around an interminable time.

My difficulty was that I could at no time really get to grips with the problem. There was plenty of innuendo and gossip, but there were never any hard facts. I had played no part whatever in Mr Poulson's professional practice and I knew nothing of his personal finances, but although this was made clear in the Bankruptcy Court suspicions lingered on, for it is always very difficult to prove a negative.

The simple facts are these.

At one time in 1975 some senior officers from Scotland Yard came to see me about an allegation that Mr Poulson had used bribery to obtain the hospital contract in Gozo. All I could tell them was that if any such bribe had been offered or accepted, it was wholly without my knowledge, and this the Parliamentary Select Committee subsequently confirmed. Apart from this one instance, the Police, throughout their five years of enquiry, never approached me for any information whatsoever. Concurrently with the Police investigations the Department of Trade were enquiring into possible irregularities in Poulson companies with which I had been associated, yet throughout the five years of their investigation no one from the Department of Trade found it necessary at any time to approach me for any information whatsoever.

This, I think, is a fair measure of the degree to which I was involved in any of Mr Poulson's affairs. And yet, once again, it is very hard to establish a negative and the fact that the investigators have not been to see you is hardly a news item.

The other problem was that in the Court proceedings in which Mr Poulson was involved, including his prosecution, a number of things were said about me which were totally untrue, but which I was unable to deny because it would have been contempt of Court to do so. I was not a party to the proceedings so I was not represented. Anything, however untrue, could be said about me without my having any opportunity whatever of denying it at the time. If I were to say in a public statement that the evidence given was untrue, I would have been held to prejudice the proceedings of the Court. So I had to put up with it. It is part of the penalty that the citizen must pay for impartial

Courts and it is, I suppose, worth paying any price to maintain that impartiality.

So it seemed likely as the years passed one after the other, that the Poulson affair would not be wound up but would peter out, that it would end not with a bang but with a whimper. How wrong I was once again. The final climax emerged when the Attorney-General announced that the criminal investigations, some of the largest in Britain's history, had been concluded, and the call then arose for an enquiry into the Parliamentary aspects. A Select Committee was appointed to enquire and report, and that meant another eight-month delay for me before the final conclusion. I could not have predicted when the Select Committee were appointed how long they would take to produce their report, nor would I ever have guessed the form it would take.

The Select Committee amassed a vast quantity of documents, and studied them with care and application before inviting the M.P.s concerned to meet them. I saw them on 22 March 1977, and spent some two hours with them, by the end of which I understood I had answered all the questions they wished to put to me, and all the possible points of importance had been covered. I then awaited the publication of their report and I was duly given a copy of it roughly an hour before it was released to the Press. I read it with mixed feelings. The Committee's description of my dealings with Mr Poulson was meticulously accurate. They made it quite clear that no question of corruption arose, and that I had not used my Parliamentary position in any way improperly to further Mr Poulson's interest. It was gratifying to have this firmly stated at last, and with authority. Then they came to the question of what I had said in or to the House of Commons. The first question was whether I should have declared an interest in the Gozo hospital when taking part in debates in the House on Malta. I had explained to the Committee that I had no recollection of making the speeches in question, but that on looking up the records it appeared to me that I had no interest to declare. If I had thought I had such an interest, I would, of course, have declared it. There was no conceivable reason for not doing so. I had already talked about it to the Press and explained it in detail to the local representative of the British Government in Malta. I had, moreover, sought the opinion of Lord Maybray-King, who had been Speaker at the time, and who agreed with my attitude. The Committee, however, did not. They thought I should have made a declaration of interest. This frankly was a matter of judgement and I did not seek to challenge their view, for they had in any case made it clear that there was no question of any impropriety or concealment and they did not suggest that in this matter I had fallen below the standards that the House was entitled to expect of its Members.

This was to come in the next paragraph which related to my letter of resignation as Home Secretary and which I read with astonishment and even with disbelief. The Committee had said that they had put to the Members concerned any accusations. The simple fact was that never in the two hours I spent with the Committee was any mention whatever made of my letter of resignation, nor had it for one moment crossed my mind that the Committee were critical of it until I read their report. It was a bitter and wounding blow. I had spent twenty-seven years in the House of Commons, most of the time carrying Front-bench responsibilities. I had been a Privy Councillor for more than twenty years. I could conceive of no accusation more cruel and biting than to suggest that I had been less than frank with the House of Commons; yet there it was printed in the report of the Select Committee, and I had to deal with it.

I pressed Michael Foot, the Leader of the House, for a very early debate, which he arranged. My intention was to explain why in my view the Select Committee were misinformed in their criticism. I do not think I could do better than reproduce from *Hansard* precisely what I had said on this point.

I come to the second point – the accusations made by the Select Committee in paragraph 33 and only about my letter of resignation when I resigned as Home Secretary. I read paragraph 33 with astonishment. Earlier, in paragraph 4, the Committee had said that before reaching its conclusions it had 'put to the Members concerned the matters that arose from the evidence they had examined' and that 'no new evidence or accusation emerged that was not fully described and put to the Members concerned during their evidence'.

The fact is that while the *Hansard* extract from the Prime Minister's statement was in the bundle of documents before the Committee, it was not mentioned in the list of questions sent to me by the Committee which it asked me to answer. At no time throughout the two hours that I spent with the Committee did any Member of it make any mention whatsoever of the statement to me.

The first intimation that I received that the Committee was concerned about my letter of resignation, let alone critical of it, was when I received a copy of its final report about an hour before it was released to the Press. So I find it a little bewildering that a Select Committee reporting to this

House can make a statement which, frankly, is not accurate. The Select Committee did not put to me the matter of my resignation letter. It did not describe to me its accusation. Not one word was said about it at any time by anyone while I was before the Committee.

The effect, of course, is simply this : although everyone has heard the charge that the Committee brings against me and although a number of people have not hesitated to condemn me, no one has yet listened to a single word of my side of the case. That is what I want to put now.

I would ask the House not to endorse this paragraph – this is what I concentrate on – for the simple reason that it just is not true. It is based on a complete misapprehension of the facts, which I shall now explain to the House and which I could have explained so easily to the Committee if only it had asked me to do so.

In paragraph 33 the Committee quotes as the fundamental basis of its accusation against me what purports to be a passage from my letter of resignation to the Prime Minister, which he read at my request to the House. It goes on to say :

'It was in these terms, therefore, that Mr Maudling chose to describe his relationship with Mr Poulson to the House.'

But that is not the case. In fact, it is nothing of the kind. Those are not the words that I used. They are just some of the words that I used, which is a very different matter. Nor was I seeking to describe, or purporting to describe, to the House my relationship with Mr Poulson. I was describing the reasons for my resignation, which is a very different matter. To resign as Home Secretary – I think I can say I was effectively Deputy Leader of the Government at the time – is no small thing to have to do.

I am always apprehensive of partial quotations, of the leaving out of words from sentences and putting dots in their place. I cannot understand why the Committee in its report did not quote my letter in full but consigned it to Appendix 65, where the House will find it. What I said in fact to the Prime Minister was :

'We discussed the assertions made by Mr Poulson during his bankruptcy hearing. Among them there was one referring to myself, to the effect that before I accepted his invitation to become Chairman of an export Company, for which post I took no remuneration, he had made a covenant in favour of a charitable appeal which had my support. I do not regard this as matter either for criticism or for investigation. However, there are matters not relating to me that do require investigation, and I entirely agree that this should be carried out in the normal way on behalf of the Director of Public Prosecutions. The difficulty arises that the task must fall upon the Metropolitan Police, and in my particular office as Home Secretary I am Police Authority for the Metropolis. We agreed that it would not be appropriate for me to continue to hold this office while the investigations are being pursued, in view of the fact that my name has been mentioned at the Hearing.'

I was referring specifically to only one of Mr Poulson's assertions, as my words show. I was doing that for a very good reason, which I will explain in a moment. I was resigning as Home Secretary solely because of my connection with the Metropolitan Police. Had I been holding any other office of State, I would not have resigned. The Prime Minister was good enough to recognize this by offering me an alternative post in his Government which, as the House is aware, I declined for reasons of a personal character wholly unconnected with Mr Poulson.

The general nature of my business relations with Mr Poulson was not before the House in any way. It was before the courts. The Committee has described my business relations with Mr Poulson. It has made it absolutely clear that there was nothing whatever about them that it had to criticize. I can find nothing in the Committee's description of my relationship that did not emerge in full in public during the course of those court hearings five years ago.

I was calling attention in my resignation letter to one particular aspect of my relationship with Mr Poulson, namely, his covenant in favour of the Adeline Genée Theatre. I single out this particular aspect for one very good parliamentary reason, namely, that it had already been singled out and put before the House in a formal motion in the name of the Liberal Party under the heading :

'Allegations of Financial Corruption in Public Life calling for investigation.'

The motion of the Liberal Party said :

'That this House, gravely concerned with the allegations made by Mr Poulson in the bankruptcy court proceedings that he had paid substantial sums of money to two Back-Bench Members of Parliament and another substantial payment to a body at the request of a Privy Councillor, calls upon the Government to order an immediate inquiry.'

As I told the then leader of the Liberal Party, who was and still is a very good friend of mine, I objected to the wording of that motion because it did not say that the body concerned was a charitable body. It gave the clear impression that the money had been paid to me for my own benefit. This was under the heading 'Financial Corruption'. I made clear in my letter that this was not the case, that the money had gone, not to me, but to a charity and that, in my view, this was a matter neither 'for investigation nor for criticism'. This point of view the Select Committee now in its report has wholly endorsed.

These are the facts of the matter. They do not appear at all in the Report from the Select Committee. No doubt the Committee was not aware of them. There is no reason why the Committee should have been aware of these facts or why it should have remembered them. If it had asked me about them, I could have told the Committee at the time. That, for the first time, is my side of the case.

The days before the debate were not easy ones : everyone had heard the other side of the case; no one had heard mine. I thought it right to reserve my position for the House of Commons. It appeared from the

Order Paper that the House were being invited to take certain decisions. The main one, sponsored by the Leader of the House, was that the House should agree with the Select Committee in their criticism of me. The others, proposing expulsion or suspension, clearly would not command general support and were of less importance. But the main Motion was a difficult one, and to defeat it meant inviting the House not to agree with the unanimous recommendations of a Select Committee, and I doubt if there was any precedent at the time for such a decision. The issue was brought to a head by an unofficial amendment to the Government Motion to the effect that the House should not agree with what the Select Committee had said about me but merely take note of it. This had been tabled by a group of Conservatives. Their leader was Ronnie Bell to whom I was deeply grateful for an action that was on his part spontaneous and designed solely to see that justice should be done. Yet, I was all the time confident that once I had had the opportunity to make known my side of the case I would succeed.

I did not think it right to canvass support. I was amused to see one newspaper article which said that on the Friday before the debate I was late at the House of Commons lobbying support. In fact I was doing nothing of the kind. The truth is that my wife, together with Lady Byers and Mrs Harold Lever, had organized a tea-party for teenagers on the terrace on behalf of the Westminster Hospital Medical Research Trust, and I was busily occupied with other friends in taking the teenagers round Parliament or obtaining tickets for them in the gallery of the House of Commons. But the journalist concerned, of course, did not bother to ask me what the facts were.

I told Francis Pym, who was speaking for the Opposition, about the Liberal amendment, which was the key to the whole matter and which everyone except for myself had until then ignored. I sent Ted Heath a draft of what I was going to say but I did not in any way invite him to support me – I left it, with confidence, to his judgement and my confidence was justified when he made a speech that was in effect decisive.

It was a long hard day in the House of Commons. Unusually I was allowed to sit in and listen to what was said, instead of withdrawing by tradition while my fate was discussed. It was difficult at times to restrain myself, and once or twice I felt obliged to make interventions, though friends did their best to restrain me, fearful that I might speak too vigorously (though that was hardly my custom).

Eventually the vote was taken on Ronnie Bell's amendment and while it was going on I sat in the smoking room brooding over a large whisky and water, and awaiting the result on the closed-circuit television. It was to be an important result for me. I had already made up my mind that if the House of Commons voted to agree with the Select Committee after hearing from me in my speech the additional and important facts which did not appear in the Select Committee's report, I would immediately resign my seat in the Commons and close my political career. No other course of action seemed either honourable or, in my own personal terms, tolerable after all my years of service in Parliament and the positions I had held. I did not say this in my speech to the House nor, so far as I can recall, did I say it to anyone privately. It seemed to me that it would be wrong to do so. The decision to be taken by the House should not be influenced either by sentiment or by consideration of the effect on any individual. It should be taken solely upon the facts as laid before the House by the Select Committee in their report and by me in my speech.

A Division of the House of Commons takes about fifteen minutes before it appears on the screen. It was a long quarter of an hour, but the result, when it came, was satisfactory.

Looking back on it I have often asked myself whether I should have spotted the flaws in Mr Poulson earlier. I do not see how I could have done so, certainly no one else did, and the activities for which he was to pay such a severe penalty were known only to himself and those who were participants in them. On the face of it his activities were much to be praised. His enterprise in building up his organization had been quite remarkable. He provided a service to many clients in the U.K. of high quality and great efficiency, which enabled the cost of hospitals, for example, to be substantially reduced. Overseas he tried genuinely and vigorously to promote British business. His contributions to the prosperity of Britain could have been considerable. Only the Inland Revenue had any means of knowing that something was unsound at the foundation of his empire. And the Inland Revenue are people whose advice no individual can seek or be given in such matters.

15

Shadow Foreign Secretary

1975–1976

TOWARDS the end of 1974 Ted Heath asked me if I would go back into the Shadow Cabinet. I said I would be very happy to do so, but I asked for a little time in order to ensure that no remaining complications of the Poulson affair would cause any difficulty. Before I could do this, however, the leadership battle was joined, as a result of which he was replaced by Mrs Thatcher. I was a strong supporter of his, and made no secret about it. Ted Heath is a man of outstanding intellectual quality and great strength of character, and his position in the world was a great one.

I knew that he was unpopular in many circles in the House of Commons. He is by nature rather a shy and remote man, and finds informal socializing difficult. I knew also, from canvassing in my own constituency during the two elections of 1974, that many people found him an unsympathetic character. On the other hand, there was no doubt that there was very strong support for him in the constituency associations, including my own, Chipping Barnet. But the real point was that in quality and stature he was head and shoulders above any possible rival. I thought the Conservative Party made a mistake in rejecting him. I went to see him immediately the result was known, to say this, and I did not shrink in any way from expressing my views.

His greatest virtue is what Nigel Birch once called his 'luminous' mind. It is allied to total dedication, tremendous intellectual energy, great self-confidence, integrity and, funnily enough, flexibility. People often do not realize that he possesses this last quality. People say Ted will never change. But he did and he was very much open to argument. There were two things over which I argued with him and about which he eventually changed his mind : first, the Incomes Policy and, secondly, Northern Ireland. He is dispassionate on fundamental issues and if he believes that things should be changed he will change them.

He was not the best delegator, but I had no complaints myself on that score. People who found him inflexible had not dug down under the surface deep enough to find out what the truth was. The first reaction might be a brush-off, the second reaction was often a different one.

He was very much a managerial type of Prime Minister, much at home in the actual running of things because he has a logical mind. It was not his inflexibility that let us down over the miners' strike. It was Joe Gormley, the miners' leader, who let us down. Joe was always saying, 'I can settle for this and that'; but when it came to the crunch he could not deliver the goods.

Ted did not decide to confront the miners. But he had no alternative but to stand up to them if he wanted to maintain any sort of incomes policy. He has been criticized for calling an election when he did. I simply do not see what the alternative was. However, I do think Ted suffered a disadvantage in being a bachelor. There is always a great advantage in a wife who says to you when you get home, 'Look, stop talking a load of rubbish, come down to earth occasionally.' Ted had no one to whom he could come home at night and who would say : 'Look, Ted, it's all very well but . . .' When he came home tired to bed his mind was still running round the problems of the day, perhaps a bit on music, but not very much else but politics. Nevertheless, he was a great Prime Minister, a man of enormous strength of character, intellectual capacity, administrative ability and a comprehension of the importance of Europe.

I think Ted's great weakness was that he gave the impression to the Members of the House that he did not care for them; that he regarded them merely as troops who were there to support him and that he was the officer in command. He was seldom seen in the smoking room, he never fraternized with the rank and file. And he did not make enough knights. If he had been a more loved leader he would have survived.

Now is the Time for all Old Boys to Come to the Aid of the Party!

A lovely job for dear old Reggie Maudling!

Super Mac

PRINCESS CHARMING AWAKENS SLEEPING BEAUTY!

"I say! Any moment now she'll be asking us to come back and save the Party!"

When Mrs Thatcher became Leader of the Party, she was magnanimous enough to ask me to join her Shadow Cabinet as spokesman on Foreign Affairs, and I had no hesitation in accepting. I am not sure, looking back on it, whether it was a wise decision but it was, in effect, an automatic one, because when the Leader of your Party asks you to accept an important responsibility, it is a simple matter of duty to say 'Yes'.

Somehow or other I never got on to really close terms with her. It was not a matter of rows or arguments, I cannot remember any dispute between us at any time, other than arguments on matters of policy, and certainly she never criticized anything that I did, or omitted to do, as spokesman on Foreign Affairs. But there were a number of reasons why we did not establish a really close understanding.

In the first place, there was a considerable difference of temperament. Margaret Thatcher is an immensely hard worker, totally dedicated to her responsibilities as Party Leader, with little time to spare for humour. I think she may have found my approach to the political issues on the face of it a trifle on the frivolous side. But I had been in politics much longer and carried Ministerial responsibility much more (and it is surprising how regularly the same problems come round again, appearing as novel only to those who have not been there to see them before) and I could not summon that total dedication to the purely Party battle which perhaps would have been more congenial.

There were also growing differences on matters of policy, both in our approach to foreign problems and more generally.

From the start, there was a tendency in the Shadow Cabinet to move away from the Heath line of policy further to the Right: to this I was totally opposed. In particular, I could not support the arguments of

Keith Joseph, who was inclined to say that all we had done in the Government of 1970–74 was wrong and not true Conservatism. I totally disagreed with this, because it seemed to me that Keith was fully entitled to measure himself for a hair shirt if he wanted to, but I was blowed if I could see why he should measure me and Ted at the same time.

I could not help recalling Selsdon Park, and the swing to the Right in our policies which occurred then, and how long it had taken in Government to get back to the realities of life. I feared that the same thing was beginning to happen again.

In particular there was the argument about Incomes Policy and Money Supply, and which was the right way to deal with inflation. I stuck to the view that an Incomes Policy was essential and had been a necessary part of the policies of Conservative Governments since it was first introduced by Peter Thorneycroft when he was Chancellor of the Exchequer. The other doctrine, the monetarist doctrine of which Keith Joseph was the most articulate and intellectual exponent, said that Incomes Policy was unnecessary or unworkable, and that inflation could best be contained by restricting the money supply. This doctrine, based on the teachings of Professor Friedman, seemed to me to be totally divorced from reality. In so far as it was a guide to action at all, it merely was a restatement in new phraseology of the old doctrine of a credit squeeze. But the tide was running strongly in the monetarist direction at that time. I agreed to accept the general line of the Shadow Cabinet and I deliberately avoided making speeches on economic policy because I could not have done so without openly disagreeing with my colleagues, and this I undertook not to do. It did, of course, mean severely restricting my public speeches and concentrating on Foreign Affairs, although as an ex-Chancellor I might have been expected to talk a good deal about economic policy. This cutting down on speech-making came to be much criticized by those who did not know the reason for it.

I did make one or two attempts to persuade my colleagues to my point of view, but they were unsuccessful. In particular I circulated to the Shadow Cabinet, on 21 May 1976, a memorandum which summed up my views on the situation and which is reproduced in Appendix 4. I do not recall that this memorandum was ever discussed by the Shadow Cabinet. Our agenda was not in my hands.

In the field of Foreign Affairs there were a number of important tasks. Our job was not in any way to try to make Party capital, but to try to ensure that so far as possible the policy pursued by the Government was on the right lines and that, when it was so, to give them our support in its achievement.

I set out my approach on the foreign policy responsibilities of the Opposition in an article in *The Times*, on 18 August 1975, in which I said :

The broad stream of British foreign policy should not be sharply diverted with every change of Government, for the national interest does not change, much as it needs to adapt to external circumstances. In these circumstances, the primary function of Opposition is to exercise vigilance, to keep a critical eye on the performance of the Government, to chide when they display tardiness or lack of vision, to suggest when new ideas are needed, and openly to support where support is justified and necessary. The role that Britain is playing now is a very different one indeed from what it was 20 years ago, but it need be no less important, and certainly no less honourable.

The full article appears in Appendix 5.

But apart from our activities in Parliament, there were other important matters to be dealt with. There were several issues on which the Party was divided, or likely to be divided, and where thought and persuasion were required. Foremost among these at the time were southern Africa, the Midde East and the dispute between Greece and Turkey. In each case very widely different views were held by individual Members of the Party, often with considerable fervour. There is not necessarily harm in this. The sort of three-way split we had had more than once on Rhodesia is, of course, a nightmare to the Whips, though less important in practical terms. But clearly it was desirable both as the Opposition, and even more so as the future Government, to get the maximum possible agreement within the Party on these explosive issues.

In fact this was part of the general task of preparing for Government. It seemed to me quite clear that one of my main responsibilities was to ensure that, when we became the Government, close connections would have already been established with Governments and Parties overseas, and that there should already be a degree of mutual knowledge and understanding between us. This was all the more important as Mrs Thatcher herself had virtually no experience of international affairs when she was elected Leader.

The other problem was that of relations between the Conservative Members in the Westminster Parliament and the Conservative Members of the European Assembly, who were, under the dual-mandate system, Members of both bodies. The difficulties of coordination caused by sheer physical distance and weight of work were very considerable, yet it was obviously most important that the Party should speak with the same voice in Strasbourg, in Brussels and in London.

These were the tasks to which I addressed myself. They involved a good deal of travelling and a great deal of discussion, mainly in private gatherings. None of the problems were likely to be solved by public speeches. It is always difficult for an Opposition spokesman to travel, because of the sheer cost that is involved these days. The funds available to the Opposition are very modest and should be used with the greatest care. Otherwise a long trip abroad either involves taking advantage of necessary business travel, accepting an invitation from a foreign Government, or making a lecture tour. At one time or another I travelled on each of these bases, but none of them was wholly satisfactory; however, if I were to do the job there was no alternative. Fortunately, I was able to visit a large number of countries – the leading members of the European Community, America, the Middle East, Africa – in most cases on more than one occasion. Without this degree of travel I am quite sure it would not be possible for the Shadow Foreign Secretary to equip himself fully for his task both in Opposition, and possibly in Government.

In all my visits I had the greatest possible help from British Embassies, who went out of their way to see that my talks were as fruitful as possible. In exchange, of course, I kept the British representatives fully informed of everything that had passed between me and the people I was visiting. Before meeting an important foreign statesman I would always take care to discuss in detail beforehand with our Ambassador the current problems of British relations with their country, in order to ensure that what I said certainly could do no harm and might be of some national value. Finally, I had regular private consultations with the Foreign Secretaries, first Jim Callaghan, and then Tony Crosland. Both of them were very willing at all times to discuss with me on a Privy Councillor basis the problems of Foreign Affairs, and indeed any matter that I chose to raise.

I am sure this is the right system. It does not inhibit the Opposition in any way from criticizing, nor indeed does it inhibit the Government from answering back where necessary, but at least the debate is conducted on the basis of a proper knowledge of the facts, and a proper opportunity to assess what is likely to be in the national interest and what can be damaging. This procedure works well in Foreign Affairs, where the interest of the Opposition is that the British Government should be as successful for Britain as possible. I sometimes wish it could work as successfully in domestic affairs. Perhaps we could be a happier country and a happier people if it could : but, no doubt, this is only a pipe-dream.

I paid an early trip to Athens and Ankara to try to assess the situation and see if there was anything that the Conservative Party could do. Frankly, I found that despite the continuing friendship for Britain, and despite the special position of the Sovereign bases in Cyprus, the U.K. had not much influence that could be exercised. Power rested elsewhere, basically with the Americans. As for the European influence, while we were certainly welcome I had the impression that the closest European influence in both capitals at that time was Western Germany.

The situation was a difficult one and it has not changed very much since. The Turks could claim some provocation for their action in invading Cyprus, but the proportion of the island which they had occupied was greater than could be justified. The Greeks, on the other hand, knew that they must concede a substantial amount to Turkey but were not prepared or able to go beyond a certain point. As one Greek Minister said to me, 'We know we have to meet the bill for the folly of the Colonels, but the cheque we are asked to sign must not be too great.'

I had a number of old friends in Athens. Averoff, then Minister of Defence, who had acted as kingmaker to Karamanlis, Papaligouras, in a key position of importance as Minister of Coordination, and also, on the Opposition side, John Pesmazoglou, who had been responsible for the negotiations with the E.E.C. I found talking to them all, and of course to Karamanlis and the Foreign Secretary Bitsios, that the understanding between our two countries had not really changed and that the friendships I had made at the O.E.E.C. and in the days of the Maudling Committee stood me in good stead. But the chances of making any contribution to the solution of the Greek/Turkish conflict clearly were small. One thing that was apparent was the importance they attached to their application for membership of the European Community. I was able to give them wholehearted support. It was not merely that they had already, in their Treaty of Association, a commitment to full membership; it was quite simply that anyone with a classical education could not fail to accept the argument that a democratic Western Europe could not possibly be complete without Greece.

Fortunately it proved possible to reach a fairly general measure of agreement within the Conservative Party on the issues involved. There were still strong pro-Turk and pro-Greek feelings. There were those who opposed Greek entry to the Community, either on the general grounds of nervousness about further dilution of the Community, or on the more specific grounds of Turkish hostility. The Turks had put it to me that they were hoping also a few years later to join the Community, and they feared that if the Greeks got there ahead of them they would be able to exercise a veto. I told the Turks that I was confident that this was clearly in the minds of the member countries of the Community, and that in my view it would be made clear to the Greeks, before they became full members of the Community, that it would be on the understanding that they would not use any power of veto to bar a subsequent Turkish admission. And so, on the whole, the turmoil relaxed a little and we all agreed within the Conservative Foreign Affairs Committee that we should support in principle the entry of Greece, and ultimately of Turkey, into the Community, but that in the meantime, while continuing to make representations about individual cases of harsh treatment in Cyprus and doing all we could to help prevent them, the political situation in reality was such that no British initiative on either side was likely to do good and could in fact do harm.

The next area of contention was the Middle East. I had been a frequent visitor to that part of the world, and I had much admiration for the Arabs and what they were trying to do. Indeed, there was some danger that I might be regarded as pro-Arab on the lines traditionally ascribed to the British Foreign Office and when Mrs Thatcher invited me to become Shadow Foreign Secretary I did mention this danger to her. She, very wisely, discounted it and added that there might be some danger that she would be regarded as pro-Israeli.

What strikes one so forcibly about the whole Middle East problem is what a tragedy it is for all the peoples who live in that area. Jews and Arabs are not by their nature all that unlike. They are both of them devout people. My friends from both sides have many similar characteristics. They have lived together in one way or another over the centuries, and now a combination of Israeli science and technology with Arab oil resources and an end of hostilities could bring benefits on an untold scale to all the peoples who live in that area. It is not merely a matter of reducing the burden of defence, though, heaven knows, this is hard enough for either side to carry. It is the fact that a positive cooperation between the two races could produce economic benefits and progress on a quite dramatic scale. You have only to look at the development of agriculture in Israel to see what could be done throughout many neighbouring countries by a combination of that technology with the oil resources of the Arab world.

On an official visit to Israel Beryl and I were taken to see many of the disputed areas, in particular the Golan Heights, and it was easy to see there how reluctant the Israelis would be to yield military control of that area to Syria once again. The remains of the Syrian gun emplacements commanding the Sea of Galilee were adequate witness of this. On the other hand, the establishment of Israeli settlements in what was still Syrian territory was extremely hard to justify.

The line I took as Shadow Foreign Secretary, on the Middle East problem, was the same that I had taken several years before after my visit to the Middle East in 1967. A settlement could only be based on the broad principles of Resolution 242 of the United Nations. This involved a withdrawal of Israeli forces from the territories captured in the 1967 War. It would have to be a genuine withdrawal.

The famous U.N. Resolution was achieved because the word 'The' was not placed before the words 'territories captured in the war', for the very sensible reason that some flexibility was required for security reasons alone. But the withdrawal would have to be to frontiers broadly comparable with those in 1967 and individual problems of a strategic character might have to be met by demilitarized zones or international supervision.

An Israeli withdrawal on these lines had to be accompanied by overt and genuine acceptance on the part of the Arab countries that mattered of the right of Israel to live as a member state of the United Nations securely within the frontiers then established, and accompanied by some form of international guarantee from the great powers.

This acquiescence in the continued existence of Israel had to be accepted by the P.L.O. as well. They were, of course, a great difficulty; their attitude was still that they refused to recognize the existence of Israel or argued that Israel should become a secular non-Zionist state, although the Arab countries were all Islamic. At that time, following the Conference at Rabat, the P.L.O. had been recognized by the Arab world as a whole as speaking for Palestinian opinion.

There was considerable controversy within the Conservative Party about the position of the P.L.O. Some believed that the Palestinians should have a state of their own based on the West Bank.

The line I took was that once a broad settlement had been reached, frontiers had been agreed, and the security of Israel had been guaranteed, it was no business of Israel or of us, or, indeed, of the United Nations, to decide on the organization of the Arab countries to the east of those frontiers; these were Arab matters. If the general view was that there should be a separate Palestinian State is was not for us to interfere. Equally, if the Palestinian territories were to be incorporated in Jordan or in some federalization of Jordan and Syria, or even a wider grouping, once again, it was not for us to interfere, so long as the basic agreement about the security of Israel within the newly established frontiers was honoured and sustained. I cannot say that I obtained unanimous agreement to this point of view, but it did in effect prove to be a basis on which the Conservative Party could reach a reasonably united view.

At the time of writing, January 1978, all these issues were in the forefront of world affairs

The other great problem from a Party point of view was of course Rhodesia. This had caused us trouble for many years, with divergent and strongly held views among different Members of the Party. It would be facile to describe them as being Left and Right, but they ranged from those who believed that Mr Smith had done no wrong, to those who believed that he could do no right. It was a divergence that had manifested itself on more than one occasion in the House of Commons, to the considerable embarrassment of the Party Whips. I thought it was my duty to try to obtain the most united view possible, not merely from the point of view of the Party but, more important, from the point of view of enabling the Party and its spokesmen to make an effective contribution to a very severe national problem.

Everyone by then had come to recognize that White minority rule could not continue indefinitely in Rhodesia, but there were very strong disagreements about the timing and methods of change, and about the new constitution that was required and how it could be guaranteed. There was concern over two main matters. The first was, of course, the position of the European Community. They had built up the economy of Rhodesia to a very high level by African standards. The country was relatively law-abiding, though based on a discrimination between Black and White that clearly could not indefinitely endure. Experience

of multiracial societies and newly independent constitutions in other
countries of Africa was to say the least of it far from encouraging.
There were relatively few examples, of which Kenya happily was an
outstanding one, where a multiracial society had endured. There were
few if any examples of democracy in the traditional Western sense.
Each newly independent African country had become a one-party
state or dictatorship. Human rights and the possibilities of political
opposition had dwindled if not disappeared. Dictatorships appeared to
be the order of the day, and while some of them were relatively benevo-
lent, others certainly were not. Many Conservative Members who knew
Rhodesia well were fearful of the fate of the European community
under Black majority rule. There was concern not only for the possible
repression of Whites by Black Rhodesians, but also about the danger
that rivalries between the two main African tribes in Rhodesia would
be fought out over a European graveyard. The fact that this had been
our fear in Kenya and it had not there materialized weighed inade-
quately in the balance against the atrocities of Amin in Uganda. It was
argued also that Black majority rule would lead to a collapse of the
Rhodesian economy, which had reached a very high standard of
efficiency in both agricultural and commercial terms, and, clearly, such
a collapse was bound to bring great suffering to all of whatever race
who lived in the country.

The other great fear that many of my colleagues felt, and with
justice, was the expansion of Communist influence. The lessons of
Angola and Mozambique were only too dramatic. If Rhodesia fell
under Communist domination, how long could South Africa last? If
the whole of southern Africa then became by a domino process a Communist stronghold, the effect on the West could be very serious. South
Africa was a focal point around which such a vast proportion of the
essential materials of Western Europe, particularly oil, were daily
moving. South Africa was the source of many raw materials of importance to the economy and defence of the West. The incursion of the
Cubans into Angola, with Russian political and logistic support, was a
new and dramatic development which added great weight to those who
feared this expansion of Communist domination.

It was not easy to know what was the right policy to pursue in the
face of this very obvious and genuine danger. There were two schools
of thought. Mr Smith was always protesting that his regime was the
main bulwark of Western democracy against Communism and he made
constant play with this argument. It was an attractive one; there were

many who felt that in the context of history the duty of the West was to support him – and South Africa – against the Communist threat simply as a matter of our long-term defence interests. There were others who thought exactly the opposite. They said that Mr Smith, far from being a bulwark against Communism, was doing the Communists' job for them in southern Africa. The Africans did not want to bring in Soviet guns; they did not want to impose upon themselves a new and Russian colonialism; but increasingly they had little choice. This point of view was strongly supported by President Kaunda, who made it quite clear that he did not want to find himself riding a new tiger. The trouble was that so many African Nationalists did not regard the struggle between democracy and Communism as vital in the same way that we did. They attached more importance to the early achievement of Black majority rule, and if the Communists were prepared to help them to their overriding objective they would then turn to the Communists, despite the dangers which many of them recognized.

It seemed to me that there was common ground to be established here. Majority rule must come within a very short time to Rhodesia – and, indeed, this was increasingly accepted, even by those on the so-called Right wing of the Party. What was vital was to ensure that it came in the right circumstances. The new Black majority Government of Rhodesia must be genuinely independent. The new constitution must provide for individual rights without racial discrimination, for a free Parliamentary system, and for independent Courts of Law. There must be, during the period of transition, which clearly would be dangerous and turbulent, some effective interim system of Government which would command general respect and smooth the transition to full independence.

None of these were really new problems, though the scale and intensity of them were greater than I had experienced before. I remember thinking the first day I flew into Salisbury as Colonial Secretary in 1962, and saw the contrast between the villages of the Blacks and the swimming pools of the Whites, and the fine things that White agriculture and White business had developed, that here was Britain's Algeria. It was our last Colonial problem, as Algeria was the last problem of the French Empire, and it had been left to the end, precisely because it was the most difficult. The most difficult issue of all was one with which I had been familiar on many occasions as Colonial Secretary: how to ensure that a new constitution would in fact be preserved. This is a matter of politics and power, not of law. There is precious little value in writing into a constitution a provision to the effect that 'it is unlawful to destroy this constitution'.

This is a problem that I had come across in many places, from Kenya to Trinidad. It was difficult to see any internal solution to it. In other countries we had succeeded partly by good fortune and partly because the necessity of living together had brought people to a sanity which provided a relatively stable basis for doing so. But could the same thing be expected in Rhodesia? Quite apart from the deep divisions among the Nationalist Parties, the whole background to Rhodesia and the European relationship to the African there was so different.

It seemed to me that we had to find some external guarantee for a new constitution. Unless we could give the European population some confidence that it would not be overthrown within six months by a Rhodesian Amin, why should they relinquish the degree of security they still had? Mind you, it was dwindling. The pressure of the guerrillas was growing, the constant call-up to the army was a tremendous strain on the morale, as well as the economy, of Rhodesia. Young people were beginning to leave in increasing numbers, for it seemed that while it might be many years before they lost the war, there was no ultimate prospect of winning it. I made the public suggestion that during the interim period there should be a return of a British Governor-General to what was still in law a British Colony, as titular head of the Government. I was not suggesting that British Civil Servants should go and administer the country. I was not suggesting that British troops should be sent in any form or role whatever. My point was that the presence of a British Governor-General in the interim period with supreme constitutional authority could provide a guarantee of the independence of the Courts of Law, and a support for the forces of law and order in protecting the interim constitution against any attempts by politicians to subvert it. The necessary condition for the success of such a proposal would be the support of the Nationalist movement as well as of Mr Smith, plus the support of world opinion and in particular of the so-called Front-line Presidents. At that time I think it was possible to achieve such a solution. It would have been extremely difficult, it would have needed much hard argument and negotiations, but the overriding interest of all parties concerned in a peaceful solution on the basis of an early transition to majority rule was so great that I believe it could have been done.

The British Labour Government were very much to blame for taking no initiative at that period. Mr Callaghan, who was then Foreign Secretary, seemed determined not to get involved in the Rhodesian problem in any way whatever. Things had reached a stalemate. The only people who had any room for manoeuvre, any chance to take an initiative, were the Conservative Party. So I decided to pay a visit as Conservative Party spokesman to the countries mainly concerned. I planned to go to Kenya, Tanzania, Zambia, South Africa and Rhodesia, in that order. Not only were these the most important countries, but it so happened that I had been personally acquainted with the leaders of all of them over a period of many years since the days when I was Colonial Secretary.

I set off and visited Nairobi first, where I was received with great cordiality, and where the Kenya Government told me that they warmly supported my initiative and hoped strongly for my success. I then went to Dar es Salaam, where I commenced discussion with the Government of Tanzania. I was due to go on from there for appointments in South Africa, and with Mr Smith in Salisbury. Maybe nothing would have come of it, but I attached the most profound importance to making an endeavour. It was, therefore, with some sadness that I received in Dar es Salaam a peremptory cable from Mrs Thatcher instructing me to return immediately for some vote in the House of Commons. I had no choice of course but to do so, and I cancelled my appointments with one President and two Prime Ministers, making the best apologies I could.

We did not win the vote and I do not suppose the Government would have fallen if we had, but certainly my initiative had collapsed. It could not be mounted again. Within a very short space of time Dr Kissinger had moved in, and the initiative passed entirely into the hands of the Americans. Great as is my regard for Dr Kissinger, I think this was a pity. I do not think the Americans understand southern Africa as well as the British do. The only British Party that could play any part at that time was the Conservative Party, but now that this had been aborted, we could do no more than sit back and wish Dr Kissinger well. He kept me constantly in touch with all that he was doing or trying to do in southern Africa. I tried to be of some use to him, from the basis of such experience as I had, and of the knowledge that the Conservative Party possessed. Alas, it was not a great success.

I think once again the Labour Government were very much to blame in staying relatively remote from the Kissinger initiative. They contented themselves with sending a British official as part of his baggage train, whereas Britain should have been represented at Ministerial level. The proposals that Dr Kissinger made seemed to us to be sensible. Mr Smith made a really remarkable move in accepting the principle of majority rule within two years. This was recognized by all points of view in the Conservative Party, and we hoped that the Geneva Conference would produce results. Alas, how wrong we were. But it was clear to us that now Mr Smith had made this move on the basis of proposals put to him by Dr Kissinger with British connivance, he was entitled to expect that we would do all we could to get them accepted at the Conference. Certainly this was the point of view of the Conservative Party which I expressed, and I said that if Geneva failed as a result of no fault on the part of Mr Smith then we would not consider the continuation of sanctions to be justified. On this point of view I think the whole Party was united.

What happened, in the event, was, as so often in African affairs, confusing. Certainly I believe that the British and American Governments let him down and that Mr Richard did not conduct the Conference in a way consistent with what the two Governments had said was likely to produce satisfactory results. At the same time, the British Government had much infuriated us by their help to Mozambique. They argued that this was no direct help to the terrorists but merely a participation in an international effort to reduce the level of suffering in Mozambique. We as the Opposition were not impressed, and I expressed, on behalf of the Party, our total opposition to any aid going from the British taxpayer to the Government of Mozambique so long as they were harbouring and fostering within their country terrorists who were making murderous incursions on the still-British territory of Rhodesia.

That was the way it was when I ceased to have responsibility. My initiative had been frustrated and progress on what really mattered, namely, a solution of the problem, had not taken place. But at any rate the Conservative Party then had a view which was consistent and could stand up to any scrutiny or criticism.

Since then the Party has become even more united on its attitude to Rhodesia. Mr Smith has been trying to arrange a settlement based on universal adult suffrage with the representatives of the Nationalist Movements in Rhodesia. At the moment of writing, January 1978, it is impossible to say what will emerge and by now the situation may have changed completely. All I can say is that there was in January 1978 a strong and indeed unanimous view in the Conservative Party that the people in Rhodesia had as much right as anyone else to agree on their own future without external interference, and that to make any such agreement subject to the veto of the terrorist organizations seemed little different from saying that a settlement in Northern Ireland would only be possible with the approval of the I.R.A. in Dublin.

The other great problem facing us, and it was as complex as it was important, was how we were to handle European problems, how to ensure a consistent line of policy, and how to develop relations with other Centre-Right Parties in the European Parliament. This was not at all an easy problem, yet it clearly was desirable that Conservatives should speak consistently on major issues of policy whether they arose at Westminster or at the European Assembly.

There were many complicated factors. The sheer pressure of business on European Parliamentarians holding a dual mandate, which called for their presence in both Parliaments, was formidable. I do not think it is yet generally realized how heavy was the burden carried by those M.P.s, and in particular by the late Sir Peter Kirk, whose contribution was quite outstanding.

There were bound to be rivalries and competition; the relative status of the European Assembly and the Westminster Parliament were not exactly defined. It was important to establish close relations with like-minded Parties in Europe, particularly with a view to fighting the direct elections, which were very much in our minds at the time. But there are big differences between European political Parties and the British Parties; even nomenclature brings its hazards. The word 'Conservative' in this country now connotes broadly speaking anything from the centre of politics rightwards, leaving out extremes. But to many European politicians the word 'Conservative' meant something close to fascist. Equally, it was hard to see how we could adopt the title of Christian Democrats in a Party that is not tied to the Church, and indeed has over the years embraced and still embraces many distinguished non-Christians.

Finally, there was the constitutional problem of the relationship between European Parliamentarians and Westminster M.P.s. A number of suggestions had been put forward. Some said that there should be a joint Standing Committee of the two groups where they could thrash problems out amongst themselves. Others put forward the idea that European M.P.s might be automatically members of the House of Lords. It seemed to me that these ideas were based on a misconception. The fundamental point is that the competence of the two Parliaments is different. The Westminster Parliament is omnicompetent save in so far as it has through treaty, such as the Treaty of Rome, devolved to other bodies certain of its powers. The European Assembly, on the other hand, has only the competence allocated to it under the Treaty of Rome, and this competence could not be extended without the approval of the member Governments of the Community. It was of the utmost importance to keep a distinction about the respective spheres of competence of the two bodies. While many of the problems that were to be discussed in both would be the same – the basic issues of economic and social policy clearly were the concern of either Assembly – the decisions must not be allowed to overlap. A link between the Parliamentary institutions would blur the distinction and make it unclear whether ultimate responsibility lay, just as an institutional link between the House of Commons and the G.L.C. might have the same effect. What was clearly needed was not links between the institutions themselves, but links between the Party representatives in the institutions.

There was a practical difficulty that our spokesmen in Brussels often had to express a view at very short notice and without opportunity for consultation. There was also a recognizable tendency for the European M.P.s to say that they must develop a policy of their own under their own leadership. This seemed to me to be a very dangerous possible development and I was anxious that the authority of the Leader of the Party and her Consultative Committee in all matters of policy wherever arising should be preserved. At the same time there were some difficulties about negotiating agreements with other European Parties, of whom the German C.D.U. were the most powerful. We wanted to concert policies, but we could not commit ourselves to a common policy agreed by a majority vote without undermining the authority of the Leader of our Party. Many negotiations took place, sometimes on parallel lines. There were continuous consultations in the European Parliament, in which Sir Peter Kirk played an outstanding role. Meanwhile the Conservative Overseas Office, ably guided by Lady Elles and Sir John Peel, were pursuing their contacts on a Party basis with the Europeans. Douglas Hurd, who was my No. 2 on the European side, was in a position to coordinate what was happening and the work he did to that end was excellent.

I wanted to set up a new machinery of consultation to deal with this problem, and in doing so I had the great help of Sir Anthony Royle. The basic point was that European policy was no longer entirely foreign policy, but domestic policy. There were differences between our policy towards Europe and our policy within Europe. Our policy towards Europe was essentially a matter of Foreign Affairs, in which the Foreign Office element should be dominant. Our policy within Europe, on such matters as agriculture or regional development or the Budget, was much more a domestic matter.

The organization of the Conservative Parliamentary Opposition had rested for years on a series of functional committees for each main group of subjects, with the respective Shadow Minister as Chairman, and the other officers elected by vote. The link that was needed was between our European Parliamentarians and our functional committees, and this we sought to provide in two ways. First, we established that every functional committee should nominate one Vice-Chairman as specially responsible for European problems, secondly, we established a European Affairs Committee which met regularly every Monday. This was to deal with the two aspects of the problem. Sir Peter Kirk was one Vice-Chairman, dealing with relations within Europe, and Sir Anthony Royle was the other, dealing with relations with Europe. We invited the European Vice-Chairman of each functional commitee to attend these meetings so as to give a regular opportunity for discussing in advance matters due to arise in the European Parliament, and to ensure that what we said in Brussels was broadly the same as we were saying in Westminster. When urgent matters arose between meetings of the committee, the arrangements would be that our people in Europe would contact the European Vice-Chairman of the committee concerned, say agriculture, and obtain from him the view of the Party in Westminster.

I think this was a logical arrangement. It was the best I could devise for ensuring coordination; of course it was not perfect. The problem was in practical terms a very difficult one indeed, mainly because of the other calls on members concerned, particularly those holding a dual mandate. But, at any rate, it gave people the opportunity of consultation. If they wanted to know what their political colleagues were thinking they could find out through this means; if they did not want to find out no one could do much about it anyway.

There is no doubt that these problems, like the problems of relations with other European Parties, will take a very long time to work out – *solvitur ambulando*. Equally, the problems of our relations with the European Parties will take time and patience. Clearly Europe will go through great transitions, and we must be ready if necessary to change our stance and our direction in accordance with the imperative of the times.

The Conservative Party's attitude to Europe is still not uniform and indeed we should have been a poorer Party if it were. Views range from the implacable opponents of the Community to the starry-eyed believers in a federal Europe next year. The great majority of the whole were in favour of membership of the Community. This came about for a variety of reasons. Perhaps by being in Europe we could find that role which Dean Acheson said we were still looking for after the end of Empire. The feelings of British industry are pretty solidly on the side of Community membership. The alternatives to membership even before we joined seemed bad enough, but the consequences of a withdrawal seemed likely to be catastrophic. I have myself always taken a fairly central view. I could not believe with Hugh Gaitskell or Enoch Powell that membership of Europe would be the end of a thousand years of history, or the end of Britain as we knew it. On the other hand, it seemed to me that a people who had built their civilization in terms of centuries must not expect miracles overnight. The economic advantages were difficult to assess. Industrially it must have been to our interest to be included in this great single market. The only objection was to say that we could not compete with the Germans and the French, but if we could not compete with them in Europe on our own doorstep, how could we compete with them, with their European economic base, in the rest of the world and how then could we earn our living? But the political arguments seemed even stronger : Britain's opportunity of influencing the course of world events would be far greater as a member of a European Community of 250 million people than as an offshore island appendage of Western Europe. These differences of view persisted, and still persist. All I can claim is that the system I established made some contribution to improving the ability of the Conservative Party to contribute to the European system as it is in the real world.

On the subject of Foreign Affairs I held very strongly the view that this was not a field in which we should seek to make Party capital. Fight Socialism at home by all means and in every way, but when it comes to the conduct of foreign policy we have only one British Government and we should hope to have only one British foreign policy, and do all we can to ensure its success. The job of the Shadow Foreign Secretary, it seemed to me, was to watch the performance of the Government, to criticize when they were acting wrongly, to make

Grand-children
Melissa and Nicholas
appraise my
'weathered head' as
sculptured by Beryl

Posing as a golfer

With the youngest of the Maudlings, Rebecca Kate, born 12 May 1977

positive suggestions whenever possible, and whenever they seemed to be acting in the national interest to give them full and open support. My exposition of it in *The Times*, which I have quoted in Appendix 6, and elsewhere was not criticized, and I was entitled to assume my colleagues accepted my views. But this, alas, was not a policy that commended itself to the activists in the Conservative Party, though it was what the national interest really demanded.

So I think there was a growing, if not openly expressed, feeling that I was not being active enough, or scoring enough runs for the Party. At the same time, it became apparent that Margaret Thatcher was developing a line on Foreign Affairs, and particularly on relations with the Soviet Union, which was, in terminology at any rate, a good deal harsher than my own.

The problem was that the contact between us was very little. I asked to go with her on her various visits overseas, but I was courteously refused, nor did I ever receive from her an account of what happened on those journeys, except when one of her assistants, Adam Butler or John Stanley, who had gone with her, was good enough to give me some account of such meetings as they had themselves attended. I asked to be told whenever she was meeting any important foreign representative, and indeed I was invited to be with her on many occasions. But there were others, some of considerable significance to me, when I was not informed at all. All this made it difficult to establish a communion of thought on foreign policy.

What was more difficult still was her method of producing speeches on Foreign Affairs. I was not consulted in advance about whether she should make a speech on foreign policy at any given time. What happened was that a speech in final form, drafted by her speech-writers (I often did not know who they were), was circulated to me without prior notice, and to a number of other people at the same time, for comments. I did not find this an adequate method of consultation between a Party Leader and her Foreign Affairs spokesman. When I did make comments on draft speeches, they were of course received with great courtesy, but it seemed to me that the formulation of ideas, and the provisions of drafts for speeches on foreign policy, should be primarily the job of the Foreign Affairs spokesman. In other words, relations within the Shadow Cabinet between Leader and Shadow Foreign Secretary should be much the same as relations within the Cabinet between the Prime Minister and his Foreign Secretary. But, alas, things did not work that way. No doubt I should take the blame for not being more self-assertive in these matters.

However, there was no argument between us, and there were never any harsh words. Rumours from time to time appeared in the newspapers, no doubt emerging from members of her entourage – for they could not have come from anywhere else – that Mrs Thatcher was disappointed by my performance. She did not say so herself to me. I am sure that if she had felt that way she would have told me. Such is her open nature.

Then, when I arrived in the House on 18 November 1976, the Chief Whip told me she wanted to see me, and I went to her room. Without beating about the bush, she told me, in the most charming manner, that she must ask me to relinquish my responsibilities. I said that was all right by me, I had not asked for the job in the first place, and it was entirely a matter of her discretion, but I would like to know why. She said that there had been a lot of pressure from Central Office because I was not making enough speeches for the Party. I said it might have been better if someone had told me about this criticism, and she seemed surprised that they had not. I then asked her to confirm that she had never in any way expressed to me any criticism of the way I was conducting my responsibilities, and she agreed she had not. She suggested that I might like to write a letter of resignation, but I said that as I had not the slightest desire to resign, I did not see why I should. We then parted with mutual, and I believe sincere, expressions of personal goodwill.

I must admit it was rather a shock, after more than twenty years on the Front Bench in one capacity or another, as Senior Privy Councillor on the Conservative side of the House, and with an experience of Government and a record of service to the Party much longer than Mrs Thatcher's, to be summoned and dismissed without any prior criticism or warning from her of any sort whatsoever. *Difficile est longum subito deponere amorem.* There we are. That is the way I suppose it is in politics, and none of us is compelled to become politicians : if we choose to do so, we cannot really object to accepting the consequences. But I had been fortunate enough to enjoy the confidence and friendship of five Party Leaders and Prime Ministers – Winston Churchill, Anthony Eden, Harold Macmillan, Alec Douglas-Home, Ted Heath – without reservation or dispute at any time between us. Perhaps that was enough. I had really no reason to wish for more.

16

Postwar Britain

IT is a commonplace to say that the years since the end of the
Second World War have been years of steady decline in Britain's
power, prestige and prosperity. Both in economic and political terms
we have lost ground rapidly compared with other countries. Two
questions need to be posed: 'Was this inevitable?' and 'Does it
matter?'

There were many historical factors that worked against our old pre-
war position; indeed, there was some evidence of them even before the
War. But how much of our decline has been due to our own fault,
above all, to our own lack of will? And how much should it really
matter? You do not have to be a great imperial power to be a happy
and prosperous nation. While other people have increased their wealth
far more rapidly than we have, we have certainly made substantial
improvements since 1945. The standard of living of our people has
gone up since then and gone up considerably, and it can be argued
that if things are so wrong with Britain then why do so many people
choose to come and live here, including many who could live in almost
any country of the Western world? There must be something special
still about Britain and the quality of life in Britain to attract these
people from so many different countries to our island.

All this, no doubt, is logical and true. International power for its own
sake, the sheer capacity to dominate and rule other people, or to
enforce your will by military means, is not essential to a nation's happi-

ness. If we can provide our people with relatively full employment and with a steadily rising standard of living then why should we care so much if standards in Germany and Japan, for example, are rising so much faster? If we choose a more leisured, less adventurous, less aggressive form of life in our society, who is to say that we are wrong? Certainly there are many who attest by their actions to the belief that we are right. And yet one cannot avoid nagging doubts about the soundness of this argument. We all know nowadays far more than we did about what happens in other countries. We visit other countries in our millions, and people from other countries come here in their millions too. With this vast increase in the movements of people and with the growing universality of the Press and the Media, we know far more than we ever did about what is happening in other countries. We know that they are doing better than we are, and while, as true Englishmen, we always know that it is the foreigner who wins by running unfairly fast, we suspect that the truth may perhaps be that we are running too slowly.

The worst thing that can happen to a nation is to lose confidence in itself, and I fear this has been happening for several decades now. I once suggested that what had happened to the British people was that they had lost their pride but retained their arrogance. I think one of the symptoms of the process of losing pride is a growing sensitivity to the achievements of others, and a growing conviction that those achievements owe less to merit than they do to good fortune. As we have declined relatively in power and prosperity, so I fear we have tended to grow querulous about our misfortunes and about the successes of other countries. If this process continues too long it can eat away at the very foundations of a nation's life, and what has been a relative decline can become an absolute decline into great unhappiness and disarray.

At the end of the War in 1945 Britain's position in political and economic terms was apparently at its height; yet already there were the beginnings of decline, if only we could have discerned them. Politically we could bestride the narrow European world like a colossus. We had not been invaded or overrun. We had stood alone against Hitler. It was British soldiers, sailors and airmen who, together with the vast power of America, had restored liberty to Western Europe. Never had we been in such a strong position politically. Never, probably, had we been greater in our self-confidence and a justifiable sense of achievement and triumph. The Anglo-Saxon alliance dominated the victorious powers. Churchill was the figurehead of victory. It was the British who had sheltered and nourished the European Governments in exile, who had returned to their countries under the aegis of the Anglo-Saxon power on the one hand and the Russian military machine on the other. As the gulf between East and West became rapidly more apparent, as Russia retreated into her own deep territories, dragging with her all that she could of Eastern Europe, so the special alliance of America and Britain retained the leadership of the Western half of the world. It did not remain so for long.

How long could it have lasted? So many changes were inevitably taking place. The growth of the superpowers, America and Russia, was bound to mean that any European country could not expect to remain in the front line of world diplomacy for long, because diplomacy is based on power, and the power of the vast areas and resources of America and Russia, with their enormous technological backing in military matters, would inevitably overshadow us. A great change had taken place with the development of aviation. We had always been a maritime power, our economic strength rested upon the trade routes, our military power rested upon the Royal Navy. In a maritime world where goods moved by sea, where armies were transported by sea, and countries had to defend their coasts against ships, we could maintain a position far beyond the confines of our relatively small population. But the growth of aviation had shifted the power to the vast land masses which could sustain this new form of transportation far better than we could possibly hope to do. Their enormous areas could justify and make possible the growth of air power. In 1945 we still ruled directly a quarter of mankind, and from that we drew much of our strength. From the independent countries of the Commonwealth had come magnificent fighting men to join in Europe's liberation, but they had come also from countries that were not independent, above all from the splendid army of India. The wind of change was bound at some time to blow much of this power away. Just as the war had shaken the political structure of Britain, because of the change in outlooks it had so rapidly brought about, so it was preparing to shake to its foundations in an amazingly short time the whole structure of Britain's Empire.

The same was true of our economic position. In many ways, it should have been strong. We had not suffered the devastation of war on the scale they had known it in Continental countries. The impetus of our trade with the world was still considerable. Our foreign investments and the income from them were still vast. But the signs of weakness were already there for any that could discern them. We had acquired great debts, disguised under the title of sterling balances, in the course of sustaining our leadership in the fight for freedom, and these debts were to hang about our necks for many a year to come.

The relative trading position of Britain had also begun to decline before the War. Germany and Japan in particular were posing for us new and sinister problems in the world's markets for industrial products. It is difficult to trace when our relative decline began. I remember they had a habit at the old Board of Trade of presenting a new President with a series of reports from British representatives overseas, all bemoaning the fact that Britain's trade was declining in the face of growing foreign competition, and it was only after you had read them with some care, that they disclosed that they were in fact a century old.

But certainly a real decline had begun by the 1930s. The War should have helped to set this right, surely? Germany's factories were smashed into rubble, while many of ours were relatively intact. But, ironically, it just didn't work out that way. We were already suffering from the obsolescence which arose from the fact that our Industrial Revolution had come before that of our competitors. As our machines grew older so competitors came into the market with more up-to-date ideas, often deriving them from us. After the War they set about restoring their industries. It was a painful process for them, but they were able to do so very often with the latest equipment which they could obtain from America or from us, and which was often financed from the U.S.A. Above all, the consciousness of defeat, like the heaps of rubble in street after street, gave to the defeated powers an incentive to restoration which passed the victors by. Finally, the steady and rapid loosening of the Commonwealth ties was bound to mean for us the loss of markets where in the past we had enjoyed special positions and privileges. It can be argued that this in itself could have been a blessing. It should have provided for us the sort of stimulus to innovation and enterprise by which the Germans snatched economic success from the jaws of defeat in war. Alas, it did not work out that way.

So there were many factors which led inevitably to the relative decline of Britain after 1945. But they were not the only factors. There were many matters within our own power in which we failed to do what could have been done. In both political and economic terms our achievements could have been so much more satisfactory if the spirit of achievement had been there. This is where we must look for the answer, not in the heads of the British people but in their hearts, not in their circumstances but in their desires, for it is from here that achievement springs. Heine said once of someone, '*Er ist dumm wie alle Menschen die kein Herz haben. Denn die Gedanken kommen nicht aus dem Köpfe sondern aus dem Herzen*' – 'He is stupid, like all men who have no heart, for thoughts do not come from the head but from the heart.' This is applicable as much to nations as to individuals.

I think that we probably made two basic mistakes in the postwar years in our assessment of and our attitude to our own position and our own problem. For these mistakes certainly the politicians must accept the major blame. But it has been said that a nation gets the politicians it deserves. Perhaps if a latter-day Churchill had arisen it might have been different, though on the whole I doubt it. The two mistakes we made were to be too deeply affected by the collapse of Empire, and to underestimate the strength of the movement towards European unity. Both mistakes in a sense derived from our prewar history and our temporary postwar position.

It is still not fully appreciated how great was the change in Britain's relationship with the Empire in the postwar years. Our withdrawal from our Imperial position, of which I think we can be proud, was one of the most remarkable achievements of history. To withdraw within a few years and with relatively little bloodshed from the position of masters of an Empire upon which the sun never set, the like of which the world had never seen, to that of a relatively small island democracy, was truly an astonishing achievement in any historical perspective : such a thing had not happened before. Empires have often fallen, but usually in bloodshed and chaos, and against the background of defeat for the former Imperial power. We were not defeated; we withdrew of our own volition. Maybe if we had tried to persist we would have been defeated; maybe the wind of change would have blown our Imperial pretensions to shreds and tatters, maybe a large part of the reason for our withdrawal was that we had lost the will to govern. So be it. But we withdrew in circumstances in which it was possible to maintain a relationship of friendship and understanding and where the best of our traditions of Government and democracy persisted.

So we are entitled to take as great a pride in this achievement of withdrawal as previous generations took in the achievements of conquest. But that does not mean that the process left no scars. A nation has a collective subconscious which does not differ all that much in its reactions from the individual subconscious. This process of transition –

so abrupt, so sudden, coming on top of the triumph of the war against Hitler – inevitably left deep psychological wounds on our nation which have taken a long time to heal. The symptoms, not surprisingly, were resentment and a collapse of confidence. We felt that as we could no longer rule a quarter of mankind, we could no longer do anything at all. We resented the fact that our former Imperial possessions showed a will of their own and a determination to pursue their own ideas and policies, possibly disregarding to some extent the fact that they still wanted to be at our side. We withdrew into our own shell, protecting ourselves with the enveloping cloak of our feeling of righteous indignation.

This same feeling influenced our attitude towards Europe. Who were these Europeans? we felt. Were they not the people who had surrendered to Hitler, the people whom we had rescued? Why should they challenge us, why should they not accept our continuing leadership? And so we failed to recognize the strength of the new Europe that was developing, and assumed too easily that we could come to our own terms with it.

Certainly we underestimated the strength behind the new concept of the European Economic Community in the early 1950s, as I can bear witness as one of the Ministers responsible for that misjudgement. We were sceptical of the results of the Messina Conference – we doubted if in fact it would really come to very much. After all our Continental neighbours had talked so often about unity and so seldom achieved it, and we had so often been forced to pay the price of involvement in the contests that subsequently took place. We felt that even if the new United Europe should develop we could claim a leading place in it on our own terms and at the moment of our own choosing. We were wrong, and we were wrong because we had failed to recognize the historical decline in our own power and our own self-confidence.

The history of our relations with the developing Community shows this well. We stood aside from what was happening, arguing, with a great deal of cogent reason, that our position was special. We were a great maritime power, we were still a great Imperial power with Commonwealth links and ties that no European country could equal. We had our special relationship with the United States. If we had to choose between Europe and the open sea, we would always choose the open sea. In many ways we were right : but history had overtaken us; this special position was steadily and inevitably being eroded. As the process of European economic integration proceeded we became step by step more aware of what it would mean to us to be left out; but we were not prepared to come in on equal terms. We wanted a special position which recognized our Commonwealth ties and our world-wide status. We were not altogether unjustified in this point of view.

It is a fact that the British Government was assured, before the Treaty of Rome came into effect, by the German and French Governments, that once that Treaty had been signed they would proceed with us to negotiate a free-trade area, which would embrace within its scope not only Britain but the other Western European countries as well, and which would not undermine either our Commonwealth position or our relations with the United States. I think we were justified in accepting these assurances and this led to the abortive negotiations for a free-trade area which I have described in an earlier chapter.

But history was against us. As each year passed our claim to a special position became weaker, and the danger of our position as an offshore island of Europe became greater. The Commonwealth was changing. Their exclusive trade arrangements with Britain made less and less sense. The Australians, for example, were looking for new trade opportunities, particularly in Japan. The ability of the London market to provide capital for economic development for the Commonwealth was declining with the relative decline in our economic strength. The present was catching up with us. And so finally we made the decision to join the Community as full members and accept its obligations. It would have been better if the decision had been made earlier. British Governments, neither that of Harold Macmillan nor of Harold Wilson, were to blame for this. Basically the opposition came from the French, who feared that our entry to the New Europe would undermine the leading position they saw for themselves. But I wonder if the French would have been so successful in their opposition if we had not sometimes given the impression of half-heartedness in our acceptance of the obligations of membership?

It was Dean Acheson who said we had lost an Empire but had not yet found a role, and British opinion was angry with him precisely because what he said was fundamentally true.

Coincident with our political decline and closely interwoven with it in a causal relationship was the relative decline in our economic power and prosperity that took place over the three postwar decades as a whole and reached its peak under the Labour Government elected in 1974. By then we had become universally regarded, and rightly so, as being grouped with Italy as the two sick men of Europe. Of course the process was not even. When Rab was Chancellor from 1952 to 1955 we made considerable progress. He declared a target of doubling the standard of living in twenty-five years, and went a long way to achieving it. In 1963–4 we made very vigorous progress, which, for reasons I have explained, was brought to a halt after the 1964 election.

But over the period our performance in productivity was disappointing, our balance of payments problems were persistent, our inflation rate accelerated to outstrip our major industrial neighbours, and we became notorious for the so-called English disease, a combination of bad industrial relations and persistent labour troubles which our neighbours regarded with deep apprehension as possibly contagious. Of course, the problem of the balance of payments was complicated by the existence of the sterling balances, and by the system of fixed exchange rates, but this was not enough to explain our failure. Yet the reason lay not in Britain's circumstances, but in Britain's heart. We could not match the productivity increases of our neighbours, we could not equal their achievements in containing inflation, just for the simple reason that we had not the will and determination to do so. It was entirely in our own hands.

It is not easy to see exactly the reasons for the malaise that affected British industry throughout those years. We did not save and invest anything like as much as our German and Japanese competitors, yet our performance in this regard was not bad compared with the Americans. It was said constantly that what we needed was more investment and more new machinery, yet the real underlying weakness was in our inability to make anything like the best use of the machinery we had. The spirit that had made the greatness in British industry appeared to have faded.

We were no longer the great innovators in the technological field. Of course there were illustrious exceptions to this which we paraded with pride, but in general the new processes and ideas, in steel, for example, or in engineering, tended more and more to be developed by our competitors. British management did not seem to have the cutting edge of managements in other countries, somehow it had been blunted. Of course, once again, this is far too wide a generalization: British management at its best can still compare with that of any country in the world, but the best was not common enough and the general pattern far too uneven. As for the workforce in general, while in many firms, particularly small ones, the record was excellent, over wide and vital areas of industry productivity certainly did not match up to that of our competitors. New machinery and new methods were resisted, disputes were all too frequent, the desire to get the best out of what was available was sadly lacking, and it must be accepted that things got steadily worse. The best measure of industrial efficiency, namely output per man-hour from identical machinery, showed that by 1977 we had fallen miles behind our main competitors, particularly Germany. Yet there was no reason whatever why this should be so. We had the same skills available and the same materials. All that really was lacking was the will to make use of them.

I believe there were a number of reasons for this decline in industrial morale. The first was the lingering feeling that after we had preserved the freedom of the world against Hitler, the world still owed us a living; the feeling that if other people wanted to work harder than we did, that was because they had to and no such compulsion rested upon us. But this is intangible. What was far more tangible was the dispiriting of management and the lamentable decline of industrial relations – and there can be no doubt whatsoever that the main reasons behind these developments were political.

Taxation was a main item. Some of the arguments used have been sound, though some have not. On the whole taxation of industrial profits was not higher in this country than that suffered by our competitors, nor necessarily was the proportion of income taken by the public sector any greater. A lot of arguments based on a general opposition to taxation and a general opposition to public sector expansion were ill-directed and damaged the real cause. The basic flaw in our taxation system was the effect upon individuals of the very high rate of progression built into our highly progressive tax structure. This meant that the extra reward coming from individual effort or success was, after tax, much less than in other countries. It affected management first of all, but it spread down the line as the volume of taxation inflicted by public spending impinged more and more on lower earned incomes, and it was then that the problem became better understood. But the simple fact remained that the penalty for success and achievement was greater in this country than elsewhere, and the successful men knew this.

You can only build a successful country on the shoulders of successful men. I know it is argued from the Left that men do not work and should not work for money alone. Of course this is true, but it misses the real point, which is that if people see the higher rewards they obtain from greater effort, the acquisition of greater skill or more enterprise, so scurvily treated by the nation's tax system, they begin to lose heart. Their efforts are clearly not appreciated, why should they bother to make them? with all the problems so often entailed. This I think is really what struck at the morale of British management, the feeling that all they were trying to do, which they rightly believed was of great value to our country, was in effect totally unrecognized because it was unrewarded.

The problem of industrial relations in its broadest sense was an even more difficult one. I have had the good fortune to know many of the leading figures in the Trade Union movement, and I have a great respect for them. But I am bound to say that the total effect of Trade-Union policy over these decades, coupled with the effect of the teachings of Socialist politicians, did immense harm to the whole country, including their own members, and the reason is quite a simple one. The idea that it was a good thing to work hard and efficiently became steadily discredited. The Trade Unions concentrated all their efforts on expanding the incomes of their members by the use of their industrial bargaining monopoly, and on seizing for themselves more and more political power.

You might say, 'Why not?' Trade Unions exist to promote the interests of their members, both by increasing their incomes and by seeing that they have a greater say in the conduct of national affairs. That might have been all right had they recognized that the first and fundamental condition of prosperity for the nation, including their own members, was to produce more and to produce more efficiently. There was little response from the Trade-Union leadership to this challenge. I can rarely recall a speech by a Trade-Union leader urging the need for greater output and greater productivity. I can recall few practical efforts by Trade Unions to increase the output from the machinery on which their members were working. This was the real industrial tragedy of those decades: all the effort that was wasted in argument and conflict about the division of the nation's wealth while so little effort was made to increase it. I am afraid the trouble was that the British Trade-Union structure suffered, as did the British industrial structure, from having been first in the field. The British machinery of the Industrial Revolution once leading the world grew obsolete, while other countries modernized themselves. The British Trade-Union structure, once an example for the world, remained conservative and unchanging while the world was developing around us and leaving us behind. It was not so much a matter of the industrial disputes, the strikes and the arguments. They were bad enough, particularly in some of the large industries, above all motor-car assembly, but it could be argued with some statistical authority, at any rate, that the number of days lost in this country in industrial disputes was less than in some of our competitors. But this missed the whole point. What mattered was not how many days were lost in disputes, they were always a fairly small proportion of the days worked. What really mattered was that when our people were working they were not working as they did in America, Germany and Japan, with a will and a determination to produce as much as possible. Pride in quality and consistency, the whole pride in efficient performance, was fading sadly throughout British industry, and with it Britain faded too.

I do not doubt that much of the blame rests with the Labour Party, and particularly with its Left Wing. You cannot for years teach people that there is a great conflict between capital and labour and that it is the task of labour, in its own interests, to defeat capital and, at the same time, maintain that capital and labour have a common interest in increasing efficiency and output. It is really as simple as that. The Right Wing of the Labour Party, particularly when in office, often said the right things about this, about the importance of private manufacturing industry, about the importance of profits; but no one very much listened to them. After all, why should they? The same people had said the opposite when in Opposition, and many of their supporters continued to say the opposite when Labour was in Government. I blame the whole Labour movement above all for destroying pride in achievement, and for creating the impression that it is not clever to do your best but better to concentrate on ensuring you get as much for yourself as you can out of the other man. This is really the foundation of the English disease which has enfeebled our whole national life and achievement for decades now.

So by 1977 the position was a very different one. However much the world admired our past they had little respect for our present. Our influence in the Commonwealth, however we might like to kid ourselves, had become very small, and we were happy when the Commonwealth Prime Ministers' Conference was diverted from its usual occupation of attacking Britain to be critical of General Amin. Our relations with America remained, despite everything, good because they are based on a rock which cannot easily be shaken, but the times when we looked to America for help outnumbered manyfold the times when America looked to us. Our position in Europe was hardly one of great popularity. We had eventually joined the Community and promptly started to grumble about it. We were asking for special treatment of such matters as the Green Pound, we appeared to many of our colleagues to be constantly complaining. That would not have mattered so much had we been one of the strong economies but we were not. The French in the 1950s had played their hand with some skill when they used their economic weakness, and the danger of Communism, as a lever to obtain enormous advantages from their European partners, but that had been a long time ago and in very different circumstances, and we did not find it easy to repeat that performance. Our inflation rate was still sky-high. The illusion still persisted among the Labour movement and the Trade Unions that the Government could somehow guarantee the maintenance of living standards in a world where the harsh truth was that competitive economic efficiency and that alone could justify any standard of living for the British people.

And yet the opportunities were still so great if we could but seize them. Our traditional skills had not deserted us, our commerce, our agriculture were still the most efficient in the world. The strength of North Sea oil, so long underestimated, was all the time coming towards us. Our friends and allies wanted to believe in us; they wanted to see us succeed; they were longing to cheer us on, if only we could summon from our own spirit the determination and resource that was required.

It is here that I come against the difficulty of the inevitable delay between writing and publication. At this moment, January 1978, a great deal is happening, much of it encouraging. There has been a sudden resurgence of confidence in sterling, probably for two reasons. First, that it has been undervalued, and, second, that people around the world have begun to appreciate the full significance of North Sea oil and the fact that this will totally transform our balance of payments prospects. Interest rates have come down dramatically, but this again was only to be expected. They had been at very high levels indeed, quite unjustified by any circumstances of the domestic economy. And, with the improvement in our balance of payments, there was no longer any need to maintain exceptionally high interest rates as a protection for sterling.

So the stage seems set for a 1978 Budget which will add considerably to purchasing power. As long as this is done mainly by the reduction of direct taxation, it seems to me wholly justifiable. The situation is not all that different from the one which I was facing in 1963, and measures similar to the ones I took are desirable. The differences are that, first, on the positive side, there is the prospect of North Sea oil revenues which were not available in 1963, and, second, that on the negative side, inflation is still at a rate that in the long term is intolerable, and over and above that, the prospects of a renewed wage explosion are grave. What gives great grounds for concern is that the Labour Government may use the revenues from North Sea oil as a temporary expedient to obtain popularity, and not as a means of financing the long-delayed but inevitable changes that must take place in the British economy.

But whatever may or may not have happened between the time that I write these words and the time when you are reading them, the fundamental position will not have been greatly changed. For it is a situation that has arisen over many years, a situation based upon the character and purpose of the British people, and these things do not change easily or quickly. The adventitious aid of North Sea oil is a great help. The relative weakness of other currencies can help us too. But nothing in the long run will provide a solution to our problems other than a change of heart. If we still go on producing far less than our competitors do from the same machinery, if we still go on arguing about the share of the national income that should go to particular groups, while disregarding the need to increase the national income as a whole, we shall make no real progress.

There is still a sourness about our industrial relations. Strikes in the public sector, or in important private-sector industries like baking, are clearly strikes against the public as a whole. It is no longer a question of organized groups of workers trying to bring pressure on their employers for better terms and more money; the pressure is not on the employers, it is on the public and no one really makes any attempt to try to hide this. So long as this attitude persists there can be no health in the British industrial scene. So long as it is regarded as legitimate to extract what you think right for yourself by the blackmail and privation of the public at large, this cannot really be a happy country.

Perhaps there may be a change before too long. It will depend largely on the Government, on their determination in matters of policy, on their ability to explain to the public at large what is really involved. At this moment I can see only one way of solving the problem, which is by the acceptance of independent arbitration in those disputes where the public interest is involved. Of course the workers in any particular industry, be it public or private, are entitled to pursue their legitimate claims, and they should not be blamed for doing this. But there can be no reconciliation between the interests of the public as a whole and those in particular groups, other than by some method of impartial arbitration. Individual claims and individual cases vary very much. A general overall rate of increase may do injustice to many who have claims for special treatment, and their claims should rest not on their ability to wield industrial muscle, to blackmail the public, but on an impartial assessment of justice. It is along these lines, and along these lines alone, that I can see any solution of this problem.

And the other great problem, of course, is the total inability of the spokesmen of the Trade Unions to recognize the need for greater efficiency and greater productivity. They talk much about claims for higher wages, about getting more money, about how to get it, how soon; there was never a word said that I can recall about how to *earn* a higher income. Nothing is said about the need for greater productivity, about the need for producing more before we start sharing it out. Perhaps 1978 will begin to see some improvement in this sterile and negative attitude. We have all been hoping long enough. Maybe some time our hopes will be realized; but if they are not, one thing is absolutely clear: despite North Sea oil, and perhaps because of it, despite any short-term euphoria about the economy, the long-term problems will remain, and, so far from being settled, they will grow inexorably worse and worse.

17

The Ever-Changing Challenge

S O much for the past. Now I turn to the future. What I have to say is based on a speech I made to the Conservative Political Centre on 9 October 1969.

I always remember Sir Winston Churchill's dogma, that it is wise to look ahead, but foolish to look further than you can see. But on this occasion I should like to cast my gaze forward as far as possible into the future, about which all that is certain is that the pace of change is accelerating, and the nature of the challenge we are facing is constantly transformed. I hope you will bear with me in this, and I hope also I may be allowed to spell out some of the ideas that have been developing in my mind during nearly a quarter of a century now of political life and activity.

I would take as my theme some words that Neville Chamberlain used when broadcasting to the nation at the beginning of the Second World War: 'It is evil things that we shall be fighting against, brute force, bad faith, injustice, oppression and persecution, and against them I am certain that the right will prevail.' It seems to me that man's fate, and, strangely enough, his happiness, is to fight against evil things. His problem may be to identify them.

My first proposition, which dominates my arguments, is the fundamental significance to human life of the speed of scientific advance, and the growth of knowledge. Despite the vast amount that is written about this, despite the volume of scientific and quasi-scientific literature from textbook to space comic, I do not believe that we yet understand or appreciate what is happening. Knowledge is moving ahead far faster than we have yet brought ourselves to understand, and, what is more, the pace of this advance is still accelerating year by year. In the next twenty years or so, which is the span of time of which I am thinking, men may learn more about themselves and their environment than they have learnt in all the history of recorded time. The seemingly impossible is being realized in a shorter and shorter space of years, and in as little as twenty years we may look back on the science and technology of today as the modern astronaut can look back on the model T Ford.

The most dramatic and most publicized advances of science may not by any means be the most important in terms of human life and progress. Take the most dramatic example of all, the flight to the Moon. What will be its long-term effect on the human race? Will it, in fact, amount to more than the technology which made the flight possible? How great will be the psychological boost to man's self-confidence, or to his arrogance? It is easy to overrate the obvious, but it is easy also to become blasé and to accept, as a commonplace aspect of life, for example, the vast destructive power of modern weapons simply because the fact of their existence is often repeated, and their mechanics are, to most of us, incomprehensible. My conviction is that scientific progress, recent, and in prospect in the near future, will produce a total change in man's economic, social and moral environment. The danger is that there will not be a similar change in his political capacity. Yet this may be decisive as to whether the course of change will be for good or for evil. People sometimes talk about the appalling responsibility that rests upon the scientist, who provides mankind with such dramatic new powers of achievement and destruction, but surely an even greater responsibility will rest upon the politicians, for whom there is the duty of ensuring, so far as possible, that the use to which these new powers are put is for the good of mankind.

Let me give some examples.

The first and most obvious is the growing power of weapons. We have seen the destructive power of modern weapons change, not merely in degree, but in kind. Modern weapons, atomic, chemical, or biological, exceed the power of those available a generation ago by more than those weapons exceeded the bow and arrow: and we should be wise to assume that this process will continue and accelerate. Certainly, knowledge cannot indefinitely be withheld. Non-proliferation agreements are immensely valuable; but just as it is now easy to make gun-powder, so it will not be all that long before the capacity to produce an atomic explosion is a simple matter for any industrial society, how-ever small. This in itself has utterly changed the face of history. It has posed the choice between mutual destruction or lasting peace. It means that war is no longer an extension of policy. It means that there is, for the first time in history, an opportunity of permanent and lasting peace between the nations. Yet this permanent and lasting peace, in itself, is likely, as we shall see, to pose its own new and perplexing problems.

Then there are the advances in the economic field. A wise American said to me, some fifteen years ago, that the two most important dis-coveries of the second half of this century, from the economic point of view, would be an economic means of desalinating sea-water, and a cheap and efficient method of contraception. I think it is becoming more and more clear that this was a good judgement. When you add to it the dramatic discoveries of high-yielding strains of wheat and rice, for example, one can begin to see the prospect of putting an end to basic hunger. Of course there is an immense way still to go; of course we are still at the beginning of the process, but it is now possible to envisage a time when no longer any large part of the world's popula-tion lives at or below the level of starvation. So long as we achieve my American friend's second objective, a cheap, efficient, and, it should be said, widely used method of contraception.

The other great economic advances are in the field of modern industry. Progress with the computer has been dramatic, and the building of computers is now one of the major industries of the industrialized West. Here again, we are still only at the beginning, and it seems important to recognize that not merely will men in the future be able to do the same things as they do now more quickly and economically, entirely new things will become possible, and the whole pattern of our lives will be changed by the computer, as it has been by the motor car.

It is not difficult to see the problems that this will bring with it. The difficulty is only to appreciate their pace and dimension. Already we can see several of them looming large : the pollution of our environ-ment; the problems of adjusting the pattern of work to be done to the working population available to do it; the real and growing problem of leisure. It may seem almost cynical to talk of leisure as a problem in a world still burdened by toil, but surely we have only to look around us in this prosperous country, or look to some of our even more prosperous friends and neighbours, to realize the problem we are building for ourselves.

Then there are the discoveries which directly affect human life and moral standards. These are not matters that the politicians can ignore. Take again the most obvious example, the transplant of human organs. Kidney transplants are already an established practice, and there seems little doubt that heart transplants will eventually follow the same course. The power of science to prolong human life may well be growing far more rapidly than we think. This brings with it problems. When are transplants justified? What is the legal definition of death? If it is possible to prolong life more easily than vigour, mental and physical, what are the social consequences?

Take another example: the sex of children. I believe it should be possible quite shortly to ascertain the sex of a baby before it is born (by methods more scientific and, I imagine, more reliable, than the old system of the wedding ring on a piece of cotton). But, further than this, it seems certainly within the realms of possibility that science will be able to predetermine the sex of children, and provide parents with a conscious power of choice. What will be the consequences of this? For many people, no doubt, it will be a blessing, but problems of a new character altogether could be created for society, if, for example, a great majority of parents should choose one sex. And a new clash between individual choice and the needs of society would arise.

I believe another development which will affect the responsibilities of politicians may spring from modern treatment of the human brain. Treatments are being evolved to cure criminal tendencies by medical measures. If we extrapolate this development where will it lead us? What power may the scientist hold to vary the character of individual men and women? Who and in what circumstances can be entrusted with such a power?

Finally, in my examples I turn to those scientific developments that affect human thought. I believe we shall see, in the next few decades, enormous developments in scientific methods of teaching. It should become possible to implant basic factual knowledge in the human mind, by methods far less tedious and time consuming than those employed today. This in itself should give new opportunities to broaden the power and the scope of human intellect. But there are other developments more disturbing. Surely scientific means of influencing human thought are liable to become more and more subtle, and thereby to put more and more power in the hands of a Government that wishes to use them. Surely, too, secrecy may become more and more impossible. Already devices are available that can listen to conversations at great distances and through walls. Yet, once again, this is at an early stage. If things progress on the present curve of scientific development, how much will we be able to guarantee the secrecy of our own conversations in our own homes twenty years from now?

These are some example of the progress of scientific knowledge to which I have referred, and I have chosen them because I think they underline the profound significance that scientific development holds for the political system, and for the main issue of politics, which is the relation of the State and the individual, the interaction of freedom and order. I have quoted examples in some detail in an attempt to illumine the immense nature of the effort of political thought that will be required of us in these next few decades.

One factor in the political equation, therefore, is the scientific circumstances that man is evolving. The other is the basic facts of his nature, with which he faces them. I think there are three persistent aspects of human nature on which we must base our thoughts. They are these :

1. Man has been committed to the pursuit of knowledge since Adam first ate the fruit in the Garden of Eden. This commitment is absolute; there can be no going back; there can be no limitation.

2. There is in human nature a deep-seated strain of aggression and violence that can neither be eradicated nor totally suppressed. Man wants to fight.

3. There is a deep-seated longing for some ideal that lies beyond everyday experience; something indefinable that cannot be satisfied by material progress or comfort alone. As the character in Capek's *Insect Play* said 'it is always the unattainable'.

Let us consider the consequences of these three basic human factors for our political problems in the coming decades.

First, it must be clear that knowledge cannot be suppressed and mankind cannot be turned aside from its pursuit on any artificial count, religious or political, and that no term can be set to learning. Dictatorial societies have often tried. The greatest crime of slaves in every slave society has been to acquire knowledge. History is littered with examples of societies that have tried in vain to suppress this thirst for knowledge. Every time they have failed; as the present-day Communist powers will fail, too. Nor can people be prevented indefinitely from using and exploiting the knowledge that science brings. It may be possible to delay matters, but I do not believe it is possible for ever to deny to people the benefits which in any age science may place within their grasp. There is probably no better example of this than the spread of birth-control methods throughout every human society, whatever the nature of the initial resistance.

And so we are facing always both the blessing and the curse of fresh scientific knowledge and of the growth of efficiency. The blessings are obvious : greater leisure, better health, longer life, greater knowledge. But the disadvantages come as well : the pollution of man's environment by the chemicals he uses; the slow suppression of the human factor and the individual unit in so many social and economic fields; the problem that leisure appears to present to so many people; the new powers that a Government can wield. These questions are being raised inevitably by the growth of knowledge and I believe that even more profound political questions will arise in their turn.

The basic strain of aggression in human nature, the desire to fight, is not removed by the knowledge that world war now can mean only mutual destruction. It is not removed, it is only diverted to other fields. Some may be harmless or, indeed, admirable. It fascinates me to see how commonly the Press talks of space exploration as the 'conquest' of space. But other consequences are disturbing. I think there is growing evidence that the absence of wars on a world scale, or wars that are major in the sense that they endanger the security of nations, has a big effect on our society, because it takes away the one obvious and historic outlet for man's fighting instinct.

Consider the evidence. First, many regimes need to manufacture enemies in order to retain their own cohesion and sense of purpose. The main obvious example is the mythology of Communism with its determination to trample under foot an already obliterated fascist enemy. But the same is true of many countries that have recently changed from colonial status to independence. Here, too, it appears to be necessary to raise the spectre of neo-colonialism and to create the fear of an external threat to the new regime in order to give it impetus. In either case, the menace is fostered long after the danger has gone.

Second, we are seeing all the time a growth of violence within countries amounting, in some cases, almost to a breakdown of law and order. Of course there are fluctuations, sometimes things get better, the tide appears to recede. In America, for example, things seem a good deal more tranquil now than they were a few years ago, and racial tensions appear to have calmed. Similarly the level of student violence which, a few years ago, spanned the globe from Tokyo to California and from London to Sydney, has receded. But despite this the general tendency for the crime rate to grow has continued.

In particular we have seen the development of hijacking, kidnapping and assassination, sometimes for political reasons, sometimes purely for personal gain. In Germany and Italy in particular this has become a grave menace and the threat of the hijacker to the international airlines is alarming. Yet the strange thing is that in many of these cases people are inspired by what they consider to be a just cause, and they are ready to justify the means by the end. As in Northern Ireland, with the I.R.A., as in Rhodesia, with the so-called freedom fighters, as in Germany, with the terrorist gangs, there appears to be a feeling that the political end justifies the murderous means. This is a distortion of what is meant by an ideal, it is a perversion springing from the aggressive factor in man's nature poisoning the third factor, the pursuit of the ideal. It would be a tragedy if this were to develop further, for the pursuit of the ideal is still, I believe, what inspires the vast majority, particularly of the young, and still represents an essential strand in human nature.

In political terms, this surely means the pursuit of freedom, not merely in its negative sense of freedom from restraint, but in its positive sense of freedom to achieve, which is the essential political precondition of the pursuit of the ideal – the pursuit of the ideal which has survived ages of oppression. It survives still – as we see – even in Eastern Europe. But can it survive generations of comfort? The spirit of idealism is sharpened by trial and challenge – it may be blunted by its absence. Without it can we mobilize the will to achieve the political feats that science will require of us?

I return, therefore, to my basic theme, that the issues of freedom and order are the fundamental issues of politics. Our purpose in trying to solve these problems is to direct these three motive forces, the pursuit of knowledge, the desire to fight, and the search for the ideal, towards solving the problems that science will pose for humanity in the coming decades.

It is a disturbing fact that all the new scientific discoveries that can be applied to human life seem to call for new controls. Because science is unleashing such ever-increasing powers, there appears to be an ever-increasing requirement for their control. The main, obvious examples, of course, lie in the field of weapons, or the pollution of the environment. Everyone can see the desirability of controlling the development of armaments, just as everyone can see the need to prevent the poisoning of our air or our rivers by noxious substances. The need for controls is explicit, though their achievement is difficult. But even more serious problems may be arising from some of the developments I referred to earlier such as the transplanting of human organs, the prolongation of the span of life, the effects on society of determining the sex of children, and the ability modern biology may give to influence the mind and character of individual men and women. The dangers involved are enormous. But what we must state with all the power at our command is that danger to freedom of multiplying controls is equally serious. The fantasies of Huxley and Orwell may not be realized in detail but some of their principles are not so far away in terms of history. They will pose for us in the most acute form the problem of how to maintain both social order and individual liberty.

Moreover, it is a fact that the old disciplines are disappearing. Different societies have, of course, reached very different stages in their progress. But in the most advanced societies the old disciplines of unemployment and grinding poverty have largely disappeared. We never wish to see them return. The problem is, what to put in their place, for no free society can exist without its proper disciplines. Wildcat strikes, social unrest, the growth of crime and irresponsibility – many features of our present society highlight the problem. The choice before us clearly is between further powers of State discipline or the growing self-discipline of a responsible society. There is no third alternative and the development of science will force us to take one course or the other. The second is infinitely the preferable in human terms. But I fear it may also be much the harder to achieve.

Where does responsibility for leadership lie in these matters? There are some who say, 'This is a matter for the Archbishops'. I do not believe this is right. Politicians must not flinch from their responsibility nor can the Churches achieve for politicians what they themselves fail to do. It is sad but necessary to record that the ability of the established religions to achieve and hold the allegiance of the young is fading. The process takes a different form in different countries but I believe it is generally the same. The Christian Church to many young people nowadays looks elderly, unreal and divided within itself on petty issues. Even Islam is losing its sway over many of the new generations of Muslims. This trend may in the future be reversed. But we cannot rely on this to solve our problems, and even less to do our duty for us.

No new religion has emerged for centuries. The nearest thing to a new religion is Maoism in China. It has many of the traditional features: a saviour who is canonized in his lifetime; sacred texts that enjoin on his followers how they should live their lives; a devil or devils, in the form of the capitalist powers or the revanchist Communists of Russia; and, as a miracle, they have the astonishing development in China of the last twenty years. Maybe the strength of this quasi-religion will fade as the Revolution recedes – I hope it will. But for the time being we should be wise to assume that, repellent as it is to us in many features, it may exercise in the minds of its followers some of the power and impetus that was achieved by the most fanatical religious explosions of the past. In fact the main world powers of the present day, America, Russia, China, are all in a sense revolutionary: but they differ in the stage they have reached. America's revolution is the furthest behind and its force the most spent. But in Russia, too, things are changing and the initial expansive force of revolution is dwindling with the passage of the years. It is interesting to see how the new revolutionaries across the world look now to China or Cuba for their inspiration, rather than to Russia.

What I believe our objective should be is to present to the people a new and positive concept of freedom: not merely the negative absence of control or regulation, not merely freedom *from* restriction, but freedom *for* achievement. We must present the new challenges to man's basic idealism and fighting spirit which replace the old challenges of war and the struggle merely to keep alive. I suggest four: the challenge of personal responsibility, the challenge of service in a world where individual service is being progressively obscured, the challenge of beauty in a world where increasing material efficiency is diverting man's attention and the challenge of truth to a political system that appears sometimes to have neglected its requirements in the battles for political power.

Our task is to ensure that the system of Government, the issues of politics and the spirit in which we conduct ourselves are consistent with leadership in the face of these new challenges. At the moment it is difficult to be confident that they are up to the task.

There is much criticism of, and cynicism about, Parliament and our system of Government. To so many people Parliament appears old-fashioned in its actions and procedures, concentrating on the wrong issues, with no real control of the Executive but with too much power of interference in the detailed running of the country and life of its citizens. As for the Executive, this draws its shape largely from the

Parliamentary system and is therefore open to much the same criticism. Above all, the difficulty is the sense of remoteness, not merely the remoteness of the bureaucrat in Whitehall, but perhaps even more important the remoteness of the municipal Government officials whose decisions may even more intimately affect our lives. If my analysis is right the reform of our system of Government both national and local appears to be an urgent task.

The political Parties, too, are the object of much criticism and even more cynicism. The first charge is that politicians are careless of the truth. Also it is widely and firmly believed that politicians generally are seeking only for power, and that they are consistently unwilling to face or admit to unpleasant facts which may hamper them in that search. So we must also seek in all that we do to restore the confidence of the public in the political Parties, who alone can provide the necessary leadership but who cannot perform that task unless they command the necessary confidence.

Man has always needed a challenge. In the past this has arisen from obvious external enemies: nature or his fellow man, war, hunger, flood, pestilence, privation. It is in facing these challenges that man has found inspiration to scale the heights. We must now identify the new challenges of this rapidly changing generation if we are not to dwell indefinitely in the lowlands of apathy. We must harness to meet these challenges the thirst for knowledge, the desire to fight and the search for the ideal.

So I suggest that the four new challenges are responsibility, service, beauty and truth.

I put first individual responsibility and all that this challenge implies. I believe it must be in the forefront of our policy to stress that scientific progress does nothing to lessen individual duty or responsibility. Indeed, as I have tried to show, it increases the need. Therefore we must set about recreating that true sense of pride, in family, work and country, which we appear to be in danger of losing. By pride I mean a sense of high standards voluntarily accepted and rigorously maintained. Without this – and without individual loyalty – our society cannot prosper. But nor can we in turn expect to recreate the sense of pride unless we evolve policies which throw upon the individual proper responsibility for the well-being of himself and his family and at the same time accord to true achievement both the reward and the acclaim that is its desert. This is surely what we mean when we talk in rather more formal terms of 'incentives' and 'self-provision'.

The second challenge is that of service, of using the opportunities presented by growing knowledge not for improving our own lot alone, but in the service of our fellow men. It must also be in the forefront of our policy thinking that the function of Government is to serve the people and in particular to be concerned with those who have fallen behind the general progress. Winston Churchill used to talk of 'bringing the rearguard in'. The rearguards in our prosperous society are still far too numerous and ill-protected. It must be our endeavour to enthuse people with the sense of purpose that can come from service both by our attitude to the duties of Government and by encouraging in every way the efforts of individuals. For again we must not allow the idea to develop that in a more organized society there is less room for personal compassion or individual service. And finally we must recognize the duties which we owe as a relatively wealthy nation to those countries throughout the world where men count in pence what we count in pounds. We have a moral duty to them, to help them in their own efforts to stand on their own feet, just as we have a similar duty to our fellow citizens at home.

Third, there is the challenge of beauty : the beauty that growing wealth should make more easily attainable but which in fact growing material prosperity so often tends to trample underfoot. So much is damaged and so little new is created in its place. Pylons march across lovely countryside, our lanes are littered with the rubbish discarded by weekend motorists, many of the remaining beauties of our cities are obscured. I have no doubt that the craving for beauty exists. You can see it in the longing for education, in the demand on the libraries, perhaps most of all in the astonishing thirst for music in all its forms. But there seem to be many strange features in our expanding material culture. Television provides a mesmeric influence in its sadly repetitive programmes. Novelists and playwrights and film makers seem to have abandoned the emotion of love for the mechanics of sex. I should be the last to seek a censorship of taste. Indeed I would fight to the end for freedom to express, to entertain and to perform. But the opposite side of this coin of freedom must be leadership, providing for more and more people, by safeguard and encouragement, the opportunity to enjoy the beautiful in nature or art, and providing through education a greater understanding of where they should be sought.

My final challenge is the challenge of truth : perhaps, some cynics would say, the most difficult challenge of all for the politicians to face. Truth has always been the first casualty of any war. It has recently become the first casualty of new revolutions and new political movements, even though they may bring with them great material benefits. I have grown to be sickened by the standards of double-think and double-talk now so often applied in international relations where the idea of telling the truth appears to be regarded as merely old-fashioned.

I regard it as the greatest duty of the Conservative Party at home and abroad to do all in our power to see that the standards of truth and honesty are restored.

So it is still evil things that we are fighting against but in the next twenty years they will be different things: apathy, indifference, cynicism, the shifting of responsibility, the philosophy of envy, and unwillingness to grasp the majesty of the opportunities that new knowledge is according to mankind. These now are the evils we must fight against, and against them I am certain that the right will prevail.

EPILOGUE

There's nothing worth the wear of winning,
But laughter and the love of friends.

I SAID in my preface that at the end of the book I would examine Belloc's words again and see how they stood up to the test of experience. I think they stand up pretty well.

You learn more about laughter as you go along. It has differing qualities, not always attractive. It can be mocking, it can be cruel, it can be insincere, but when it is spontaneous, as on the awakening face of a baby grand-daughter, or in the sudden recognition of friends, it remains one of the unsurpassed joys of life. As for the love of friends, you learn to distinguish between those who are true and those who are false, though to do so is not always easy. I find myself driven back always to the advice that Polonius gave to Laertes:

The friends thou hast, and their adoption tried,
Grapple them to thy soul with hoops of steel.

And what are the alternatives? What are the other things that are worth the winning? I must still distinguish, as I did before, between the wear of winning and the wear of doing. There are so many things that are worth doing, great and small, for the sake of what they produce. A Budget, a new system of education, a new international treaty, are worth doing for the sake of the benefits they will bring to individual men and women. Equally valuable are the smaller things. The help you can give to an old lady whose pension is not being properly paid; finding accommodation for a harassed family; helping to provide some sustenance for the ill or the handicapped. Whether it be that what you are doing is on the grand scale that affects millions, or on the humble scale that affects only individuals, it is still worth doing and profoundly worth doing for the results it produces.

But the wear of winning is something else. Some end product that you seek from your own efforts. What are the other things that may be worth the wear of winning? Money is clearly the first example. It is easy to despise the value of money, and it is particularly easy to do so if you do not suffer the privations or discomforts that come from its absence. The people who denigrate the desire to earn more money tend to be either those who have enough already, or those who know their chances of success in its pursuit are very little, or those who merely wish to revel in the joys of discomfort. For most of us ordinary men and women, money is a natural objective, not for its own sake, but for what it can buy, because without money we face discomfort and insecurity, because with money we can do many of the things which we wish to do and, even more important, help our families and our friends. But there is a limit. I would have thought that the pursuit of money for its own sake would become increasingly sterile. It is extraordinary to me how many people who have already amassed substantial wealth are so vigorous in the pursuit of even greater riches.

Fame comes next. There is no doubt it is exciting, stimulating, almost intoxicating. This has always been so. The difference in present day conditions is merely that the dissemination of fame has become more widespread and more facile through the Press and the Media. But it is a hollow achievement, it is in itself of no value whatever. If it arises from the love of friends, if it represents the reward of achievement, then it is satisfying. That is true fame. The fame that is adulatory is an illusion.

Then there is power. How far is power worth the wear of winning? For men over the ages it has been perhaps the greatest attraction of all. It is inherent in human nature (and in this perhaps Adler was more accurate than Jung or Freud), the pursuit of power is not of necessity harmful in itself. Acton said, 'Power tends to corrupt, and absolute power corrupts absolutely.' I have never been quite sure that he was right, nor do I see how a Christian can reconcile this view with the absolute power of God. There is no such general principle. All depends upon the nature of the individual and how he seeks, and why he seeks, the possession and use of power. You can use power in two ways, one to exert your will over your fellow men, the other to bring them benefits, and these two ways interact and overlap. I still believe, though perhaps it is starry-eyed of me to do so, that the motive which should bring men into politics and which, in this country at any rate, does bring most men into politics, is the scope and opportunity which political power at any level gives to exercise what talents you may have for the benefit of your fellow citizens. Of course it carries its consequences. The greater the power a politician wields the greater the benefits he can achieve for his fellow citizens if he is wise, and the greater the damage he can do them if he is foolish or mistaken. The danger is in the belief that 'The man in Whitehall knows best'. There is nothing more dangerous than the arrogance of virtue be it conscious or subconscious. If power is not balanced by humility it is a continuing menace.

What else remains? There is pleasure, there is happiness. They are closely related but not quite the same. Both are things that one feels, yet pleasure is something concrete, while happiness is a state of mind which pleasure itself may induce. You enjoy your pleasures, you are happy. Aristotle said of pleasure that, 'It supervenes upon activity like bloom upon the cheek of youth.' You take pleasure in doing things. The form in which it comes may be either physical or mental. It can range from the pleasure of diving from a high place into a cool sea, through the satisfaction of a No. 4 iron laid two foot from the pin, through the savouring of the great vintages of Bordeaux or Burgundy (and is that physical or spiritual?), to the enjoyment of Mozart or Beethoven. All these are pleasures but they do not add up in themselves to happiness, though, strangely enough, providing pleasure for others is one of the greatest sources of happiness.

But are they in themselves a final objective? I think what Aristotle was saying was that if you pursue either pleasure or happiness as an end in itself, you will not really achieve it. Bentham said that, 'The greatest happiness of the greatest number is the foundation of morals and legislation.' For a long time I believed this and it is not a bad rule of thumb in Government or in life, yet I doubt if it is really enough in itself. My old clerical schoolmaster, Billy, disagreed. He thought happiness a rather vulgar objective and argued that man's goal should be not happiness but content. I would rather share the view of Cervantes, *'Todos los contentos d'esta vida pasan como sombra y sueño, o se marchitan como la flor de campo'* – 'All who are content with this life pass as a shadow or a dream, or wither like the flower of the field.'

This leads me to my final conclusion. There is no such thing for human beings as content. Man can never be content. He would very soon find himself bored in Paradise. Eternal happiness would soon pall. No doubt this is our weakness but it is our nature. It is the mystery, the uncertainty, the conflict, the divine discontent that still pluck at the human heart-strings more than anything else, and this is as true of the politician as it is of the artist, the businessman, the house-wife or the farmer. One of the tragedies of the modern world is how so much of the magic and the mystery is being dispelled by the advance of science. The moon of Beethoven or Debussy is being replaced by a dusty planet occupied by crawling scientific devices and occasionally golfing astronauts. To misquote Mme de Staël, *'Tout expliquer, c'est tout détruire.'* The world of certainty is a dull world, and Meredith was right when he said that those who seek it receive a dusty answer.

So I come to the conclusion, final for the time being at any rate, that I have found so far nothing more worth the wear of winning than laughter and the love of friends. But I am still not content that this should be so. The business of political argument and controversy and bickering becomes increasingly wearisome with the passage of years, of experience. One longs to think that this is just a means to an end and that a better means can be found. One longs to think that the problems of international peace, of maximizing production, of extending welfare, can be solved and that man liberated from them can turn his mind to more positive values and positive achievements. But it will be a long time indeed before that can happen. And if it should come about, would it really be acceptable to the human race? That is a question that some day will have to be answered. But as of now I should not like to predict what the answer will be.

> 'And now abideth faith, hope, love these three;
> But the greatest of these is love.'
>   — *First Epistle of Paul to the Corinthians*

APPENDICES

Political Writings

1943–1976

1 CONSERVATIVES AND CONTROL
From *The Spectator*, 12 November 1943

In the last century it was the parties of the Left that unfurled the banner of individual liberty in their assault on the stronghold of privilege manfully defended by the Right. Now it is the party of the Right, still on the defensive, that is fighting in the cause of individual liberty against the threatening collectivism of the Left. What is the cause of this drastic transformation? What, at the same time, are the reasons underlying the virtual disappearance of the mighty Liberal Party? Are they the same? Has the social need that the Liberal Party met now passed, and has its place been taken by a fresh need that Socialism is better fitted to satisfy? The answers to these questions should provide some clue to the natural development of Conservative policy.

The main political issue of the nineteenth century was the struggle against political privilege. That struggle, in which the Liberal Party were the protagonists, has now to all practical intents been decided. But the people, in whose names it was fought, and who gave generous support to the Liberal extenders of the franchise, have come to realize that this alone is not enough. The 'century of the common man' has seen the emergence of two political facts : the first, that political and economic liberty are interdependent, so that the achievement of the one is valueless without the other; the second, that whereas in the political sphere liberty and equality are complementary, in the economic sphere they seem to be ultimately irreconcilable. It is against the background of these two facts that the regrouping of the parties and the reshaping of their political philosophies must be viewed.

In the campaign against political privilege the individualist doctrine of *laissez-faire* Liberalism was an admirable weapon, and in that cause the Liberal Party flourished. Yet with the advent of victory the party succumbed. What other explanation of this dramatic political dénouement can there be than that the social need which the party had expressed had been satisfied, giving place to a new need for which the doctrines of Liberalism would not suffice? This new need is not far to seek. The people, their struggle against political privilege won, turned next to the complementary struggle against economic privilege. But the Liberal Party that had drawn much of its strength from the political affinity of equality and liberty, and had won the former in the name of the latter, was inherently incapable of facing a situation in which they were incompatible. The trumpets of individual liberty might have caused the fall of the mighty walls of political monopoly, but it was soon apparent that they would echo in vain against the stronghold of economic monopoly. A new and more powerful weapon was needed; in Socialism it lay to hand.

Socialism recognizes the ultimate irreconcilability of liberty and equality in modern economic organization and makes its choice, for equality. Further than this, if the sacrifice of economic liberty entails the sacrifice of political liberty as well, Socialism is prepared to accept this as well in the supreme cause of the abolition of economic privilege with all the misery and frustration of human life that it entails. Socialism is an authoritarian creed, and as such is diametrically opposed to the Liberal political Left of the nineteenth century. But it can offer precisely what Liberalism is incapable of offering – a lead in the new struggle against economic privilege which is to be the feature of the present century as the struggle for the extension of the franchise was the feature of the last. So the reversion to the title of the popular party passed to an organization that offers to the electors economic equality at the expense of economic and ultimately of political liberty. The hard facts of the prewar world lent attraction to the offer.

The twentieth century has seen a radical alteration in the political philosophy of the Left. The chances are that it is soon to see the effects of equally radical changes in the ideas of the Right. The Conservative Party has already declared itself as the champion of individual liberty; but the form that this championship will take is not yet apparent. So far two alternative lines of development have emerged. The first is an appeal to emotion, the second to reason. The emotional appeal attacks State control in any shape or form, and it generally runs something like this: 'Have you fought this bitter war for freedom only to resign your personal freedom absolutely to a totalitarian State of your own creation? Have you not had a bellyful of orders, regulations and restrictions, most of them devised only for the amusement of their perpetrators? Do you want to have your entire existence, private as well as public, from the cradle to the grave ordered and controlled by the hordes of State bumbledom?' No one can doubt the power of this appeal, presented usually with eloquence and often with wit, to a naturally independent people chafing under the unnatural restrictions of five years of war. Yet can anyone of intellectual integrity maintain that it represents a serious contribution to political thought?

The second alternative rejects this blind and indiscriminate opposition to control. It recognizes the justice of the struggle against economic privilege, while clinging fast to the cause of individual liberty. It says, in effect, State control is not a good thing in and for itself, but a measure of such control is a manifest necessity to the modern nation. Private enterprise and public enterprise, freedom and control, each have their virtues and their drawbacks; each has its own proper sphere of operation which we must determine in the light of experience. With good will on all sides and a readiness to give and take and to subordinate selfish interests to the common good a satisfactory solution can be achieved. The adherents of this second view are, in fact, appealing to the British and peculiarly Tory tradition of compromise in politics. But their polity suffers from the very fact that it is a compromise : for while compromise in matters of practice may be both laudable and expedient, compromise in matters of principle is fatal : and in this case it is not even necessary.

These two lines of political thought have one thing in common. They have both taken over uncriticized from the Liberal movement its conception of the meaning of freedom. This Liberal conception is in its essence purely negative – a definition of freedom as the sheer absence of control, an assumption that freedom is always freedom from something or somebody. So far both wings of the Conservative Party seem to have taken it for granted that this is the only possible definition, and that freedom and control are absolutely and inevitably opposed. The result is that they have to choose between arbitrary opposition and dangerous compromise. The needs of a new age have outgrown the Liberal idea. For all too many of our people freedom from control has meant nothing more than freedom to be poor, to be workless, to live in discomfort, insecurity, squalor. They have been free to vote, free to a remarkable degree from the interference of the State in their lives : yet their lives have been circumscribed and dictated from the moment of birth by economic necessity, and they have been condemned to a perpetual struggle against poverty and the threat of unemployment. The truth is that to speak of freedom in such circumstances is a travesty. Freedom for civilized man is not a mere negative, not just freedom *from*; it is freedom to live as a member of an organized society, freedom to think, speak, work and worship and to develop his individual personality in conditions that befit the dignity and greatness of the human race.

Who is the more truly free, the savage who obeys no law and knows neither security nor opportunity of self-development, or the citizen of an organized community who is controlled by law, but who gains thereby the right to live unmolested and the opportunity to develop his natural talents? If, with the Liberals, we maintain that freedom is negative, we must answer 'the savage'. But if we feel that such an answer is a denial of all significance in human life we must admit that true freedom is not negative, but positive, not the opposite of control but the purpose for which control exists. Freedom means nothing if it is not freedom to develop to the full the individual personality : a man, as a social animal, can achieve this only in and through membership of a community, of an organized and controlled community. Control is part of the machinery of freedom and in the freedom of civilized man control is absorbed and transcended.

So far the Conservative Party has shown no signs of working towards any such positive conception of freedom. Like the Socialist Party it accepts the apparent irreconcilability of freedom and equality, and with this acceptance it is compelled either to reject equality or compromise freedom. The country is unlikely, either by mood or experience, to accept the former : though the latter may provide temporary stability it involves a compromise of principle which will render it incapable of protracted resistance. The best hope of the Conservatives lies in the rejection of an outmoded conception of freedom, and the adoption of a new and positive conception of man's freedom to develop his individual personality in and through his membership of an organized self-governing community, in which the purpose of State control and the guiding principle of its application is the achievement of true freedom.

2 COLONIAL SECRETARY
A letter to my constituents published in the *Daily Mail*, 21 June 1962

We are now witnessing a period of sudden and rare political turmoil.

Not so many months ago it seemed even to the most experienced observers that with the weakness of the Labour Opposition the pendulum of politics had stuck, and the Conservative Party could look forward to decades of power.

Then at Orpington the ice broke under our feet and all could see for the first time how thin it had become.

I am convinced that there is one fundamental reason which underlies all the individual complaints and grievances that are the substance of by-election controversies. It is this. We are seeing the close of one political era and the opening of another.

The problems and the needs of our country will be very different in the 1960s from the 1950s : they call for a new outlook and new policies.

This does not mean that old policies have failed : indeed it may even be proof of their success. But it does mean that in many ways they are no longer adequate or even always relevant.

It is a natural temptation to politicians to keep advocating solutions of the familiar and even comfortable problems of the past. This has been the great weakness of the Labour Party and it is one that we must avoid if we are not to run out of steam in the 1960s as they did in the 1950s.

But to do so we must first identify and then tackle the problems of the

60s. The present disillusion of the electorate with the main parties springs, I believe, from their feeling that none of them has yet done this.

In 1945 the voters chose the Labour Party. They felt instinctively that the country needed something other than a return to the *laissez-faire* of the 20s and 30s. The time had come to tackle decisively the problem of unemployment and to make a major step forward in organized social welfare.

The war had shown what could be achieved by strong central planning (though the cost to individual liberty was overlooked) and it was natural to choose the party whose policy was based on strong and purposive Government action in the economic and social fields.

The electorate in 1945 chose between freedom and order and chose order. History is unlikely to say that they were wrong.

But by the early 1950s two things had happened; the Labour Government had worked itself out of ideas and the electorate had come to realize that the nation's needs had changed.

This was no mere coincidence. The reaction from order to freedom, the longing for more individual liberty, the desire to break away from the drab and austere aftermath of war to a freer and gayer society in which individual enterprise could lay the foundation of a new and modern affluence – all these feelings posed problems that Labour policies could not solve. And so we were given our mandate in 1951.

We have tackled and solved the problems of the 1950s. But the 1950s have passed and taken their problems with them. Unless we turn to the problems of the 1960s we may find that we have worked ourselves out as the last Labour Government did.

I believe that the new national mood which is developing is based on two factors.

First, there is a realization that liberty in a purely negative sense is not enough. Man's basic instinct for freedom is not satisfied by merely being free 'from'; he needs also to be free 'for'.

Secondly, there is the growing sense that material affluence in itself is not enough.

What is lacking in both cases is a sense of purpose, a purpose for the free individual, a purpose for the affluent society.

If you study in the Press the complaints of today – and in this the Press mirrors the views of the people – they range from criticism of the Government for failing to 'give a lead' and to explain the problems of the nation and the reasons for our policies, through the boredom of modern life in comfortable suburbia to the listless follies ascribed to modern youth and even the inadequate determination of our representatives in the field of sport.

There is one constant factor : loss of sense of purpose and even of pride.

We are living in the most dangerous and the most exciting times that man has ever seen. The prospects open to the world range from the disaster of nuclear war to an age in which science can provide liberation from poverty and squalor and the basis for a new advance in the dignity and value of human life. The choice is there to be made. The nation is looking for a party that will reflect this noble purpose in word and deed.

Freedom without order is meaningless in the economic field as it is in the political. No one save an anarchist believes that the right to individual liberty includes the right to destroy society.

Nor does it include the right to undermine the economy. When old disciplines go new ones must be found unless freedom is to destroy its own purpose.

No one wishes to return to the old, harsh disciplines of unemployment and grinding poverty; but unless their place is taken by the self-discipline of a responsible society the whole basis of a free economy – and therefore of a free society – is in jeopardy.

It is the responsibility of Government in the 1960s to drive this fact home by constant explanation of the rights and the duties of the free individual in a free economy and by determined action if powerful groups or organizations attempt to override them.

To do this may be inconsistent with classical *laissez-faire* Liberal doctrine. But it is essential for true freedom and a sound economy in the 1960s.

I believe the people as a whole know this in their hearts and are waiting to be told it. There is nothing negative about an 'incomes policy' in this sense : indeed it is a positive challenge to buttress prosperity with moral responsibility.

Our further object must be to paint a clear picture of how much there is in this world, at home and abroad, that needs urgently to be done, that is profoundly worth doing, and that can be fully done only by a country that has a sound and vigorous economy.

This must be the sense of purpose for an affluent society. To clear up the remaining areas of poverty and squalor in our own society, to take a lead in the long process of freeing the impoverished majority of mankind from the material shackles that stand in the way of decent human existence.

I believe that our people want to take a new pride in Britain and her achievements past and future. Pride is no mean emotion. A man who takes no pride in his work is living only half a life, whatever his material reward. So it is with nations.

The pride that swells into arrogance and brutality can be disastrous, as we have so often seen. But it can be equally pernicious when pride gives way to cynicism and self-satisfaction, the cynicism that tears down old values without erecting new, or the self-satisfaction that says, with the chaplain in Shaw's *Saint Joan*, 'an Englishman is never fairly beaten.'

There is too much evidence of both reflected in the Press, from our attitude to politics to our attitude to sport, to let us be complacent.

To sum up, the Conservative Party will regain its supremacy if, and only if, it can find the answer to the real needs of the 1960s. They are not the needs of a country haunted by Jarrow and the Rhondda, nor any longer the needs solely of a country breaking away from the austerity of war and the meshes of Socialism.

They are the needs of a people conscious of the greatness of their past, enjoying the affluence and freedom of the present but feeling in their hearts the lack of a sense of the purpose of this freedom and affluence.

3 INCOMES POLICY

A memorandum submitted for discussion by the Cabinet but withdrawn (see page 191) and subsequently published in *The Times*, 12 September 1972

I must ask my colleagues for their forbearance if I put to them again a thesis they have already heard from me more than once in the past. But in the light of the T.U.C. Conference, and the present economic outlook, we seem to be approaching a critical time.

The last two decades have seen profound changes, both economic and political, in the whole capitalist system. All Western countries have been affected in varying degrees. All of them are trying in different ways to find a solution to the same phenomenon. I am beginning to wonder whether we have recognized how profound are the changes we are facing and how far we may have to pursue our search for remedies. I suspect that the problems we are facing are not economic but political. Economic factors operate within a political framework and the old orthodoxies of economics, however coherent and self-consistent, may not apply in a changed political situation. What determines the course of a country's society and its economy is fundamentally political power and how it is used.

The capitalist system within which we have been operating is based on certain principles. The first principle is the maximum of freedom and of competition so that the highest reward should go to those who prove their merit in competitive circumstances. This has led inevitably to wide disparities in living standards and to the concentration of a large amount of wealth in a fairly limited number of hands. The justification for this has been :

1. that competitive conditions have produced major advances of human prosperity, and

2. that a system which combines incentives for success with welfare provision for those who have not succeeded is morally and politically justifiable.

By and large this pattern has been accepted, albeit subconsciously, by the great bulk of the people of the Western democracies.

But we must recognize that this has only persisted because the majority have not been prepared to use their potential economic and political power against the prosperous minority. It has been tacitly accepted until recently that to do this would be harmful to all.

I believe that the fundamental situation is now changing. We have seen in the last two decades an arising consciousness of the power of organized labour. One can speculate at length on the reasons. They are many and varied : the growth of relative affluence in our society and the consequent diminution of sanctions, the diminished prospects of international war. Whatever the compound of reasons it is the facts we must face.

There seem to me to be two main factors. The first is the rather belated effect of universal education and the way in which this has taken away from the minority the power of exclusive knowledge which they previously enjoyed. The second is the growing organization of workers and the growing realization, with the complex interrelation of modern industry, of the indispensability of relatively small but organizable groups. It is basically a question of monopoly power. Some groups of employees, organized into unions, now possess the power to bring any capitalist economy to a halt. Knowledge and skill have contributed to this. The days when the community at large could provide skills to replace those of a striking union, e.g. of electric power workers, have now passed. Society's defence is now political, not practical.

We see the result of all this in the problem of cost inflation which has bedevilled this country for many years and it is now infecting the whole Western world. This is a new problem : it is a political problem. The old traditional economics cannot begin to cope with it.

The argument is still made that proper demand management is the answer to all inflationary problems, including those of cost inflation. It is argued that if the volume of money is kept in relation to total output there can be no problem. It is argued that responsibility rests on governments and if they will control their expenditure all will be well. I think both these arguments have now been exposed for the nonsense they are. You cannot deal with a cost-push inflation other than by means directly relevant to its source. To restrict the volume of money only means in modern conditions that, while the socially powerful continue to expand their incomes, more and more of the less powerful lose their jobs altogether while the economy stagnates and investment collapses. Nor do I believe that there is any truth in the theory that more competition could provide the solution. The more competitive the economy, the stronger the power of the unions. Squeezing the money supply does not encourage firms to resist wage claims, it forces them to give way.

Many attempts have been made in recent decades to find an incomes and prices policy. None have been wholly successful. This was hardly surprising. You cannot solve the problems of a major social upheaval by economic mechanics alone. We have perhaps underestimated what could have been achieved because we expected too much too soon. Our attempts at an incomes policy produced only limited success. Labour's attempts produced even less. But surely we should see clearly by now that the argument whether or not a government needs an incomes policy is sheer semantics. Any government in a democracy must have an incomes policy in the sense that it must attempt directly to influence the sources of cost inflation.

I agree, therefore, that no final solution has been found to the problem either of restraining the totality of income growth or of settling the relativities between individual incomes. But I have no doubt whatsoever that we must return to the search as a matter of urgency. Unless we do this and unless we are prepared to cast aside all previous political and economic dogmas in order to meet a new political situation to which they have little relevance, we have no chance of success.

It seems to me that there are two possible approaches to the problem of incomes control or, in other words, the problem of suppressing cost inflation. The one is a policy of conflict, of fighting it out and of defeating the inflationary forces. The other is a policy of seeing how systematically we can encompass these forces within a modern economy.

I do not believe that policies of conflict will or can work. I do not think we can now redress the balance between the monopoly power of labour and the interests of price stability by individual measures. We can do a few things here and there to make striking less attractive. I do not believe this reaches the fundamental problem. We have in the past to a considerable extent succeeded in damping down individual wage settlements in the public sector but this is a catch-as-catch-can solution dearly bought and, as we now see, precariously balanced. It is not a permanent answer.

I conclude therefore that in modern political circumstances a capitalist economy must be prepared to accept a far greater degree of systematic control over the level of incomes and prices than we have ever contemplated before. My colleagues will no doubt point out all the difficulties and I am aware of them. They are formidable. Our views on statutory control of incomes and prices have often been expressed and the practical difficulties are considerable. We have seen how dusty is the road to agreement with the unions on some systematic approach to wage increases. No country has yet found the full answer, nor shall we for many years yet. But of one thing I am absolutely convinced, that the old classical economics are no longer relevant to a wholly new political situation. We must find a mixture of voluntary agreement and government supervision which will operate to restrain the political springs of cost inflation. If we cannot do this none of our economic policies will succeed.

I have no doubt that as much as possible should be done by voluntary agreement. This is the best way, most in accord with our traditions and our temperament. But the lesson of experience seems to be that we must be vigilant to detect the practical limits of voluntary action and ready if necessary to extend them by the use of legislation. One thing is certain : we cannot just go on as we are. And this, I am convinced, virtually the whole country now realizes.

4 INCOMES POLICY
Memorandum circulated to the Shadow Cabinet, 21 May 1976

During our discussions of economic policy I have not taken the scarce time of the Shadow Cabinet to expand my views on the need for an incomes policy. After all, I have been saying the same things consistently since I was Chancellor of the Exchequer and my views may well therefore appear to be either repetitive or out of date, or indeed both. But I thought I might set them down in this necessarily sketchy paper.

All economic problems are basically political problems, and politics are about power. The sole and overwhelming reason why an incomes policy is needed is to deal with the monopoly power which the Unions now possess and, even more important, are now fully conscious that they do possess. So long as they continue to wield power to destroy individual businesses or, indeed, complete industries, and the threat of bringing the entire economy to a halt, any talk of a return to 'free collective bargaining' or the operation of a 'free market' is meaningless. The simple fact is that for years now the Unions have increasingly demanded, with effective menaces, excessive wage increases which have inevitably led to excessive cost and price increases. That is what has happened. That, and the other side of the Union coin, their total unwillingness to cooperate in raising productivity, constitute the 'English disease' which has become the despair of our friends and the bane of sterling.

There are apparently only three ways in which this problem can be tackled.

1. It would help if we could reduce by law the power of the Unions, but we have tried this and it has hardly been a great success.

2. We can endeavour to bring pressure on the unions, through education, persuasion and public opinion, to exercise moderation in their demands; which is what succeeding Conservative administrations have meant by an incomes policy. (Strengthening the influence of our own supporters within the Unions is becoming an increasingly important part of this policy.)

3. It is argued that the power of the Unions to put up costs and therefore prices can be restrained by monetary measures, which I take to mean the restraint of effective demand or, in old-fashioned terms, deflation or a credit squeeze. It has also seemed to me that this fails because (a) the big battalions still get their demands while it is the rest of us who suffer; (b) it condemns the economy to stagnation because no businessman is going to invest in increased capacity while he still cannot find employment for the capacity he already has; (c) such a restrictive policy must be permanent for, with respect to Enoch Powell, whose logic on this point is more formal than real, experience shows that once you relax restrictions income growth rapidly starts again, as indeed commonsense seems to indicate that it always would.

I have remained very sceptical of the effects of monetary policy on inflation. There are after all two types of inflation: cost push and demand pull. If I am a manufacturer of kettles and my wage bill goes up I have to increase my prices or lose my profit. If, on the other hand, demand for my product rises, my prices will rise too, initially because my profit rises, but later because of the effect on the demands of labour. No doubt these forms of inflation can coexist and indeed interact but it is a fundamental mistake to try to deal with one form by measures appropriate to the other.

I do not see how reducing the money supply can help combat a cost inflation. Of course, there are many other reasons for reducing public expenditure, above all the need to restrict the public sector's share of the economy and to provide incentives by reducing taxation. What I am thinking of here is solely 'effective demand management'. (What a pity we cannot use Erhard's favourite single word, *Konjunkturpolitik*.)

The questions to which I have not yet seen satisfactory answers are :

1. What actual measures do we intend to take in practice to maintain a tighter monetary policy?

2. How does the money supply, whether it be M_1 or M_3, affect the economy, save through its influence on demand? What people spend is limited by the amount they can earn, borrow or dissave and is determined by the extent they wish, at any given time, to approach this limit. In the past, flexibility of demand management has always rested on the credit base and I doubt if this has really changed.

How can a credit squeeze and the consequent reduction of demand effect prices? Take the two components of prices :

Profit. Low demand can certainly reduce profits. As we all know the present trouble is that profits are too low already .

Cost. Taking very crudely the main components of costs, the results seem to me very much as follows : (a) it can have little effect on basic raw-material prices; (b) its effect on overheads is to spread them over a lower output and therefore increase rather than reduce unit cost of production. This seems to me to leave only the largest component of cost, i.e. incomes, wages, salaries and to a small extent dividends, and the argument therefore boils down to whether a general deflation of demand is a better way of holding down Union pressure for higher incomes than an incomes policy.

For the reasons I have given above I do not think it is an effective way of restricting the monopoly of power of the Unions.

Of course, effective demand can be expanded too rapidly and lead to demand inflation which will then interact with cost inflation. But I find it hard to believe that effective demand is too high so long as the economy is running as far below capacity as it certainly is now (remember the three-day week), and a permanent policy of keeping effective demand well below potential capacity is a policy designed permanently to confine this country to industrial stagnation, inadequate growth and continuing economic decline.

5   THE CONSERVATIVE APPROACH TO FOREIGN POLICY
From *The Times*, 18 August 1975

It is very rarely that the official Opposition divides the House against the Government on an issue of foreign affairs. It has not happened in the present Parliament, and apart from divisions on the European Communities Bill, which was rather a special occasion, it has been rare.

This does not mean that the Opposition is under any obligation to give automatic support to the Government, nor, I would hasten to add – lest Mr Callaghan should object – is there any obligation on the Government to produce a policy to suit the Opposition. But what it does mean is two things.

First, that for many years now there has been a general custom of trying to reach an agreed approach on the British national interest in our dealings with the outside world : and second, that the deep divisions on these issues lie not so much between the parties, as between the Left and Right wings of the Labour Party.

For many years now, from the days of Ernest Bevin, we have seen the spectacle of Labour Foreign Secretaries at Question Time harassed and attacked from their own back benches by their extreme Left, and, let it be said to their credit, hitting back with vigour and effect. The reason, I think, is simple. Labour Foreign Secretaries in office have recognized the two basic facts of British security : first, that our safety depends upon Nato, and upon the United States in particular; and second that any threat to our safety that might arise, could only arise from the Communist camp. These principles are definitely not accepted among the Left wing of the Labour Party, where anti-Americanism has taken the place of the old tradition of pacificism, and has combined with the fellow travelling supporters of the Communist regimes.

Any attempt to assess the fundamentals of British foreign policy has to be made against a background of dramatic change. We live in a world where more has changed in one generation than in centuries before, and it seems reasonable to expect that the expanding discoveries of science will impinge ever more drastically upon the physical and social environment within which diplomacy must operate. Let us consider some of the factors that affect Britain particularly. First, there is the loss of the Empire, the change in our status from a country that ruled a quarter of mankind, to an island state of Western Europe.

This decline, coincident with the growth of the superpowers, has meant a drastic decline in our ability to influence affairs abroad. The relative decline in our gross national product has further undermined our influence. It is difficult, although impossible not to face this decline if we are to be realistic in our policies. But we must avoid the easy temptation of thinking that because we can no longer do everything we want to, there is nothing that we can do and it isn't worth trying.

And there is the nuclear stalemate. The balance of terror remains an effective shield against a new world war. It is certainly better than no shield at all, but it cannot last for ever. Such a weight of potential mutual destruction must not for ever overhang mankind with its consequent dangers of accidental conflict, and possibly more sinister, the proliferation of atomic capacity in many less responsible hands. This is the basic reason why the search for détente and disarmament is fundamental, though it must be pursued, if it is to be successful, with complete realism.

The third factor is the emergence of the concept of a concerted foreign policy on the part of the members of the E.E.C. Every month that passes, and every incident that occurs, underlines the limitations on the power of individual Western countries, and the need for them to work in concert if they are to exercise the influence that their united economic and political power could sustain.

Fourthly, there is the new-found unity and confidence of the developing countries, particularly the raw materials producers. The oil producers have pointed the way; others are likely to follow. The situation is not unlike the position in this country, where the power of monopoly Trade Unions has grown so fast, not only because it is technically greater in modern industry, but even more because its possessors have begun to realize what power they really wield. Unions of raw materials producers are clearly not in an identical position with Trade Unions, but the potential exercise of monopoly power on a world scale could make profound changes to world economic conditions. Indeed, one of the other changes is the growing emphasis on economic problems in international affairs, and the way in which traditional diplomacy and economic diplomacy have become intertwined.

Finally, I would suggest that the absence of war on the world scale, and the relative freedom from international conflict enjoyed by many countries has led to greater internal instability, as aggressive instincts, normally released in international conflict, now explode in internal ones. The resulting instability in many countries leads, as we can see graphically in the case of Portugal, for example, to new opportunities for intervention and to instability and threats to peace on an international scale.

Against this background, what should be the objectives of British policy? First and foremost, of course, the furtherance of British interests, both political and economic – and these, broadly speaking, mean the maintenance of peace, freedom of trade and access to the raw materials and markets we must have for our prosperity. This surely is unarguable.

But the sheer pursuit of Britain's interests narrowly defined cannot be everything. We must have regard for what we believe to be fair in our dealings with other countries. In the Middle East it would serve our narrow interests best to espouse the Arab cause wholeheartedly, and abandon Israel. Yet succeeding Governments have refused, and rightly so, to do any such thing, believing that it would be unjust and immoral to do so, and that British interests must be based on an attempt to find a just and lasting solution.

Then there is also the question of how far, if at all, we should attempt to intervene in the internal affairs of other countries, particularly those whose regimes are repugnant to our ideas and democracy. Here clearly conflict arises.

We must remember that parliamentary democracy has not been a very successful export, and we cannot expect every country to adopt our particular philosophy. Our power of action in the modern world has been drastically reduced, and expressions of moral outrage are often deluding to the victims or actually counter-productive.

On the other hand, persuasive as is the call for minding Britain's business, it is not wholly convincing. It is one of the heartening features of our society that people do express their sense of outrage at what they consider to be persecution : for example, the very strong feelings about the treatment of Jews in the Soviet Union. This was raised by Conservative M.P.s when we recently met a delegation of Soviet parliamentarians, and we claimed then that in our view we were entitled to raise these matters.

But we must recognize that we cannot live alone, defended only by the integrity of our own principles of government. We have to have friends and allies. Above all, we have to seek, in the long run, agreement with other systems, which we find repugnant, because the alternative of mutual destruction would help no one. Certainly we must be specially aware of cases where developments within a country can threaten our own security, and of cases where there appears to be not only a different system of political practice from our own, but also departure from accepted standards of fundamental human rights.

The difference between the Labour and Conservative parties in their approach to foreign policy often appears to be one of degree rather than kind, though it is surely true, as I believe Collingwood pointed out, that the two merge into one another. Certainly there are a number of matters in which there is a clear difference of emphasis. In defence matters, for example, we have criticized the Government and voted against it, because we believe their defence cuts, particularly in the naval field, are going much too far.

In the case of Europe, our support for the Community has been earlier and more consistent than that of the Labour Party, and with certain notable exceptions, such as Mr Jenkins, their enthusiasm has been notably less convincing. We feel sometimes, also, that there is a tendency to double standards in the Labour Government's choice of attitudes to differing countries throughout the world, a charge to which Mr Callaghan, in his engaging manner, jovially admitted the other day. But the truth is that Opposition spokesmen have inevitably more freedom of expression than Government Ministers. While we must never forget that we hope to become the Government soon, and that what we have said in Opposition will be remembered by countries with whom we will have diplomatic relations, there is the possibility of expressing sometimes more frankly and freely, opinions which often Ministers may share, but are constrained from expressing by the niceties of diplomatic practice. Mrs Thatcher, for example, was able to call attention to the dangers of excessive optimism about Helsinki more bluntly than the Prime Minister was able to do. This is a clear advantage.

Our main foreign policy objective is the maintenance of our national security, with the long-term purpose of mutual disarmament and détente. We stressed, and the Government accepted during the recent debate, that the Helsinki agreement in itself would not justify the standing down of a single Nato soldier. In fact, détente, if it is achieved, will in itself be the greatest justification of Nato. Now what we must see is whether, in the

M.B.F.R. and S.A.L.T. talks, the Soviet Union applies the principles of Helsinki, because if it does, real progress in disarmament and towards peace can be made. We have to concentrate, as our first priority, on strengthening Nato, and on developing the E.E.C. in a political as well as an economic context, and these problems the Conservative Party is studying.

The first problem is the question of direct elections to the European Parliament. There is a clear but undated commitment to this in the Treaty of Rome. The problems involved in the mechanics of the election, and the type of franchise are considerable and while we must respect the commitment, it is important to proceed with deliberation. Beyond this, the main developments on which we should concentrate appear to be twofold. There is within the framework of the Treaty of Rome, basically an economic treaty, provision for concerting policy on such matters as exchange rates, expansion and inflation, and energy.

Beyond the treaty we can see the development of a concerted approach to foreign policy problems. This I regard as being of the utmost importance, as each new problem we face tends to stress the common European interest. Whether, in the long run, it is better to operate through common institutions is less important, what matters is to develop the will to work together, and the habit of doing so. There are some encouraging examples already, for example, in the eastern Mediterranean. The more the better.

One of our difficult problems is the attitude to be taken to the United Nations. No one, I hope, would deny that it embodies the ultimate ideal of international cooperation. Equally, I hope, no one would deny that practical results to date have fallen far short of that ideal. Our policy must be not one of despair, but one of trying to make the ideal progressively effective. There are two simple truths that must be faced. The first, that double standards do tend to operate within the United Nations, albeit for very understandable reasons. The second is that the founders were realistic in recognizing that a system which gave any member the same voting power, from the smallest to the greatest country, needed to be tempered with realism – hence the Security Council and the veto.

The truth, regrettably, is that in all major matters of international concern it is the great powers and not the United Nations that call the tune. We must recognize this, and the implication it has for our partnership in the European great power, while maintaining our long-term desire to see the United Nations reestablished on the principles on which it was originally established.

Then there are areas of special interest, because of British history, tradition, or direct economic interest. For example, the Middle East, the eastern Mediterranean and southern Africa. In all there appear to be differences of emphasis between Conservatives and Labour. It is said the Labour Party are more pro-Israeli, more pro-Greek, more anti the white governments remaining in Africa. I suspect that these differences once again are less between the two Front Benches, except possibly in the case of Simonstown, than they are between Back-bench and Front-bench members on the Government side. I have thought it right, as Opposition spokesman on foreign affairs, to stress, where possible, in these parts of the world, the extent to which there is agreement, not complete, but substantial, between the Government and the Opposition.

The Middle East remains one of the most dangerous areas. Peace there still remains tenuous. There are overlapping conflicts : Israeli versus **Arab**, Right versus Left, the Soviet Union versus the United States. There is also the essence of tragedy, the conflict not of right verus wrong but of right versus right : because there are rights and wrongs on both sides. Successive British Governments have based their policy on United Nations resolution 242. The concept to which we have adhered is that Israel should return to the general position of the 1967 boundaries, and that the military advances thereby surrendered should be compensated by an Arab recognition of the State of Israel, and a United Nations or other effective guarantee of her frontiers. A Palestinian state could within this context be established on the West Bank of the Jordon. Whatever emphasis may be placed on either side, whatever the long-term arguments of rights denied, or rights threatened, it is hard to see any other solution that in the foreseeable future will enable the peoples of the Middle East to live together in peace and prosperity.

There is cause for deep concern about the position in the eastern Mediterranean, and Britain has a special responsibility in Cyprus. The threat to the integrity of Nato, arising from the Greek reaction and from the Turkish dispute with the United States, is a very serious one indeed. So far as possible we should try to play the part of mediators. In Cyprus itself, it seems that a solution can come only from agreement between the two parties on the island.

In southern Africa, too, there appears to be movement. Our interests here involve not only our traditional and trade relations but also the Cape route to India and the Far East. No one in the Conservative Party has defended the concept of apartheid. As the world has moved on, so the inevitability of majority rule in Rhodesia has become more apparent. But it is right for us to point out that Mr Vorster seems to have changed the emphasis of his policies, and is making a real effort to achieve an agreement with neighbouring African states, which must be in the interests of everyone who lives in that area. It is also not unfair to point out that parliamentary democracy does not mean a lot in African terms, where the concept of an official opposition is, to say the least, indifferently understood, and where the remaining number of democratic regimes are few indeed. Our policy, while recognizing the reality of ultimate majority rule in Rhodesia, must be to try to help in achieving agreement on a transitional period, and in ensuring that the arrangements for such a transition can be ones in which all communities can have genuine confidence. But we must be realistic and recognize that our contribution – though potentially important – is certainly limited.

Finally, there remains our special position in the Commonwealth. It is one of the most fascinating examples of the illogicality of the British tradition, that the Commonwealth should have persisted in the way it has. On any crude calculation the Empire should have been swept away without any successor (as should have been the House of Lords), yet the fact is that there still remains within the Commonwealth a common sentiment of very considerable importance. I believe both parties recognize this, and increasingly this common recognition is producing a fulfilment which, if modest, is nevertheless important. The world would be the poorer if the Commonwealth system were to disappear, and it is the mutually accepted responsibility of Government and of Opposition to try and maintain it.

The broad stream of British foreign policy should not be sharply diverted with every change of Government, for the national interest does not change, much as it needs to adapt to external circumstances. In these circumstances, the primary function of Opposition is to exercise vigilance, to keep a critical eye on the performance of the Government, to chide when they display tardiness or lack of vision, to suggest when new ideas are needed, and openly to support where support is justified and necessary. The role that Britain is playing now is a very different one indeed from what it was twenty years ago, but it need be no less important, and certainly no less honourable.

6 THE CONSERVATIVE PARTY'S RESPONSIBILITIES IN OPPOSITION
From *The Times*, 21 and 22 January 1976

In an article last August, I said : 'The broad stream of British foreign policy should not be sharply diverted with every change of Government, for the national interest does not change, much as it needs to adapt to external circumstances. In these circumstances, the primary function of Opposition is to exercise vigilance, to keep a critical eye on the performance of the Government, to chide when it displays tardiness or lack of vision, to suggest when new ideas are needed, and openly to support where support is justified and necessary.'

The months that have followed have only strengthened my conviction that this is the right approach. An Opposition should not seek to exploit foreign policy solely as a stepping-stone to power. When it obtains power, it will have to wrestle with the self-same problems. An Opposition is bound to do all it can to frustrate the Government in domestic affairs, particularly when, as is true at present, the Government is committed to a disastrous partisan course.

But when it comes to Britain's dealings with other countries, the Opposition must wish to see the Government succeed, so long as it is defending British interests, and doing so in a manner which takes into account not merely short-term expediency but long-term necessity and the needs of national security.

We are right to point out how much the Government's economic policy has weakened Britain's stance in foreign affairs and has muted Britain's voice and how its repeated and ill-judged reductions in defence expenditure have gravely reduced our ability to protect our national interests. Our purpose must be to try to ensure that, so far as possible, the Government use what influence Britain still wields for fruitful ends.

The two great events of 1975 were the Referendum on membership of the E.E.C. and the Helsinki Conference. On both these issues the Opposition found itself ranged alongside the Government, or, at any rate, the majority of the Government. The Conservative Party probably made the greatest contribution to the highly successful result of the E.E.C. Referendum. As for Helsinki, we welcomed the purpose of détente, because to do anything else would have been crazy, while warning very clearly that nothing that happened there could possibly justify the West in letting down its guard. The proof of the Helsinki pudding came in the eating thereof.

Since the summer, a surprising quiet has descended in some of the world's trouble spots, while others, especially Angola and Lebanon, have suddenly emerged. Portugal now seems more stable than at one time it seemed we could hope. Little has been heard recently of the dispute between Greece and Turkey, or of the position in Cyprus. There is no sign of real progress, but on the other hand I think we can draw comfort from the well established principle that it is the things that go wrong that are newsworthy and solid, if unspectacular, progress seldom gets the headlines.

In Rhodesia, there does seem to be a more genuine attempt at discussion and agreement between Mr Smith and Mr Nkomo than seemed likely a few months ago.

Two new and disturbing developments have been the renewed dispute with Iceland, and the very dangerous situation in Angola. In both cases the Conservative Opposition has endeavoured to play a constructive role. It is difficult to criticize the Government for protecting the interests of British subjects, and there is no doubt that it has been doing its duty in providing protection to British fishermen who are harassed by the Icelandic Navy when peacefully pursuing their perfectly legal occupation. But it was right also for us to point out the long-term dangers of deadlock between Britain and Iceland, and the alienation of international sympathy involved in a dispute between a very large power and a very small power.

We suggested that it might be helpful to appoint some distinguished international figure to act as a mediator between the two countries. How much better for Britain if they had accepted our suggestion then. How much conflict and apparent climb-down would have been avoided.

We also put forward a proposal designed to help in Angola. We pointed out that American policy had been paralysed by the dispute between Congress and the Administration, and that in these circumstances a very special responsibility devolved upon Europe, and we suggested that Britain, together with her E.E.C. colleagues, should try to set up a conference of all interested parties in Africa and elsewhere to find a solution. Alas, there has been little or no sign of any Government response or of any Government action while the situation has grown steadily more critical.

There is considerable evidence that a gap has been developing between Government and Opposition on a number of issues of foreign policy. In its attitude to the Soviet Union, post Helsinki, its tactics in the European Economic Community, and the double standards shown in protesting about the actions of some foreign governments, it seems that the Government is yielding to increasing pressure from its own Left-wing supporters.

Without in any way departing from the plain commonsense of the issue, that peace between East and West is better than war between them, it cannot be denied that Russian policy since Helsinki has been disappointing. There is very little evidence of any progress in that broad range of human issues, inelegantly described as 'basket three': the reuniting of families, freedom of movement for individuals, and access for journalists. Yet these are some of the things where the Russians could most easily have made some moves, and where they know that Western opinion is particularly concerned.

But what is more disturbing has been the continued build-up of Soviet strength, coupled with the apparent deadlock in the S.A.L.T. and M.B.E.R. talks.

The Government appears unwilling to recognize these facts. It is under heavy pressure from its Left wing to make further severe reductions in defence expenditure, and if it is to justify these to any extent at all, it clearly must play down the extent to which Soviet power is continuing to increase. It does not, thereby, serve the cause of peace. *Si pacem vis bellum para. . .*

When there was the great protest about the executions in Spain, we made our position clear. We thought it hypocritical to protest about the death penalty for those convicted for murder when so many people in this country think it is right. Where we considered that protest could be justified was if people were condemned without proper trial, but we argued that if it is applied to Spain, it should apply to all the Communist countries as well.

There is little evidence that the Government is prepared to accept this view. Indeed, its reaction to the matter of Dr Cassidy is a case in point. If her charges against the Chilean authorities are true, then their behaviour was clearly outrageous and totally unacceptable. But where is the evidence that the Government shows the same vigilance in following up similar charges of outrageous behaviour in the Communist world, or anywhere else?

It seems likely that the main arguments of 1976 will be concerned with the development of the European Economic Community, and how it can fulfil the world role that American hesitations are making steadily more important. There are two reasons for this. It became increasingly apparent in the course of last year that individual member countries had much less chance of exercising influence in international affairs, acting on their own, than they could have acting together. At the same time, partly as a result of world recession, progress in the Community itself came to a halt, and there were growing and disturbing signs of drift.

In this situation, the publication of the Tindemans Report is timely. Decisions must be made this year about the future course the Community is to take, and in particular about the holding of direct elections. It is a sad fact that Britain's influence in the Community has been reduced by some of our Government's recent manoeuvrings, combined with our persisting economic weakness. It is all the more important, therefore, that we should not be seen to be dragging our feet now.

Nothing is more likely to encourage Communist pressure, with all the dangers that involves, than the impression that Western resistance will crumble.

Opposition spokesmen inside and outside Parliament have been warning the Government on these lines, and voting against it in Parliament for some time past, and Mrs Thatcher herself, in her speech on Monday, gave an authoritative statement of the Conservative Opposition's attitude and the criticism it has to make of the Government.

We were severely critical of the way the Government had handled the question of British representation at the Paris energy conference. Mr Callaghan started off by demanding a separate seat for Britain. While no one can blame a British Foreign Secretary in principle for standing up for British interests, and the Opposition did not make the mistake of doing this (I suspect Mr Callaghan rather hoped that it would), we pointed out that the way it was going about it was unwise, because it underrated Britain's long-term interest in harmonious relations with the rest of the Community, and because in any case it would not succeed.

We were proved right, and our unfortunate Foreign Secretary had to be protected by the Prime Minister from the wrath that came not merely from the Opposition but, sadly for him, even from the Labour Left wing, who, having revelled in British intransigence, felt sadly let down by the outcome.

Then there has been a growing feeling on the Opposition side of the House, that the Government applies double standards in dealing with other countries, and that what it condemns violently and in public when done by Right-wing regimes, it conveniently ignores when done by the Left.

The Conservative Party has been conducting a close study of the difficulties involved, particularly in direct elections, to which in our view Britain is committed, and it will be our purpose to have constructive and practical proposals to put forward. There have been mixed reactions to the Tindemans document, both between parties and within parties. This was hardly surprising. He wrote as a self-proclaimed federalist, and the tone of some of his arguments grates on the pragmatic English ear. But it is, nevertheless, a very important document, and I hope that it can be the basis for further progress towards European unity.

One's immediate main reservation must be, of course, about the proposal that the Community should be divided into two classes of members, the hustlers and the laggards (and how sad is the automatic assumption throughout Europe that Britain is one of the laggards). I do not think this can be acceptable as a permanent proposition, and in fact it is doubtful whether that is what Mr Tindemans meant. Maybe it is bad for the convoy if its progress has to be restricted to the pace of the slowest ships, but I know of no other method of keeping a convoy in being.

It follows from this that the responsibility on the slower movers to increase their pace, in the general interest, is a very great one. Mr Tindemans rightly points to increasing cooperation in the field of foreign affairs, and the success it has had in enhancing European influence. I am sure there will be general agreement about this, though there will be less agreement with the idea that a concerted policy should give way to a common policy determined by a majority vote, which the minority are bound to accept. This seems to me to be moving rather rapidly in the direction of a federal Europe with a single federal Government. I believe experience has already shown that the objectives of common action depend upon the will to work together as partners rather than on the imposition of institutional rules.

No one can foresee how the East–West confrontation will develop in 1976. Will Angola make progress towards détente impossible? Do the Soviets really want détente? Will American policy be hamstrung by domestic politics throughout this election year? What role will China play under the guidance of the new Prime Minister?

No one can map the likely progress of the discussions on vital economic matters between the industrial countries, the oil producers and the developing world. No one can be certain whether 1976 will see growing sanity in the Middle East, with further progress on the basis of the Israel–Egypt agreement, or whether it will bring progress to a halt, with all the dangers inherent in that.

One thing, however, seems to me absolutely clear : in all these matters, Britain has a vital interest, and the whole of Europe has a vital interest. Nothing can be more important for us than to ensure that the European voice is as united and effective as possible.

INDEX